Joseph Wesley Donovan

Trial Practice and Trial Lawyers

A Treatise on Trials of Fact before Juries....

Joseph Wesley Donovan

Trial Practice and Trial Lawyers
A Treatise on Trials of Fact before Juries....

ISBN/EAN: 9783337158910

Printed in Europe, USA, Canada, Australia, Japan

Cover: Foto ©Suzi / pixelio.de

More available books at **www.hansebooks.com**

TRIAL PRACTICE

AND

TRIAL LAWYERS.

A TREATISE ON

TRIALS OF FACT BEFORE JURIES,

INCLUDING

SKETCHES OF ADVOCATES, TURNING POINTS, INCIDENTS, RULES, TACT AND ART IN WINNING CASES, CONDENSED SPEECHES, A BRIEF SUMMARY OF THE LAW OF ACTIONS, EVIDENCE, CONTRACTS, CRIMES, TORTS, WILLS, ETC. ETC.

BY J. W. DONOVAN,

Author of Modern Jury Trials, etc.

ST. LOUIS, MO.:
WILLIAM H. STEVENSON,
LAW PUBLISHER AND PUBLISHER OF THE
CENTRAL LAW JOURNAL.
1883.

St. Louis, Mo.: Printed by the Central Law Journal.

PREFACE.

Twenty questions of fact to one of law, are contested in ordinary trials. Often the wrong side prevails when adroitly managed by a keen, clear spoken counsel, who detects the weakness of witnesses; and very often has the faltering story of a timid plaintiff been sustained and strengthened by an eloquent illustration in an argument: so that jury trials are *won* or *lost* by *management*.

There is a fine art in practice, that comes to one by experience, to another by a series of blunders, while others learn much of it by reading and observation. The great majority will never know it. They are not willing to pay the price. Many victories that are credited to counsel, belong equally to witnesses. The vivid story of a single witness, told in a winning way, will leave an impression that no eloquence can remove. The potter has no more power over the clay, than good evidence has over an intelligent jury.

It is the *art of putting things*, saying things, and doing things in a way to enforce conviction, that this volume relates to. It is made up of turning points, sketches, references to means of *winning cases* by incidents and illustrations, drawn from the varied experience of advocates in different sections of the country, who have learned and mastered the science of stating facts with clearness.

Success in practice depends so much upon the number of clients that one can make himself agreeable to, that the art of gaining business like that shown by Chief Justice Waite, or of winning verdicts by stories like Judge Holmes employed, and that made Abraham Lincoln successful, as well as President, has been carefully explained in numerous chapters.

The experience of successful men, forms the foundation of all rules of practice, sketches and incidents here reported. The merest mention of counsel without some illustration of their methods, consumes but a small space in any chapter; but wherever a name can add authority to a rule or statement, it has been given. The majority of lawyers mentioned are known to the writer; a few are reported from others. It is conceded by all whom I have conversed with on the subject, that in trials of fact before juries, trifles often turn the verdict, and men can learn much from each other on turning points of practice. This is what I have attempted to show in these pages. And as for the effect of eloquence — I have heard Gen. Butler in his powerful Philippic on an Indianapolis editor, when hundreds stood upon the seats and shouted, "Hit him again! Give it to 'im!! (smiting their hands together,) Give it to 'im!!" until I realized the force of "fighting" eloquence. I have heard Gough give his nineteen rewards to the faithful, looking up toward the heavens with expanded nerves, and eyes dilated, face all ablaze with magnetism, hands charged with electricity, and tones tuned with the finest melody. I have seen Benjamin F. Taylor when he marched the forces up the sides of Lookout Mountain, and pictured the battle above the clouds with lifelike energy — pictured it so graphically that we could almost hear the final shout of victory that shook the hills of Tennessee, when the boys in gray retreated from the boys in blue. I have heard the echoing shout receding over Cemetery Hill, caught up by Union forces and carried through the ranks of the entire army of the Cumberland; I saw the audience sit spell bound at the close, dismissed by a waive of the chairman's hand, so touched by the grandeur of the scene that they marched out in silence from College Chappel, and I called that eloquence, but it was imaginary. I have heard Phillips describe the conduct of a heroic general till he called before us the mighty dead, like Napoleon, Wellington and Alexander, and "dipping his finger in the sunlight," wrote on the blue arch of Heaven the name of his brilliant hero, and I was thrilled by his graphic description, and even that was *imaginary*. And when a *real* picture came before me in a New York court room, and Beach was the champion of a discarded wife by a wealthy husband, and when I heard him rehearse her wrongs, and tell her simple story to a jury, and listened to their verdict of heavy damages, I knew, and felt, and realized the power and force of eloquence, and thought it would be instructive to repeat it, and describe it as a lesson to advocates.

J. W. D.

Detroit, July, 1883.

INDEX.

A

ABOUT TRIALS, 62.
ACTION, 3.
ADROITNESS, 47.
ADVOCATES, 246.
ATKINSON, 303.
ARGUMENT, 37.
ARNOLD, 238.
ASSUMPSIT, 194.

B

BEACH, 260.
BLACKBURN, 295.
BLACK, 296.
BLACK, W. P., 280.
BLISS, 266.
BOOTH CASE, 175.
BRADY, 4.
BRADBURY, 299.
BREAUX, 292.
BRIEF, 99.
BROWNE, 308.
BUTLER, 249.

C

CAMPBELL, 294.
CANDOR AND DIGNITY, 102.
CARLISLE, 289.
CARTER, 294.

CARPENTER, 20.
CHEEVER, 304.
CHICAGO BAR, 268.
CHIEF JUSTICE WAITE, 41.
CHIPMAN, 302.
CHOATE, RUFUS, 253.
CHOATE, JOSEPH, 264.
CINCINNATI BAR, 282.
CIRCUIT COURT PRACTICE, 142.
CIRCUMSTANTIAL EVIDENCE, 117.
CONKLING, 249.
CONTRACTS, 196.
COURAGE IN COURT, 155.
CORWIN, 21.
CRIMINAL CASES.
CRIMINAL DEFENSES, 65.
CRIMINAL PROSECUTIONS,
CROSS-EXAMINATION, 70.
CURTIS, 264.

D

DAMAGES, 197.
DAVIDGE, 286.
DEXTER, 268.
DICKINSON, 15.
DICKINSON, DON. M., 303.
DILLINGHAM, 16.
DIVORCES. 172.
DOOLITTLE, 278.
DOUGHERTY, 296.

E

ELOQUENCE. 6.
EVIDENCE. 198.
EVARTS, 258.

F

FIELD, 267.
FINE WORK. 71.
FISHBACK. 235.

FORCE, 56.
FORGERY, 201.
FRAUD, 199.

G

GENERAL AGENCY, 200.
GENIUS, 84.
GIVE A LITTLE, 152.
GORDON, 308.
GREELEY'S TREE, 99.
GRIFFIN, 303.

H

HALE, 299.
HANCHETT, 305.
HARRIS, 295.
HARRIS, OF ALBANY, 298.
HARRIS, IRA, 299.
HARRISON, 307.
HARRISON, 234.
HENDRICKS, 305.
HIS FIRST CASE, 119.
HOADLY, 282.
HOMICIDE, 201.
HOWE, 292.
HUMAN NATURE, 31.

I

INDIANAPOLIS BAR, 305.
INGERSOLL, 236-288.
IN THE PROCESSION, 232.

J

JOHNSON, 283.
JUSTICE CASES, 132.
JUSTICE STORY, A, 140.

K

KIRCHNER, 221.

L

LARNED, 302.
LAWYERS' ADVICE, 37.
LAWYERS NOT ON TRIAL, 60.
LETTER WITNESSES, 130.
LIKES AND DISLIKES, 136.
LINCOLN, 19, 250.
LINCOLN, ROBERT T., 271.
LINCOLN, T. D., 283.
LOTHROP, 302.

M

MacLEAN-SCRIPP LIBEL CASE, 221.
McDONALD, 307.
McSWEENEY, 284.
MANAGING CASES, 37.
MARSHALL AND CRITTENDEN, 9.
MARSTON, 302.
MAXIMS, 173.
MAY ON LINCOLN, 250.
MEMORY OF LIVES, 312.
MERRICK, 287.
MICHIGAN BAR, 302.
MILLS, 273.
MISER'S HAND, 310.
MISTAKEN IDENTITY, 219.
MUNN, 280.
MUNN IN CLARK MURDER CASE, 241.

O

O'CONNOR, 257.
ON HIS MERITS, 109.
ONE OPINION, 96.
ONLY ONE WITNESS, 230.
ORATORS AND ORATORY, 210.
ORDER OF TRIALS, 165.
ORDER IN OFFICE, 25.

P

PARTNERSHIP, 205.
PECKHAM, 298.

INDEX. xi

PECULIAR ADVOCATES, 15.
PERSONAL PROPERTY, 206.
PHILADELPHIA LAWYERS, 295.
POND, 304.
PORTLAND BAR, 299.
PORTER, 259.
PREPARING TRIALS, 23.

R

REMEMBER LITTLE THINGS, 160.
RESERVE FORCE, 58.
RIGHTS AND REMEDIES, 193.
RUSSELL, 304.
RYAN, 13.
RYAN, 180.

S

SEMMES, 291.
SEPARATING WITNESSES, 43.
SEWARD, 11.
SHARP PRACTICE, 112.
SHAFFER, 261.
SHIPMAN, 228.
SHORT SAYINGS, 169.
SOLDIER'S VERDICT, 157.
SOUTHERN BAR, 289.
SOUTHERN LAWYERS, 293.
SPECIAL VERDICTS, 83.
STANSBURY, 18.
STATING CASES, 34.
STORRS, 270.
STRANGE DEFENSES, 147.
STRANGE SUCCESS, 168.
STROUT, 300.
STYLE OF SPEAKING, 244.
SWETT, LEONARD, 271.

T

TACT AND SKILL, 45.
TAKING WRONG POSITIONS, 79.

TALKING TOO MUCH, 106.
TEN TRIAL RULES, 29.
TENDER AND TROVER, 208.
TOTTEN, 287.
TREMAIN, 11.
TRIAL ELOQUENCE, 234.
TRIAL LAWYERS, 1.
TRIFLES THAT TELL, 81.
TURNING POINTS, 68.
TURNING VERDICTS, 113.

V

VALLANDIGHAM, 17.
VAN ARMAN, 269.

W

WAITE'S START IN LAW, 41.
WASHINGTON BAR, 286.
WEBSTER AND CHOATE, 248.
WEBSTER, 254.
WESTERN JUSTICE, 135.
WHEN TO STOP, 158.
WILLS, 208.
WINNING CASES, 54.

TRIAL PRACTICE.

CHAPTER I.

TRIAL LAWYERS.

THEIR ART, MANNERS, SKILL, AND ELOQUENCE.

Trial lawyers, commonly called advocates, generally show a natural genius in lawsuits very early in practice, whether vivid, graphic, powerful, or eloquent speakers, their first efforts reveal their style, and future prospects of success. A real advocate is a genius; he may be an excellent trial lawyer with but very few of the graces of an orator, but he can never become a real *advocate* without natural faculties, warm sympathies, keen knowledge of human nature.

The skill, art, character and arrangement of speeches give them force and effectiveness. Gifted speakers are rhetorical and logical by nature; their words flow spontaneously and apply to the subject and the hearer with very little effort in selection. But the greatest advocates have added to nature's rare gifts, the polish of learning and acumen, anecdotes and illustrations, with a wealth of excellent quotations to clothe and adorn their arguments.

Good arguments are not made by accident—occasional bursts of eloquence may come without forethought, but speakers like Clay and Everett relied upon careful study and thoroughness of research, and so, in the history of American advocates, the leaders, the trial lawyers of power and influence, have been naturally gifted and highly cultivated; their arts of practice are full of interest and instruction to all who follow similar callings.

Within the era of thirty years, and especially since the American conflict, a greater variety of subjects have been argued to juries, and, on the whole, a better line of arguments have been made than the average of any previous years in America. True, in England, there have lived but one Erskine and one Burke, in Ireland, but one O'Connel and one Curran, and in America, a single Webster, a single Choate, but one O'Connor and another Prentiss, whose places are never filled by recent rivals, but, in the main, a succession of brilliant men have brightened the pathway of modern trials with excellent examples of wit, humor, sagacity, and effective eloquence.

With the examples of success in the practice of the advocates mentioned, the world is already familiar. They were like sun-light to their brethren, and need neither comment nor coloring to enhance their brilliancy. But there are others, more modern and less understood, that seem a closer connecting link with our generation, whose career it is well to remember, and whose well-won victories will form a part of the

Trial Practice, discussed in this volume. As all trials are presumed to be managed by advocates as much as plays are dependent upon their chief actors, it may be well to glance occasionally at some of the past leaders of the American bar, who have been head-lights to their followers, and may remain so for generations. To this end, I will assume to mention whatever is instructive in the career of men in different States, believing that an actual example will be more effective than mere theories of practice.

ACTION.

When a great master said that the first, second, and third requisite of oratory consisted in *action*, he evidently knew that the action of an orator was better understood than their average speeches. The dumb brute can detect his master's look of pleasure or unkindness. The child can comprehend a motion and a gesture, and of all things clear, the simplest and clearest are looks and actions combined. The native Indians and frontier foreigners use limited words and "wink with their hands," as the Germans say, to convey their meaning. It is not strange that men are muddled on a jury, when even court and counsel often find it difficult to settle a legal controversy.

Actions attract more attention than words. The eye is wiser than the ear and wiser than the head. It is never satisfied with seeing. The curious motion that reveals some new plan of argument, is sure to be noticed, especially if graceful and appropriate. Besides, gestures are always original: they can never be studied; therefore, they are newly born in view of a jury. To secure such attention as to make an audience follow with their eyes the upward and onward gestures, is to be eloquent. Actions are eloquent, often pathetic or strong and determined, or faltering and courageous or even weak. They reveal emotions, and express truth or dishonesty. Often has a pause like that of Patrick Henry, in the midst of his greatest of speeches, been more effective than twenty sentences: " and George the Third,"—" may profit by their example."

The power of Judge Ryan's arguments consisted in his command of excellent English and force in gesture.

Webster's remarks of Bunker Hill Monument, " let it rise, let it rise, till it meet the sun in his coming," must have been majestic in sight of a vast concourse to see him rear the great figure in the air before his hearers. If the jury can read from a counsel's actions, they may read from a witness and a client, and the case is often won or lost by the straight-forward actions of the witnesses and parties, to say nothing of counsel's candor.

BRADY.

James T. Brady was, next to John Van Buren, the greatest criminal lawyer of New York City. A born genius, equipped with a fine form, size, voice, and engaging manner, brimfull of wit, humor, anecdote, knowledge of human nature, pathos, and an attractive delivery.

His speeches were bristling with points from end to end. He was fertile in resources, ready in debate, tolerably well versed in law, highly rhetorical, and generally eloquent. Mr. Brady was a great after-dinner speaker. Like Tom. Corwin, his natural tendency was toward wit, but his brilliant imagination never ran long in one groove. Engaged in the Sickles–Key cases, the Cole–Hiscock trial, and many more of great prominence, he became known as a great criminal lawyer more than a general counsel. He had pleasing and expressive eyes; a warm, cleanly-shaven face, curly hair, and small mustache, and seemed very young; in fact, he died in his early prime, but gained the reputation of a master advocate.

The efforts of Mr. Brady throughout the Empire State were ever pungent and powerful, thrilling in interest and extremely touching in many passages. His keen ingenuity and mastery of human passions was a marvel to the bar, and an entertainment to every jury before whom he appeared as counsel. He had piercing eyes, and attractive manner, and won by strange resources that seemed always his own. He was admired for his wit, and loved for his generous nature. His appeal to the court in defense of General Sickles, in Washington, will never be forgotten by any who were fortunate enough to be in hearing when he pictured the father's first meeting with his child after hearing of his wife's dishonor. The statement of Mr. Brady was so vivid and life-like, that General Sickles was completely overcome, and argument was suspended till he could be removed from the courtroom. Seeing its effect, Mr. Brady rested without a word to the jury, and won easily. He died young in years, but ripe in honor as an advocate. I cannot refrain from adding a brief passage of his

ELOQUENCE.

In closing, Mr. Brady said:

"He seemed," said this distinguished witness, his own heart filling up and overflowing, as he recalled the scene; "he seemed particularly to dwell on the disgrace brought upon his child." These words set free the tempest that had so long been pent up. As they fell from the lips of Robert J. Walker there occurred here in this very court a scene which from the memories of those who witnessed it never will be, never can be, blotted out. All eyes were turned to the dock; every eye was eager, fixed, dilated, quivering; and there was he, he who from the first hour of imprisonment down to the utterance of those words, had borne himself with heroic calmness, suddenly overcome and racked with relentless grief, stricken down as though he were himself the motherless and houseless child for whom he wept, smitten to the quick and beaten to the dust; drenched in the gall and wormwood of a tribulation, the depth of which no mortal hand can sound, and over the subsiding flood of which no arch of peace can ever shine. There was he, the avenger of the invaded household of the more-than-murdered wife, of the more-than-orphaned little one; there was he, in an appalling moment of parental agony, subdued at last. Talk of the mind diseased — talk of the circumstances that unhinge, upset, and madden it — talk of the distraction into which a ruthless perfidy had plunged my client and my friend — talk of his condition of irresponsibility when he dealt the fatal blow — talk of this, and with your worrying interrogations strive to elicit the recollection of it from those who, themselves the witnesses of it, who were themselves agitated as they never were before. Nature, heaven, God himself, in his heart-broken image here, became here, in this very court, the witness of the torture by which on that terrible day, the 27th of February, the prisoner was inflamed.

"You beheld the scene of the 12th of April. It was the same as that to which Robert J. Walker testified. Recall this scene. Think of how the proceedings of this court were suddenly arrested by the sobs of the prisoner when the beautiful image of his poor child was revived by the words of Robert J. Walker; how he was bowed to the earth, and how he writhed as though an arrow were buried in his heart; how, supported by his friend, he was led from this court, his vision quenched in scalding tears, his limbs paralyzed, his forehead throbbing as though it had been bludgeoned by some ruffian, and his whole frame convulsed. Recall this scene. Think of this; think of the tears you yourselves shed as this stricken victim was borne by — think of this — and then may we well say to the jury: if your love of home will suffer it, if your genuine sense of justice will consent to it, if your pride of manhood will stoop to it, if your instinctive perception of right and wrong will sanction it, stamp murder upon the bursting forehead that has been transpierced with the thorns of an affliction which transcends all other visitations; and for the scandal, the dishonor, the profanation, and, in the end, the devastation which provoked this terrible outburst, this tempest of grief, this agony of despair, as Robert J. Walker described it; for this incalculable wrong, I say, and for this ir reparable loss, declared by a verdict for the prosecution that so many thousand dollars, an appropriation from an economic or swept right off from a lavish jury, can afford a soothing compensation. Do this; do it if you can, and then, having consigned the prisoner to the scaffold, return to your homes, and there, within those endangered sanctuaries, following your ignoble verdict, set to and teach your imperiled wives a lesson in the vulgar arithmetic of a compromising morality, and let them be inspired with a sense of womanly dignity by a knowledge of the value you attach to the sanctity of the household, to the inviolability of the wife, to the security of the hospitable roof, and last of all, but above all, to the inherited tradition of an innocent, but ruined, offspring."

STANTON.

Edwin M. Stanton, the companion of Brady, and great war secretary, was no less artful and logical, and often more powerful in debate, but opposite in build, manner and plan of advocacy. He won his cases more by adroitness of management and soundness of reason, than by pathos or appeals to passion. He was the associate of Mr. Brady in the Sickles trial, and ably did his work, fully consenting to drop the defense after the court-scene already described, as a wiser measure than further argument. He was large, tall, and dignified, and never forgot the gravity of an advocate's high calling. His manner was impressive and his methods ingenious. In a famous trial near Cleveland, before the war, he was given a $1,000 retainer to save a young man from the gallows, who had stabbed a rival in a ball-room, after having threatened in the hearing of companions to do so, with only jealousy for a motive. Mr. Stanton's management of this defense was masterly. Reaching the county-seat, he early learned that public sentiment was deeply aroused, and still a few were opposed to hanging in general. He was cool and quiet, said not a word, and noted the evidence carefully. He was opposed by the eloquent statesman and lawyer, John A. Bingham, and knew too well Bingham's power with the jury. The junior advocate concluded a short address for the people, and referred to his associates who should follow. Silence became intense. The court room was packed with listeners. "Proceed, Mr. Stanton," said the court, gravely, and a ruffle went round as the strong man arose and said in measured tones, "I have no remarks to add, your Honor." Bingham was white with rage. This cut him off entirely. He tore his notes in shreds, muttering imprecations at Stanton's trick. Deep disappointment followed. The case was duller now; the jury said, "Murder in the second degree," and saved the young man's life. But this was Stanton's sagacity.

MARSHALL AND CRITTENDEN

Were another pair of brilliant Kentucky advocates, within this range and period, who stamped their characters on the Southern bar, as lasting monuments of fame and forensic eloquence. They were quite unlike in build and language, yet greatly similar in their management of cases. Tom. Marshall was tall, slim, a Henry Clay build, and sparkled with wit and repartee in jury trials for years; at times grave, severe, chaste; always original and effective; in manner somewhat excentric; a full master of human nature; trained and cultivated, but born eloquent. His speech in the Matt Ward case is a model of rare passages.

He never met the fullness of success in political life that came to his associate in the Ward trial mentioned, but it was difficult to say which one, Tom. Marshall or John J. Crittenden, moved the jury most or best pleased the audience. Mr. Crittenden was a refined, though bold speaker. His dignity as a senator, governor, and statesman followed him in trials, with signal effect, everywhere. But he never rested on such resources. He was well-read, and persuasiveness seemed his art of winning juries. The candor, high sense of honor, rare knowledge of men, firmness, and courtly bearing did much to enforce attention. He had a fine presence, rich voice, modulated like sweet music. He was clever and candid, and brought tears to his hearers by a beautiful quotation read from a German author, where justice, truth and mercy, came and pleaded with the creator, saying (of man's creation): "Make him not, father: he will defile thy temple; make him not: he will trample on thy law;" and, finally, mercy kneels and says: "Oh, make him, Father, and I will follow him, and at last bring him back to thee." From this beautiful selection Crittenden will be remembered long after his statesmanship is forgotten. It is known as Gov. Crittenden's allegory. He and the genial Tom. Marshall are gone, but their eloquence is not forgotten.

SEWARD.

The genius of William H. Seward as advocate, is not easily overestimated. A man of small mold, neither large nor commanding, but intensely original and bold in his thought and action, he needed no counsel and preferred to try his case alone from the beginning. His sentences were measured, but pithy and full of logic. His art was work with a system well directed. He was ripe in learning, courageous in the belief of victory, and zealous in all his undertakings. In speaking, he seemed to grow taller and larger, and expand with his theme to a force hardly looked for in a man of his proportions; more a statesman than orator, yet once enlisted for a client, his efforts never flagged till victory relieved him of his burden.

It is believed that his conscience prompted his action as an advocate more than his retainers. Possessed of means and a large clientage, he could command any amount of ideal cases in which to exert his eloquence, but the poor and rich, friendless and influential, received alike his best legal services. Like Lincoln, his great and successful rival for the presidency, he had a heart that beat for all humanity, and slighted no one who commanded his talents. Unlike Lincoln, he was elaborate in his efforts before juries and clothed his language in the flowers of classically-quoted learning.

TREMAIN.

Lyman Tremain was another of New York's great advocates, whose wit and logic, eloquence and skill, will long remain in the minds of his juries and clients.

Tall and commanding in person, grave and determined in manner, powerful and sublime in reasoning, he embodied all of the rare requisites of a master advocate. He cut his arguments as if out of solid marble, first rude, then shapely, then polished. His thoughts were inspired by great events. His dark complexion and Websterian manner needed an occasion to stir his nature to its real depths. He struggled with his juries like an athlete in an arena, trying first one means, then another, to meet and overcome their opinions. He was an ideal advocate in this. That he mastered the law and facts fully and presented both thoroughly, and yet his style was individual. He had but little of the pathetic, and, unlike Brady and Marshall, he needed thorough preparation and great trials to draw his fire, as soldiers express it. In his defense of Stokes, that is a monument to any advocate, he based his argument equally on four grounds; self-defense, poisoning, probing and insanity. All ably sustained and eloquently urged. His effort was his last of capital defenses. Before this, he had often appeared for the people. Not a statesman, he goes into history purely as a great advocate, and a ripe counselor.

RYAN.

Ryan and Carpenter, long the great rival advocates of Wisconsin, attained national eminence during the war. Of opposite dispositions, but natural genius, they reached the summit of fame in jury cases in their native State before Mr. Carpenter became the brilliant senator of the West, and Judge Ryan adorned an honored seat on his State Supreme Court bench at Madison. Both men were learned. Judge Ryan believed that every word in our language had an appropriate meaning, and sought through varied dictionaries to search it out. Every faculty great, every passion intense, every undertaking mastered, but himself he could never rule. Erratic, high-tempered, and easily nettled, his career was somewhat marred by his bursts of anger and lack of genial bearing. Born a genius, like Webster, his politics differed from the average sentiment of his State, and no open opportunity ever led him to national eminence, like his competitor, the genial Matt Carpenter, whose career was so busy that he even declared he never had time for society. Judge Ryan made a study of the reason of things. The happy harmony of his sentences is noticeable in all his speeches. He revelled in the style of Addison and Burke. Even in his intensest anger, he was sublime in expressions; full, ready and exact, without fear, and with distinguished ability, never popular. He feared no man's argument when he was grounded in the right. At the bar he was a giant that crushed all little obstacles. His size was not unlike Webster's, with a warmer and more impulsive nature. In Webster's seat, at Washington, who knows what a name he may have carved in history. Surely in a court room he never would have feared the greatest of New England's advocates. It was largely his location and lack of a field for fame, that robbed him of glory and renown. He had read and mastered languages. He could reason with the greatest. He lacked no art of eloquence, neither from fire, fervor, nor beauty of modulation, and yet he passes into history as a great judge, and his speeches are rarely seen in print. As high as $50 a copy has been offered for Ryan's speeches. His language was always fine and forcible, and often eloquent and beautiful. His feelings were strong and temperament ardent; his manner earnest, often vehement and denunciatory. His power of sarcasm unequalled. He abounded in metaphors. His figures were brilliant. His replies salient. His appeals all powerful, persuasive, and convincing. America has not produced an advocate with greater command of language. And from this we learn the value of *urbanity*.

CHAPTER II.

PECULIAR ADVOCATES.

Daniel S. Dickinson, of Binghampton, N. Y., was a genius in oratory, and a rare advocate. To have "Dan" Dickinson was almost a victory from the first. His first case was tried about 1384, when he drove a one-horse wagon into Binghampton, himself barefooted and ragged, with his worldly goods, his wife and child, and little or no means to provide a living. It happened the same day that a suit was set for trial at the hotel where he was stopping for dinner, and a banker, seeing his bright look and poor apparel, engaged to pay him a small sum to help in the case, which he did cheerfully. It was arranged that he should close, and so great was the expectation to hear a barefooted lawyer speak, that men left their shops, children ran away from school at recess, and even the banker had a seat within the railing. Dickinson never made a better effort to reach a jury. He was young, impulsive, full of quotations and warm argument. He talked directly to each juryman, one at a time. He seemed to guess their calling, and opened with the remark that law is the shield of the poor man's rights, as well as the rich man's possessions. That a simple change in circumstances; a death of a partner or a father, might soon scatter the earnings of a lifetime, and leave dependent children at the mercy of a charitable community. He quoted a verse of Burns that "man was made to mourn." He touched on the means and struggles of earning a living, and turned to the tenant case only when his voice had reached the real melody of a song, saying: "And this is the house you are to carry from the heads of his children, and this is the family you are turning from their home, and this is the mercy that our friends would have you show." "But we will not," broke out a juryman, with a resolute look and a face well wet with involuntary tears. Instantly rejoined the speaker, "Then I am done," and cries, "go on, go on," came from the banker and others, and confusion followed a verdict for the barefooted lawyer, who was made attorney for the bank, and became a statesman.

DILLINGHAM.

Governor Dillingham, of Vermont, was, in his day, a powerful advocate. A man of good presence, medium sized, educated in books and men, thorough in law, and equally so as a real student of human nature. He early acquired fame and fortune, with a fine clientage, in Vermont, where he was long known as Governor Dillingham, and a great favorite as an orator. He had a wonderful memory, a fund of rare humor, a keen, incisive way of *cutting legal knots*, and happy surprises in his conduct of trials that are always attractive. Merchants would close their stores, and farmers would quit their fields, to hear him. At one time, in an interior town, he was detained over night at a hotel where a lively law suit was in progress — suits were held in bar-rooms then. The Governor grew uneasy, called defendant's counsel aside and asked permission to aid him in closing to the jury, which request was granted. Quietly suggesting occasional points, he waited his turn to speak. Addressing the jury as a neighboring farmer who had dropped in to hear the fun, he gradually reached the real pith of the contest, and suddenly burst forth in a volume of such eloquent thoughts, stories, and copious reasons, that the jury sat spell-bound to the close. The plaintiff's counsel, up to this time confident of victory, was so completely captured by the apt words of his adversary, that his reply fell flat and unnoticed. The jury found a verdict for the gray-haired farmer, whom counsel congratulated as "a mighty good talker, anyway," and later, learned, to their great amazement, that he was the State Governor. His art was in his human-nature style of reasoning.

VALLANDIGHAM.

Clement L. Vallandigham was the most brilliant advocate of his day in Ohio, where he had an immense court practice, and excelled as an advocate before juries, in both civil and criminal cases, for a score of years. He was tall, slim, with sharp features, Roman nose, and eagle eyes, magnetic in tone, power, and expression. His speeches abounded in illustrations, wit, and skillful setting of all the minor details. He was an exhaustive reasoner, a real volcano when aroused in heated discussion. His arms, hands, and body, seemed in harmony with his rapid thought and earnest conviction. He had intuitive genius. He was utter self-oblivion in all his gestures, bitter in speech, and determined to win all victories. Graphic and dramatic in style, he suited his words and actions to perfect harmony. His sentences were cut in short, spicy sayings, that rang in the ears of the jury, and were intensely powerful and convincing. His art was in his *clearness*. Every particle of testimony illustrated, while in manner he was as vivid as Choate, and earnest as Seward. He died young, by his own accident, in showing how a woman could shoot herself with a pistol, in a famous murder trial, soon after the rebellion.

STANSBURY.

Henry Stansbury, leader of the Cincinnati bar for years, who died since '75, was a literal Cyclopedia of legal knowledge and acumen. Tall, spare, slim, of the style and manner of Chief Justice Marshall, he possessed, in a marked degree, the genius of reaching a jury by other means than eloquence. He was a pioneer in Kentucky, and lived at Newport, near Cincinnati; grew wealthy in heavy cases in all branches of legal practice. The sturdy sense, courtly bearing, and natural aptitude for legal discussions, were the forces employed to carry his arguments. Juries believed him. They took what he said as a child would take food from a parent. He was a giant in law, by reason of his commanding abilities and admirable character. For years he drew around him the best elements of his adopted city, and stood at last as a venerable and venerated monument in the courts of Ohio.

ABRAHAM LINCOLN.

Honesty, integrity, candor, and clearness in speaking, were the chief characteristics of this wise, shrewd, far-seeing man, who won nearly all his jury cases for years before his election to the Presidency. He was logical, and had such a fund of clear illustrations, that his conclusion when reached, seemed the only one possible to contemplate.

He was utterly wanting in low cunning, and yet crafty by his candor. His reasoning was founded on his unerring judgment of human nature, and first compared with some simple object that he, and his hearers, could not fail to agree upon. His marvelous fund of humor, was never better used than before a jury. A good, clear-cut joke was to him, an excellent argument—it always is to a jury. Like Seward, he relied upon himself, and depended on his own judgment. Appearing to waver, he was self-asserting when it best served his purpose. He believed in his points before making them, and soon made others come to the same conclusion. His instinctive knowledge of men, taught him that either side might have minor rights; but only one central controversy should be settled in a suit, so he waived the less to gain the greater. He was a thinker, and carried his plans in deep silence to and from his office, gaining strength by revolving them in his mind.

Great and noble in his natural sympathies, he never forgot his nobility by elevation as head-servant of a mighty nation. The same counselor, friend, and advocate of right and justice, went to mold and make the martyr that first made the man. With such qualities added to a warm, friendly feeling, a sympathetic and often eloquent voice, with a will to do equal and exact justice, with an inclination to speak and act, and do his part in absolute rectitude, what wonder he succeeded! He had every requisite of an advocate, form, life, voice, fancy, logic, honesty, ambition, knowledge of men, knowledge of law, mastery of facts, clearness and belief in his cases—having selected for trial, only such as were morally certain to bring him a victory. Even with Webster such a mind would have shown no weak comparison in a contest before a jury. The reader will see more of Lincoln in a separate chapter.

CARPENTER.

The brilliant career of the genial and ever busy Matt Carpenter, is quite generally known. His law practice during the last years of his life, was mainly in the Supreme Court at Washington. But we will notice his earlier career as an advocate. His presence was fine and imposing, large, tall and graceful; smoothly shaved, save a mustache; heavy hair and large eyes; rather a broad head and sinewy frame; musical voice of great power; witty and clear in his replies; a real orator in court or Congress. He saw a case in the center. He framed his speeches like a rare bouquet, adding flower to flower until they were beautiful. He was logical and strong, full of ingenious devices and captivating in the terseness of illustrations; one of those sweeping orators that carry an audience like Garfield did, by sublime passages to the height of sublimity. Carpenter was great with juries, great with courts, and at home with witnesses. Every inch an advocate, and genial enough to attract a host of personal admirers, who crowded in to hear his closing speeches. He early adopted a plan of terse reasoning through stories, illustrations, but his style can not be said to be at all trifling. He died young while United States Senator. In his contests with Judge Ryan, he was about evenly matched.

CORWIN.

Tom Corwin, the wit and genius of Ohio, twenty-five years ago, was a man of wonderful ability, and gifted as well as brilliant, as an advocate; tall, large, dark hair, dark eyes and complexion, large forehead, smoothly shaven face. In style, varied, at times logical—again humorous, then brilliant and rhetorical; vivid in imagery, graphic in descriptions—a master of men and eloquence. His career, as an advocate, is scarcely equalled in any country.

While Senator, in Washington, the Ohio Ten Mile Valley R. R. Co. was formed, and Mr. Smith made president. Suit arose and no one but Corwin could answer for opponents of the scheme. He came on to argue a dry demurrer. A lawyer, for a joke, sent word that Tom Corwin was to speak in the court house. He found the court yard and court house filled with people. He walked in and shook hands with lawyers in a friendly and surprised manner. The one who had formed the joke was among them. "How is this?" said Tom. "They heard you were to be here; they came from the hills and valleys, to hear you." Corwin took it all in a glance. With great dignity, he said: "May it please your honor, I am pleased over this large array of people; I am honored; I am delighted." He expressed his surprise. He touched the demurrer five minutes, then touched the crowd. They laughed, cheered, till almost uncontrolable.

Corwin went on: "I dreamed last night, your honor, that I stood upon an eminence and saw wagons coming from the valleys of this beautiful county of Miami. I stood under a tall sycamore tree. There was a table spread with the luxuries of the fields, by the husbandmen and their wives. When everything was completed, and the tables were so crowded with good things that they seemed ready to break, I saw at the head of that table, the president of the Ten Mile Valley R. R., at the foot, the vice-president. The father and mother, side by side; the lovers and brothers all eating of the delicious fruits; and one man proposed this toast: 'Here is to the father of his country, Washington; first in peace and last in the hearers of his countrymen.' Then one said: 'I propose a toast, 'President Smith, *of the 10 Mile Valley R. R. Co.*' Instantly the concourse vanished; tables disappeared. It was a dream; now, your honor, *had it been built, the dream would have been a reality!* But the whole paper road is a dream!" He won his case, amid rounds of applause.

CHAPTER III.

PREPARING FOR TRIALS.

When a case is taken for examination, and witnesses are tendered to sustain either the theory of prosecution or defense, something may be gained from first hearing his own story, told in his own way. It may need pruning to come within the rules of evidence. Most witnesses are inclined to bring very much hearsay, which is not only a waste of time, but causes them to be tripped and confused during delivery. If a witness is told that such objections will be common, and must be borne with, and should not be a cause of anger or short answers, he will be more patient and reasonable on the stand. The machinery of trials will run with far less friction if witnesses and counsel understand each other in advance. A good trial lawyer will please a court and jury, by even an orderly arrangement of facts and circumstances.

Some witnesses are too low voiced to be heard, and told to speak louder, at trials, will be confused by it, who, if made to understand that their story is to be told in all respects as clearly as they would explain it to a family circle; that to be pert, cranky, or too independent, will lead opposing counsel to greater severity. Human nature is such, that persuasion is most likely to please, and kind answers to beget kindness. It is a mistake to instruct witnesses to be over positive, or attempt to vary from the truth. Truth will tell the same story a thousand times without variations. It is such an armor of strength; it nerves one with such supreme confidence that counsel can safely reassure all his witnesses to a certainty that in telling the clear truth they are never likely to be tangled, or to cross their stories, and become a subject of ridicule.

I can better explain this by an incident: A lady was suspected by a clerk of shop-lifting, and invited into the private office by the merchant, who abruptly explained that she had been caught in the act. Her conscious innocence did not desert her for a single moment, and she asserted it openly and boldly. The merchant insisted on a search being made, and she readily consented, adding, "What have I taken, sir?" "Handkerchiefs," he replied, "there is one in your reticule." This she handed out boldly, and it contained but one handkerchief, which the greedy man held up in gratified delight. "But, you goose, you," said the now indignant woman, "that *has my three initials plainly marked in ink, and was bought here months ago.* The three I bought to-day will be here in a moment, with my change, which I was waiting for, when you invited me here with such impertinence." Just then the cash and parcel boy arrived as she had stated. The woman's look of triumph was a sharp contrast to that of the confused merchant, who had lost a good customer and gained a large lawsuit by his hasty guessing. This illustration shows how strong and brave one always is with right on his side. There is no better witness, no better counsel, than *a just cause*, and the *right side to contend for* before a court and jury.

ORDER IN OFFICE.

Law practice begins in the office, matures in the courts, and ends in disappointment — to one side or the other.

The most expensive offices are rented by New York lawyers, but by far the best libraries and best preserved files are in western cities and large country towns. The recent improvement in office furniture, together with fine ceilings and rich carpets — an innovation of the past twenty years — is a move in the right direction for those who can afford it. They beget a just pride of business surroundings, and a love for the profession.

Order in offices denotes care and attention to details, and neglect is a mark of indifference that leads to forgetfulness. It takes no more time to keep things in right places at all times, than risk the anxiety of hunting them up in seasons of use, when their loss may be most keenly humiliating, if not a positive injury to business. The best merchants keep all goods in order. Trade is increased even by the appearances of a proper location and tasty arrangement. Doubtless, men of slovenly habits may draw around them a certain class of clients, but order and system are never likely to discourage custom. Good practice demands fair surroundings. As men are less embarrassed in clean boots and dressed to suit their calling, so the office of a lawyer need not seem like that of a coal yard. Nothing need be used for appearance, and yet something will be gained by having a pleasant home to work in. Many hours are spent in an office that few could afford to lose out of their lives any portion that could be enjoyed in pleasant quarters.

To live up to one's highest privileges is not only a pleasure, but a duty. To respect and honor one's business, is to dignify and brighten its surroundings. What if it requires a care each year to be neat, orderly, and have pleasant quarters, with some outward signs of prosperity? It was an extreme view, yet half full of truth, that a real estate owner mentioned in connection with his personal experience: "It is not half so much what we have, as what men think we have," was his reason for building a fine brick, and driving to his office in a neat carriage. "If I consulted my income," he said, "I would drive a plainer turnout, and live in a cottage; but, I find it pays better to live in a good house, in order to set other people to buying better homes, and increase the profits of real estate business." A similar statement was made by a leading physician, who struggled for years in semi-poverty, until, by a visit to Chicago, a friend advised him to spruce up, get a first class location on a rich street, and charge accordingly. He tried it, and says, "I can't afford to rent or keep a poor office. It pays twice as well to be located and ready for rich customers." There is no disguising the fact that no one will place a higher estimate on one's services and ability than he is willing to demand. It is better at all times, purely as an investment, to keep an office up to the highest average standard that is known to be in use by the prosperous portion of the profession.

LAWYER'S ADVICE.

To become a rich and influential lawyer, one must guard well his counsel and avoid bad suits. It was an easy matter to nickname Seward "Small potatoes," but Seward had too much sense to be bowed down in practice by such little slanders on his character, and showed clear courage in outgrowing the malice and becoming a master advocate and conscientious counsel. He had the courage to do his duty to all clients, and not risk a wrong verdict even to gratify temporary feelings of triumph. He made it a rule of his practice to win just and lasting victories for his client by honest means. His great forte was candor and sincere attachment to his client's interest. His defense of Freemen against public opinion, and his fidelity to the alleged railroad conspirators, whom he defended during an entire summer, is but a chapter of his history, and displays his ability and determination. Many a man would have wavered and halted in a course so unpopular. The struggles of Seward in early life were the real foundation of his progress in the profession. Similar crosses in life came to Shaffer, to Porter, and Beach, and many more who have served clients through a long life of candor and usefulness, and earned a lasting name in legal history.

It may not bring so large fees for the first few years, but, in the end, honest work, well done, is amply rewarded. The hardships of early life are remembered by thousands as training schools, in the life of many a lawyer. Many a young man now starting in practice, may point to the long list of illustrious advocates who began poor, and grew to eminence on the fair merits of good counsel, accepting small fees up to an age when a demand for their talents and services commanded large salaries in trusted positions.

The care of estates, the loaning of money, and counsel of corporations, with much of the businessman's legal work, falls to conscientious counsel; and when such a reward comes, the fees are larger and labors less irksome, while the employment is constant and highly respected. When such lawyers reach the end of life and stand as leaders in their States, they may well be envied by the rich, and mere money makers, of any station.

In every community there are business men who have longed to be lawyers—longed for the luxury that an advocate enjoys, as he speaks for his neighbors at public gatherings, or settles their disputes with wisdom and honor. Many a man's liberty is secure by the work of his counsel; many a business enterprise stands on the caution of its confidential adviser; many a farm title or costly contract is planned and executed by the silent brain-work of an unknown partner—for the counsel is the partner, in a large sense, of every client whose confidence he possesses. The business of a lawyer, more than that of any person but a doctor, depends on the candor of his dealings, and the soundness of his advice.

TEN TRIAL RULES.

1. Select young jurymen, with warm, intelligent faces; exclude ex-officers of every kind. Become early familiar with the winning facts on both sides. Conceal them, and instruct parties and witnesses to keep silence, and let counsel do the planning of theories.

2. Find what opponents are likely to prove, and how probable will be the showing, and, if false, how it can be denied or met by fair explanation.

3. Nothing takes so well as common sense. Be reasonable. Never weary a court with technicalities, nor a jury with quibbles, nor offend a witness by browbeating, but know what you need to make a case and stop when it is established, so that the jury may see the sharp end of your evidence.

4. Cross-examine only with an object—bring out the point and don't cover it; avoid all abuse of counsel or parties; such quarrels draw attention from the issue, and cause disagreements, while kindness and fair play win a lasting victory.

5. Explain the reason of the law to the jury, or in their hearing. The average mind is wiser than many suppose. But be sure the jury know the *consequences* of the verdict.

6. Counsel, and not clients, should control cases and trials.

7. In opening an argument, select first the points on which there is least dispute, and, if possible, those nearest with your position. Pass to the others with confidence, and carry the jury with you by reason, not by threats, not by bombast. Leave appeals until after

the convincing is accomplished. But feel what you say, and believe what you say, always.

8. Treat a jury with unbounded confidence. Like begets like, under all circumstances. Men are not driven by threats, but pursuaded and convinced by reason and common sense when it is clearly illustrated. Jurymen prefer to do right. Show them the right road in a plain, clear manner.

9. The strongest of reason is: What would you have done under like circumstances? Human nature finds excuses for wrongs that lead to good results and are justifiable. Men generally do on a jury what seems most reasonable, if it is shown to them in a sensible and convincing manner.

10. There is no opportunity better than the earliest. Let the jury know from the beginning that you believe in your rights and will fairly enforce them, while their minds are clear as *white paper.* "Write it on their hearts and engrave it on their bones," that your client has the rights you contend for, and will ask for none other. But insist upon justice. On this, be so full, so determined, so fortified with law and reasonable evidence that it will stand like a mountain, unshaken either by quibbles or appeals.

CHAPTER IV.

HUMAN NATURE.

Human nature is the instinct of reason. It tells what is right, what is wrong, what is probable and what is unreasonable. It is something like intuition and yet separate from all other faculties. Each nature being, in one sense, the likeness of other natures, feels, sees and understands best the parts of life in which it has had experience.

The lady that looked angered at Napoleon, in his attempt to fondle her child, was pleased and quieted by his remark, " I am a father. " Instantly she felt the touch of nature responsive to her own. The advocate who speaks of parting lines, or reefing sails, or knots an hour, port side and fathoms deep, attracts the sailor juryman's notice as readily as the one who speaks of braces, beams, base or moulding to a joiner juryman, while to another, some keen reply in the language of cards, would touch his fancy sooner than either.

Human nature, then, is understood by the reference to the condition of hearers. Men listen to, read about, and seek after things that fill their ideals. The Mexi can is as well pleased with a bull fight, as a New Yorker would be by a change of stock, a Chicagoan at a rise in grain, or a Bostonian with a lecture. The pleasure of a theatre-goer may be distasteful to the deacons on a jury and even a reference to church or religion will often *lead* to a disagreement. In selecting a jury some heed must always be paid to these sympathies, including nationality, for, trifling as it may seem, five Englishmen in America, matched with four Germans and three Irishmen, would hardly be harmonious in a land case. The men to be avoided on juries, are leaders, ex-officials, and unyielding debaters, unless they are debaters for your side. One such is equal to five ordinary men.

Take a political gathering, and how many will govern and control its action? Less than a dozen to a thousand will rule a convention, and, in many cases, one man can manage a multitude. So with juries; they are actuated by motives and go so much by instinct or prejudice and leadership, that it is well to avoid danger in advance by a wise selection of even-tempered gentlemen.

How will you know their prejudices? By comparison. Having excluded enemies and officers (not officers, if for the plaintiff) survey the balance; turn off the hard men, men who have frozen into ruts of reason; exclude low-headed men, they generally get stubborn. Look for the Burnside heads, with veneration, intelligence, and capacity to comprehend matters. Remember men of 30, 40 and up to 50 believe in life, in enjoyment, in fair play, and have a hatred of meanness and mean acts. If your case is desperate, lean on discordant elements to secure a division of opinion. The defense should like a disagreement.

Fair men have warm blood. The milk of human kindness is not crushed out. They can be reasoned with. Old men may be deaf; many are fixed and rigid in their notions, and take prejudices that reason can not conquer. The very best means of selection is a measurement by the eye. I never knew dishonest eyes in an honest head. Honest eyes are wonderfully telling. They are the windows of the features, that light and stamp them indelibly.

Often during a trial some tender touch will bring silent tears to the good men, and aid in a verdict when a stubborn one, in his stead, would have been stolid as iron and unmoved by any touch of nature. Sympathy is to be neither courted nor despised. It is a two-edged sword, and should remain in sheath till drawn by actual use, or in self-defense. To excite sympathy, do it but once. Strike when the iron is hot. Seize some point that has been hinted at from the other side. This is a case: A sister sued for breach of promise. Her main stay through the trial was her brother, who was berated by counsel for " neglecting business and advising his kindred into a muddy law suit."

"Counsel has seen fit," said the other in reply, " to murmur at the attentions of this kind and tender-hearted brother, who neglects business to attend a sister's lawsuit. Muddy law-suit! Muddy, how? By the slimy touch of a coward's perfidy! One who has not stolen in at nightfall, and carried away her jewels and her wardrobe, and her years of loving industry; but one who stole into her affections, and taught her to regard him as her destiny. Then, while in possession of her character, and the jewel of her existence—a heart's first love and confidence—he has thrown in the dust to make her life dismal, and soil the current of her life blood forever. And of whom could the poor girl hope for comfort? To whom could she turn in trouble? To one who had grown with her growth in this big, friendless city? And to him I say, and you say, God bless the young man for his confidence in his sister! God bless them both for their mutual confidence! God bless *any young man for such nobility, who sees the sister's wrong, and yet has the steady courage to stay his hand from personal assault, and help her to seek redress in a lawful manner!* Where should she turn but to him, her only living relative? Could she speak and tell her confidence to her faithful father? No answer could be heard in that far-away home above the stars, and so with mother gone, and father gone, and an only brother as her refuge, counsel must throw that poisoned arrow through the heart of this unfortunate orphan creature, and open anew the wound his client had left unhealed.. O, gentlemen, am I misjudging human nature when I say you will resent that insult with your verdict?"

I could see the jury moulded and united by that sentiment which, more than any one thing, turned the verdict to *heavy damages.*

STATING CASES.

I have never heard a better statement of a claim than in the form of a story. To say at the beginning of your statement, "The story of this case, gentlemen, is romantic," at once fixes attention. Then, without any circumlocution, go forward, keeping dates and events in logical order. "It will appear by the evidence that the plaintiff was formerly an actress of New Orleans, noted for her charms of manner, as well as personal beauty; that she attracted the attention of a wealthy young gentleman, now the defendant. That a day was appointed for their marriage; that a sham form was used by a pretended minister, and she surrendered herself and her life to the husband of her choice, and ever afterwards remained true to her marriage relations. It will appear the priest was only a pretended clergyman, probably an hireling for that purpose; that after the birth of two beautiful children, and the death of defendant's father, and he had become a millionaire, and after this, his young wife turned to a silver-grey-haired mother, and head of his household, he suddenly decided to seek another and a younger love, and actually brought to his home such a creature, whose presence was mildew and poison to their home and happiness; and, when she could endure it no longer, defendant seeks to cast her off, and treat the marriage as spurious from the fact of his own perfidy. Believing in the validity of such marriages under our statute, and believing that the wife and mother is entitled, at *least*, to the poor pittance of her share in the husband's property, and to a declaration that shall vindicate the character of her children, we have brought her action in this manner for damages. The case needs no comment. It appeals to the sense and reason of mankind to grant the wife and mother her demand in the declaration, which we believe you will do on a full hearing of the circumstances. If it shall be attempted, as letters threatening as much would indicate, to malign the character of plaintiff, to further add infamy to injury, then we shall be ready to set up the real facts in that matter, and show how the husband, by connivance, sought to get room for a divorce by acts of collusion with designing men, versed in the handicraft of flattery and soft promises, but this will, we think, but intensify the wickedness of the defendant, if attempted. We are here on the merits, and ready for a hearing of the whole matter."

Follow such a statement at once by one of the truest and best-tempered witnesses, and show, by clear courage, step by step, in the order of the evidence, how all matters happened, in the clearest possible form, clearness being itself eloquent in such matters.

If the statement is attractive, you rivet the attention of the jury. If borne out by the evidence, you weld it, step by step, and, after a few hours' work, you have converted the minds of the jury to your theory, for they had rather believe that such a person had such a reward in law, than dream of a theory of a wrong side triumphant.

The evidence being in, rest promptly, and guard your client's rights from the other side. Should a half-dozen villains dare to swear to mean and unreasonable stories about the plaintiff, pass them with just enough cross-examination for impeachment—they generally impeach themselves by bad characters and evil faces—and do not depend too much on destroying such testimony. It is worthless, generally.

ARGUMENT TO THE JURY.

The argument should begin by treating of the points least disputed. Brush away a few unreasonable things; correct a few mistakes; pass a few bad witnesses, and say: This, then, is the real controversy, whether such a marriage is a marriage, and whether such a wife is a legal one, and, if deceived, what she deserves in damages. Argue fully, review fully and tersely, briefly (Burr's best rule was thirty minutes), and clinch the whole with: What would *you* expect for a sister, or a daughter, in such cases? Then, in the intensity of personal belief, be in deep earnest, and demand a verdict, using eloquence enough to impress the importance and value on the hearts of a jury, in words that the Chinese Emperor used to Governor Seward, " Write it on their hearts and engrave it on their bones," that your client deserves a liberal verdict.

MANAGING CASES.

Counsel seldom blunder on making their cases out of court. The story sounds so plausible, told by one without oath that it sounds like the only theory that could be imagined or established. Soon enough he will find his mistake in the trial; much will fall off by a timid delivery; much will be forgotten under oath, and on hearing a few witnesses sharply questioned, others grow cautious and conceal what may possibly lead them to contradict others, and that they fear may bear on their credibility.

There is no need of the slightest apprehension to a truthful witness. Truth told on the hill tops of all the different countries on earth, if *truth*, is identical everywhere. The witness should know this. It is a counsel's duty to tell his witnesses that *truth* is always alike, always safe, always powerful.

But the best witness may not always be situated so as to give the right fact in the right way.

A case happened in A. like this: In the absence of a gentleman at Saratoga in July, a telegram came to his secretary to pay a certain bill, not exceding a sum named. The next day a young man called and presented such a bill, and received a check for it, and departed. Soon after the gentleman returned, and denied both bill and dispatch, and caused the arrest of one positively identified by two persons as the person who collected the money on a check to bearer. The bank was unable to aid in identification, which turned on the secretary and book-keeper. The latter was careless in answers, and left a decided doubt, from inattention to details. He merely remembered of a spruce young man, very polite, calling and getting a check, after a telegram in their letter-box, and was not certain enough to secure conviction. The secretary began by quite a show of certainty. He had known the prisoner eight years before, and was reasonable, candid in description, etc., seeming to make a case without question.

"You were a busy man in the office?" began the cross-examiner. "Yes."

"And shaded your windows at that hour of the day?" "Yes."

"And often burned gas in dark days of the year?" "Yes."

"And took no special notice of defendant that morning?" "No, sir."

"And could not quite be certain about this particular person getting that check, as you would be if you had made it to your own employer?" "Oh, of course not."

"The matter passed off and no questions were asked?" "None whatever."

"No parley?" "No, sir."

"Your bills are paid promptly?" "Yes, sir."

"This was no exception?" "No, sir."

"In your busy, methodical way, you don't stop and question people who bring receipted bills for payment?" "No, sir."

"That is your reason for not being quite as sure about the transaction?" "Exactly."

"Then you would be more certain if your father, brother or employer had called?" "Yes, sir, I think I would."

"So on your oath now you state it as a belief and not so much an absolute identification, beyond all possibility of a doubt?" "I think so, yes sir."

"You are not willing to swear to a positive certainty that you could not be mistaken?" "No, sir; I may have been, but don't think I was."

"Do you swear you might have been?" "Yes; possibly."

This is the stopping-place ordinarially (but beware, he may know it and brace up), so go on. "I think you did not even stop to call the young man by name, did you?" "No."

"Nor notice specially more than generally a man resembling defendant?" "I turned half round and glanced at him and went on and wrote the check."

"To bearer?" "Yes."

"And he left?" "Yes sir."

This dulls the edge and helps in the argument, which is, of course, that it is not who may have called with the check and perpetrated the swindle, but *who did* call beyond all reasonable doubt. The reasonable doubt is here made by the people's witness, who has been coaxed by a series of easily-answered questions, to answer and tell the real truth and probably no more.

CHAPTER V.

CHIEF JUSTICE WAITE AND HIS CLIENTS.

Chief Justice Waite was once a country lawyer, with a small practice, but a resolute will to do justice to his clients. He lived in Maumee, Ohio, and first collected accounts and bills for New York, Boston, and Cincinnati merchants. It was a time of long credit, and exchanges of produce for goods was the country merchants' chief means of payment.

They required time to turn themselves, and young Waite accepted their installments and gave them their extensions. It came to be known that if any one could collect a debt Waite could do it. This was his Eastern reputation, but his character at home was still stronger. His word was a bond of indemnity that needed no surety. His promises were rigidly kept and he firmly insisted on like treatment from others.

Gradually he became active in Justice practice, then in Circuit Court cases; then a strong counselor to firms of importance. His manner of treating clients was admirable. When one called with a case, and stated the circumstances, he would urge him to repeat the points on the other side, and what they claimed to be just in the matter. Then, before advising suit or defense, he insisted, as a deciding point, that he must know the case as it really was, and not as the client wanted it to be.

Seeing themselves practically placed in a lawsuit before Judge Waite—for he first made himself judge of office cases—they confided their facts and relied upon his judgment, which went throughout Ohio, and later, won him national fame in his excellent work in the Geneva award case, over the water. It was there his lucid argument was much admired for its mastery of details and the ingenious propositions sustained. He is said to have made the most eloquent address of any lawyer on that contest of two nations. His appointment as Judge was a reward for that high service and his strong qualities of common sense.

Such is the career of a lawyer whose conduct is a lasting law lecture on method of dealing with clients. In point of success there is but one higher rank than Chief Justice of the Supreme Court of our Union, and that rank is *true manhood* to fill it honorably, and the good name and loving favor of his friends and neighbors. His character for honesty at home and uprightness in practice gave to M. R. Waite the name of *deserving the place he fills* with such honor and credit. This is more valuable than to lead the highest court in America, in which he is first in questions of trial practice.

He began poor, but soon became proverbially reliable in this way: he became, first, efficient; second, considerate, and always reliable. He had a fine family residence in Toledo before his appointment, and lived very nearly upon his income. Having early secured a paid-up insurance of $20,000, he expressed his confidence in the future of his family, and said his life should be devoted to his profession, without regard to money-making beyond his expenses. But he took great pride in all upright and successful practice. When appointed by President Grant to the Supreme Bench he had already made a bright record in jury cases.

He is both a just Judge and a great advocate. The real lesson in the life of Chief Justice Waite is his rectitude in little things. He never wanted trial practice on the wrong side of litigation. He was willing to begin low, by collecting commercial claims, but even in this he was just and reasonable. Many a merchant was tided over a dark pay-day by his kindness, and all these acts of justice will be so many marks of greatness,—for it is always true in law that the *good*, alone, are great.

SEPARATING WITNESSES.

The following incident, abbreviated from the Apocrypha of the Bible, is of great benefit to many in practice. It should be read in full, but this summary will explain the salient features with clearness and interest: Joachim was a rich man of Babylon; Susanna, his wife, had two children—was good and very beautiful. They had all that heart could wish. In their garden was a rare park, and through it ran pure water.

This garden was the place of holding court in Babylon. The elders then were judges. There were two priests—a large and small one. Both admired Susanna, and loved her. At noon-day she often bathed in the garden stream, and one day, after sending her maids for towels and wash-balls, she was left alone by the water, when the two priests saw her alone, they sprang from a thicket, and one seized her by the shoulder, and turning, he saw the other in confusion.

Both remained. "Consent to us," said the larger, and she consented *not!* They threatened to report that they found her with a young man, and such an offense would mean death to her. Susanna cried out aloud, "O, what a strait am I in! If I consent not, I die! If I consent, I sin against God! *I will not consent!*" And she burst the fence doors and flew away, and they cried out against her. And the people called for a trial.

She came to the court-yard attended by her father, mother and kindred. She was delicate, and very beautiful, and she was deeply veiled. The priest said, "Remove the veil," and seeing her beauty the people wept. She looked up to heaven, and trusted the Lord.

They told their story of finding her at high twelve with the young man, who embraced her; that they seized her, and he sprang away. The people believed it, for elders were judges; and they condemned her to death. Then she cried with a loud voice: "Lord, Thou knowest it is all false! Deliver me from mine enemies." But they proceeded to the place of execution.

Then Daniel, a young lawyer, said: "What fools, to condemn on such evidence! Come back, and try the case legally." They went back, and Daniel said, "Separate the witnesses." Then the priests testified one at a time. The big elder was sworn first, and, when leaving the stand, Daniel said: "Under which tree in the garden did it happen?"

"Under the holm tree."

"Stand aside," said Daniel, and called the little elder, who told the same story through, and was about leaving, when Daniel said: "Stay! Under which tree did you see them together?" He hesitated, and said: "Under the palm tree" (in an opposite side of the garden).

"Thou hast also lied," said Daniel. And the people arose and put both priests to death, they having convicted themselves of conspiring to kill an innocent woman. Then Daniel became a great advocate (with a splendid practice) in Babylon. Susanna was all the more respected as a virtuous and upright woman—even one who could resist temptation from her priest.

This incident is doubtless Shakespeare's foundation for "A Daniel come to judgment," in the "Merchant of Venice." It forcibly illustrates the power and use of separating witnesses on a trial, better than a dozen pages could define. It applies more to criminal than civil cases, but in all assaults and general accident cases, should be used and remembered.

TACT AND SKILL.

All that can be read in text-books will fail to describe very many little things that happen in a court trial. Books never foretell of ill-temper, blunders, and halting witnesses. The best that can be learned of the ablest-tried cases will leave an unwritten history in every lawsuit, where some little thing, happily used, has, or may have, turned the verdict.

Tact in management will foresee evil, and avoid it. Watch with alertness for a lucky turn, and use it to the right advantage. Most people learn soon enough afterwards what would have benefited their case, if aptly applied in season. Skill has more to do with arrangement and order of happy things, and keeping them in form to use with a jury in argument, but the lack of experience and careful study will allow many a point in practice to slip by unnoticed that the artful would apply to advantage. This little difference in skill is what people pay for. Little dark places cleared up, little impressive acts or words of witnesses noted, little circumstances or sayings that stand out from the rest with emphasis, need grouping like a coiled cable, and italicising with force by skillful usage, that trained thinking and long practice gives to the diligent. Genius may reach all at a single bound, but most lawyers learn, in good season, that genius at the bar is found to be like a keen razor, of excellent material and superior finish. Genius, in anything, is generally crude, and gains by experiment. The greatest genius may have poor application, and turn out badly. There are more studious plodders on the bench and in the upper story of law than men of original brilliancy.

The nature of law labor is such that skill, learning, and tact are all qualities requiring study. It is not the study of books alone. How few, indeed, could be read in a life-time. It is the study of men, of things, scenes, effects, causes, and results, that grow and follow naturally from consequences. A lawyer, of all men, must think, and think constantly, through every stage of his case, and train his mind for adverse turns of evidence.

ADROITNESS AND ACUMEN.

Some time in the course of every trial will come the fine turn of the scale-balance, where a little thing said or unsaid may unite or divide a jury. I never had much confidence in tricks and arts deceptive, but there are turning points, like guide-boards, that mark the progress made, and show the true direction. A man that saves his points is like one who saves his grain for use in winter, rests his team at a hill-top, or feeds them for strength in their journey. Many lawyers explode their wit too soon, and, like hunters firing at random, scare away their game. It may be wit, it may be eloquence, possibly, in the examination of witnesses, but it will be somewhere that the ripe fruit will show between the leaves, and can be saved for a client if picked in season.

Just what to do and when to do it, is something that a *sixth* sense must teach a counsel. It comes to the lawyer through practice, but practice must be polished to discern it. The sense of fine work in lawsuits is a cultivated gift that increases with use like the skilled surgeon, the trained musician, or the accomplished scholar.

URBANE DEPORTMENT.

The long-used habit of polished language and chaste expression, with grace of gesture, ease, and deference of manner to superiors, and general courtesy to all, is a branch of legal training that belongs to the law, but only a few lawyers ever attain it. Manners are not well-taught in books; they are learned by experience and observation. It is that mysterious something which denotes gentleness combined with strength. It need not be feminine or weak, nor too soft, nor very yielding. This is quite the other extreme. The force of a blow is not increased by a rough-edged blade. The voice of a speaker may be penetrating and forcible without wounds or injuries.

All that we admire of speaking, singing, or acting, is grace, force, tone, and naturalness. The mirror, held to nature, need not reveal a giant in muscle to show a rare musician or a Grecian athlete for an eloquent orator. Small instruments make sweet music.

Demosthenes, the father of oratory, was a striking example of one lacking in form, but equipped in style and finish. His brilliant successor, Cicero, was more graceful and accomplished, but only after years of training and the daily study of words, arts, and subjects beyond the rules of other orators. Cicero and his successor, Erskine, attained greatness by the polish of their genius, the subtlety of their sayings that pierced to the hearts of their greedy hearers like the words of Mark Antony over Ceasar's body; a speech fit for a model of all times for its caustic urbanity, cogent in reasoning, powerful in argument, eloquent in pathos, deep in logic, powerfully convincing and couched in language even unoffensive to those it would annihilate. Urbanity rules the tongue, and tempers the hands and actions of a speaker. The man that rules his temper, and controls his manner, has a better prospect for long life and peaceful prosperity, than one whose selfishness leads to constant friction. But few lawyers ever acquire a razor blade polish in court room deportment.

Sooner or later the majority of men, tried by contests of an exasperating nature, yield in debate to trials of sarcasm or side remarks, which are trifling in themselves, yet telling on their constitution, and creating enemies. It was the bitterness of Blaine, that overcome him with enemies. It was the urbanity of Garfield, that made him a leader; the imperial bearing of Conkling, that let his enemies walk over him in victory; and this is a lesson to all advocates. To reach a happy medium that will neither excite bitterness, nor show weakness, force with gentleness, power without arrogance, intensity without irony, and finish without affectation, strength, symmetry and beauty, either of which omitted will render the other less effective.

STARTING IN LAW.

Training, courage, patience and aptness for the business are the essential elements of success in law practice. If one has not discernment enough to know how well he can fill these requirements it is better to wait awhile, or learn from another what is lacking.

With a thorough training, courage should follow easily, for no one is strong without knowing it, and

(4)

strength comes of confidence in ability to do what we undertake. Then with energy and work well done, new cases will follow, and business will grow like a tree, with new branches from every limb. If one is willing to wait the growth of an orchard, the development of an enterprise, or any ordinary matter that requires time, he should be willing to take law business as it comes — thankfully. Actors are all willing to play subordinate parts many years in starting till suddenly called in to replace their seniors, when they often display their earliest talents by accident.

Lawyers are watched in court trials very much like actors in a play, and, indeed, many are superior to actors, and the real tragedies shown to juries are superior to the imitations of the mimic stage. A few well cut knots of controversy, a few well turned periods of argument, a clear insight into the puzzling problems, will soon place a lawyer in his proper rank before any community. Learning, language, manner, familiarity with facts, and ingenuous handling of half-a-dozen witnesses will do the work. The best talent of a lawyer is common sense—a basis to which all cases finally must come before the last court leaves them. What is good sense is always good law, and counsel who act and advise on this principle must succeed in keeping their clients out of petty litigation, which is invaluable.

The next best gift is foresight — the gift of telling how reasonable men will judge of a contract or controversy— the ability to frame a correct theory of a defense or prosecution. Without this intuitive knowledge, few can reach the right beginning in practice.

It is born with a lawyer. If not, he was born for another calling.

The third gift is clearness. Things that come clearly to a teacher can be as clearly explained, but we never know well what we cannot tell to others. The very fact that it is not clear to the speaker, renders the listener all the more muddled. Some are so gifted in clearness that they send, as it were, a ray of electric light through their trials, and satisfy court, jury and client of the certainty of their positions. Memory goes to make up clearness. So many details are to be kept track of that memory is a rich gift in trials, and one that cannot be over cultivated. It grows by use, and strengthens by practice. With all eyes on the actor, his lines are important. Neither wit, grace nor appearance can replace matter and memory of the points in contest. As the actor wins a recall, so must the lawyer by influence on all in hearing. His form, manner, voice, matter and ingenuity, each form a part, and aid in victory.

AN INSTANCE.

In a Kentucky murder case great excitement prevailed, and hundreds of armed men thronged around the counsel. Judge Curtis defended ; he felt the sentiment of conviction in the air. The danger of lynching was not trifling. With subdued tones and careful diction, he opened in an eloquent tribute to the character of women, for charity, long suffering and love of mercy. Tears fell freely, for on that ground no one disputed the speaker. The court was hushed and silent, till snow flakes could be almost heard to fall. The crowded house grew to a house of admirers of the modest beauty of statement, as well as of the doctrine taught. All eyes met the speaker. He stood in the crowded court room like an athlete in an amphitheater. His danger increased when the second passage was reached, where his client had been berated for acts of conduct in his early love, and a fair chance come for a strong turn on his adversary. The speaker wisely foresaw two answers, the bitter and the sweet; he chose the latter; he regretted that his noble brother should so far forget his high calling as to make sport of the early affections of his client. True, he stood solitary and alone, a childless man, and when he died it would be the last of his line. True, he had years before met and won a fair Kentucky lady, and but for her parents' wishes, they would have been united, and great God, said the speaker, can it be that to please a miscellaneous audience, this holiest of earthly affections is to be held up to scorn and ridicule. In a State of chivalry and bravery like Kentucky, can it enter into the heart of a man humane, to trifle with the most sacred affections of man or woman.

The ice melted, the audience were his. The influence of courtesy and nature was sublime. The defendant's life saved by it. This silent influence that brings out a recall, a half cheer, a sentiment of belief in the audience is, after all, the art of oratory. It conciliates, captures, convinces, wins and controls the judgment of a jury. It is superior to questioning and brow-beating bad witnesses, and, coming from one of known integrity and sincerity, it weighs with a court and a

AN INSTANCE.

court room. For the court is one of an audience, and wishes to do about the fairest thing after all that the case admits of. He may pound with his gavel at the crowd's applause, but his heart applauds with the rest. The responses of heart to heart are the same with judges as with auditors. Strong argument, earnest and eloquent words, are never lost in the hearing of reasonable men. It may not always secure an acquittal, and may lead to a disagreement or sympathy enough for a lighter sentence. A man whom the people love and respect is not likely to have a long punishment inflicted as one with few friends and a weak advocate.

CHAPTER VI.

WINNING HARD CASES.

Man never met a more difficult case to contend with than the Buford-Elliott defense in Owenton, Ky. in 1879. The life of Col. Buford is strangely romantic. His family, habits and home troubles all form a background of the fearful deed he accomplished, and yet he is free and clear to-day as any Kentuckian. Skill and will of counsel cleared him. His deliverance came from absolute determination of counsel. Other men have been saved from the gallows by fortuitous circumstances, but Buford's case was marvelous. Time without limit was spent in preparing for trial and shaping public sentiment, or rather dulling the first intense bitterness to the accused.

Knowledge was used in the smallest detail, and no stone left unturned on the insanity defense which finally resulted in Buford's release. It would be impossible to detail each step, but think of ninety days in preparation?

Underwood, in Michigan, actually killed Charlotte Pridgeon, and within a year crossed to England, having first been acquitted of murder by reason of insanity, and later released as not liable to be so held in bondage when no jury had been sworn to convict on such a charge. Underwood was English, and had an English jury.

Tremain cleared Stokes by an over-mastering speech and a determined effort to bias the jury, which worked on the theory that the slain was a dangerous man to inhabit the earth. In fact, the victim was on trial more than the accused. The amount of work in trial after trial is wonderful to display on a single charge. Ingenuity of counsel cleared Gov. Scott, and appeals to what the jury would have done placed where Sickles and McFarland were, cleared both prisoners. The single period of James T. Brady in defense of Sickles was enough to melt the hearts of a dozen juries. The masterly appeal and able argument of Graham in McFarland case, is admitted to have saved his client. In it are four great speeches, condensed in a single effort, which clearly shows the value of accumulated arguments. In the Sullivan-Hanniford case, at Chicago, defense relied upon an attempt to strike Mrs. Sullivan by deceased, and so skillfully was it placed before the jury, that not guilty was the verdict.

In the trial of Garfield's assassin, excellent ability was displayed for the people. When Judge Porter, in an ingenious cross-fire with the prisoner, belittled himself that he might show off the sagacity of the accused, who thought more of his passages at arms with counsel, than saving his life by a little more foolishness and less ability. A rare point, too, was turned by Judge Porter in overcoming the inborn prejudices of several jurors who cared very little more for Garfield than other citizens, and objected to capital punishment.

To this, counsel closely addressed the argument that while chivalrous men like Booth, might in a moment of some curious freak, kill a human being, still, Booth was not like the creature before them, who was held up in all his littleness, meanness, wickedness and utter lack of manhood; all the names and things that could cover a creature with infamy were used with wisdom, and when finally every juryman had learned to hate the crime and criminal, Porter rested and won.

These are large cases, took high priced talent, and resulted generally as they should.

The defense of Beecher was about as ably made as that of either instance mentioned. The cool and considerate effort and excellent temper of Mr. Evarts, the artful array of circumstances, were often conclusive with the jury, while the great heart of Mr. Beecher made him too noble in the eyes of the jury to brand with crime, and he was practically acquitted.

FORCE AND MODULATION.

A low tone in statement, a low tone in asking a verdict, a medium tone in explaining away objections to your theory, brings a strong and forcible vindication of your side. Reserve force is best shown by cool determination. Men of iron never need to bluster; they assert their views and execute them. Grant, Napoleon, and Wellington, were of this class. It is evidence of weakness to express all of one's feelings at once in an argument. It is often said of a great speaker: He begins very low. This shows his desire to gain close attention. Again, he talked like a whirlwind at such a point, and when he closed you could hear a feather fall, he was so intensely interesting. I have even known of speakers that seemed to chain the audience to their seats for several seconds after they were at liberty to separate. The spell-bound speeches are always best in law suits. When one can reason in whispers and be heard, he and his hearers are not far apart. It is a magnetic method, and raises no resentment. It is the height of eloquence so to use it in moderation and reserve.

At a murder trial, in southern Indiana, an eloquent counsel had left a jury in tears — in fact, all in the court room were moved by his touching appeal, and when his opponent arose and began a reply, his emotion was shown so distinctly in tone and manner, that every one seemed to believe in the prisoner's acquittal. But the sublime moment had not come, and counsel was only building a bridge on which he could carry over the jury to the other side. He knew, as salesmen know, that it is unwise to be too hasty in persuading customers to take their wares. He knew that he must first show his opinions were not so far from theirs. He knew that human nature was aroused, and he must go with it to a reasonable turning point. From low tones of kindness and sympathy, he gradually turned to questions of duty, and the reason of trials like the one they were engaged in hearing, and about to determine. Of its effect upon the community, and upon their own rights as citizens. In a few moments he had taken them home, and showed them the value of personal security—of the necessity for the law's protection. Then he suddenly drew a picture of the danger if laws were violated, and tears should be allowed to screen the guilt of the offenders. Then with touching words, he regretted his duty and theirs to lead one possibly, who himself had in moments of anger brought sorrow and disgrace upon those who must now bear the natural consequences; and in such a strain ended his excellent argument, winning a case for the people by force and moderation, that he could easily have lost by over zeal in his closing address to a jury already predisposed to acquit the defendant.

RESERVE FORCE.

In a discussion before a court of judges it is a good plan to start with a striking and important case, one on which there can be no question or dispute, and as the argument advances other less positive cases may be examined for and against your position. This brings attention to a merit on your side, and compels attention, while a few weak cases may prejudice the court, and lead to a bias too early in the discussion. In the end and beginning of every law argument, one or more good cases should be cited. Trifles turn a case in such matters, and the last words said may be impressive. There need be no fawning or cringing, and yet great respect to court's discussions. Let it be known and follow the rule, that one evil ruling will reach the court of last resort before you surrender.

Right here, let me say, that every lawyer is in duty bound to follow the side he honestly believes to be right through the highest court for settlement, not for spite, but for victory, and respect of courts themselves.

Counsel who insist on their rights generally secure them. It need not be done in the spirit of vengeance or malice, but should be a rule of practice to win every case that has a winning side to it. To do this, the first step is, *caution in taking cases;* the next thing is to see that the witnesses are such as *you* believe and can depend upon, and men or women who will tell the whole truth, and having told it, stick to it. Then, in the very best of temper, with a handy brief, in which not only cases are cited, but the nature of the case and the principle decided. Attend to each point as it goes in evidence, for the impression made as witnesses testify is even more lasting than argument. It is a first impression, and one that juries are inclined to remember. Think of a half-dozen supervisors, read and intelligent at the age of sixty, all having an abiding belief, and asked to change it! This is a great expectation. Men of fixed opinions change them reluctantly. It is very much better if they have not said "no" mentally to your position before they listen to an argument. If you have been keen enough to hide your best points and reserve them for argument, so much the better for your success.

There is a kind of fascination in a well planned trial that leads to constant discovery of new truth, as if it came out unawares. An art that conceals the art of trying to, and yet reveals the plainest truth.

Take a bad witness half way to his seat; recall this way: "One moment; what was the condition of the four when you first went in? or, what was the condition of the room as to being shaded with blinds?" "Shady." "That darkened it a little?" "Yes." "Not so light as the court room now?" "No, sir." "You could not tell quite as certainly who called, as if one had called whom you had long known?" "No, sir." "That leaves it just a little uncertain, that is, you are now not swearing to a positive certainty?" "No, sir." "*Then you* admit candidly that there may *possibly* be a mistake about this being the real person whom you believed to have called with the check?" "I think he was the one." "Yes, I know, still you swear that you may have been mistaken?" "Yes, sir." This is the finest of work. The reserve force, the unconscious work, the foundation for an argument that *if* a witness may have been mistaken, then the jury can't take the risk of *mistakes*.

LAWYERS NOT ON TRIAL.

It is a mistake to abuse a brother lawyer in trials. He may have his client's story, and believes it. He may have the close of the case, and turn a bad point on you when you are powerless to answer. He may represent the people and have great discretion in right to *nolle pros*. He may have personal friends on the jury who but for the attack, would be with your side, and now will stand out and disagree, causing great expense and annoyance, and, in any event, *he is not on trial*, and abuse will not win your victory. You believe in your theory; he, in his, and each has a right to his own opinion. In fact, he is hired to enforce it by all laudable means at command, therefore it is more pleasing to a jury to do as Judge Perrin always advised: treat opposing statements as possible mistakes, and seek to show which side is mistaken. Juries had much rather hear this argument than a personal wrangle and a bitter controversy.

CHAPTER VII.

ABOUT TRIALS.

DIRECT EXAMINATION.

State to the jury what occurred, is the clearest possible direction to testify. State what next occurred; what was said, if anything, or what was done by the parties. Go on, and tell the jury in your own words what happened in your presence.

This is the natural road to truthfulness. The truth is stronger, when most direct. Keep to the line, as hewers say—never mind the chips. Look well to the timber you are making. Unless the several timbers, bricks and stones of a building are well made separately, they match badly. Every witness is a timber to be used in building your case. The case itself is its own foundation. What you do is to build it out of materials that join and become symmetrical. As a builder discards bad timber, so should a lawyer keep away all bad witnesses. They color a case dreadfully. Three or four good witnesses are often better than a half a score of indifferent ones. Never put on a man (if you can avoid it) whose face will carry discredit to a jury-box. Select and arrange proof to be interesting. If a few fine looking witnesses are seen to support one side, and double their number the other, it has an influence in forming opinions. Really, cases are won as you go along, and not by the arguments. The jury hardly wait to hear the facts rehearsed. They take stock in a case as it goes along. It is not in numbers, but quality and candor that tells the story. One truthful man may be believed against many. Order your forces well, always with a view to clearness.

CRIMINAL PROSECUTIONS.

To convict one of crime, it must be shown clearly (1) that a crime has been committed, (2) that defendant could have done the deed, (3) that he had a motive. Crime—opportunity—motive. Human belief is such that some crimes are too shocking to be credible. This must be remembered, but with it bear the fact that Prof. Webster, of Boston, could and did commit a most dreadful murder. That kings and queens have committed cruel crimes, that seem most unreasonable. Seek first the means of killing or robbing, as the case may be. Analyze the deed fully. Study the possible motive and opportunity. One to two witnesses on any point is sufficient, but beware of over numbers from the defense.

A single witness to an important conspiracy case was positive that he overheard a man tell his wife, after retiring for the night, what he accomplished, and how far certain steps have been taken, and proceeded to state facts, apparently, in their natural order to compel belief in his story. He was cross-examined with skill and caution by Wm. H. Seward, and grew rather hurried and impatient. Later in the case this link was completely broken by the fact that the wife was not at home, but a hundred miles away at that season, while the husband and wife slept in the chamber, and the supposed bed-room was a meal-room, full of barrels and boxes, but totally void of bed or bedding. As a chain is no stronger than its weakest link, this defendant was acquitted.

Another rule is, never to rest a conviction on the unsupported evidence of a bad witness, or an accomplice. Some one is sure to learn his weakness, and make the most of it. The conviction of criminals should at least be honest and fairly sustained by evidences. In the words of Senator Jacob M. Howard, "it is enough for counsel to deprive one of property, or rob him of his character in a contest for his client, but when it comes to the point of taking away his liberty for a number of years — which is in effect his life — and deprive his kindred of his protection, and brand them with the stigma of a felon's name, it is far more creditable and honorable to lose a case, and go to one's judgment hereafter without the tarnish of human blood upon his garments, for committing a higher crime than the accused was charged with."

I conclude this theme by the single remark, that an industrious investigation of causes, and a faithful story of the crime, is enough, and the whole duty of the prosecution. Things that may be urged, and arts that should be employed to defend a criminal, would be often cruel to apply in a doubtful conviction.

In the famous Stevens Poisoning Case in New York, near 1856, Chauncey Shaffer, for the prosecution, was forced to analyze the earth around the coffin, the metal nails in the coffin, the shroud and the body, nearly a year after interment, and actually found arsenic enough to poison three men, in the stomach of the victim — the wife of the defendant — to convince the jury of his guilt. This was one of those cases of mysterious death from short sickness, and on the surface no motive of guilt to confirm suspicions.

In a similar northern Michigan case, the deceased was a consumptive, whose wife had received attentions from a neighbor before her husband's case was given up as hopeless. A neighbor noticed a small paper of poison on the mantle, and wondered why it was left carelessly in reach, when soon after she saw it was missing, and remarked about it. A little later in the day, the wife said, "Why, you were mistaken, here is the rat poison, right here before your eyes, on the mantle." (Lately placed there.) The circumstances, placed with the recent death of the husband, led to investigation, conviction and life sentence for murder. It need not be urged that circumstances are swift witnesses, but they require minuteness in detail to place them in an unbroken chain of evidence. A missing link destroys their potency.

CRIMINAL DEFENSES.

Crimes are usually surrounded by mysterious circumstances. These must be well learned by defendant's attorney. To learn them *go at once, and measure every spot with the eye, and take in the situation.* This will be convenient in drawing out evidence, and may lead to an acquittal. Take an instance: Two men quarrel; they threaten each other; they separate. After many days they meet, fire shots, and one is killed. A witness says he saw the killing. This with the avowed malice is a strong case, and requires an ingenuous defense. Counsel visits the ground, sees the unevenness; finds that to witness the shooting, one must be in the right position. He gathers from one who came early to the scene what words were said, and how each acted—slayer and slain. This is very important. It may reveal revenge, and may show self-defense.

Trial is called. The accused is young, a blonde, full of warm impulses. The first care is that he shall be truthful, and surrounded with as much influence for good as possible. If his character is shady, let it alone. If good, enlarge upon it, and show by ten or more that it is *good*. The presence of six good citizens, flanked by friends and relatives, is a strong force at such a critical period. The jury will assume that every witness for the defense wants an acquittal. They are right. Juries read best between the lines. They calculate on public sentiment. In all trials the public view is often the hasty one. They are shocked by the crime, and have not weighed the circumstances. This, of course, is not a crime for money. That must appear early; the jury should be selected from men as near the age of accused as possible, and something near his nature and nationality, if convenient.

Now comes the order of trial. In this case, beware, and say nothing. After the people state and begin to prove their case, draw by one or two questions a slight discrepancy or difference of location, but do not dwell upon it. Do it in kind tones, and pass gently to the witness who saw the transaction. Note where he stood. How well he could see and hear. Make him admit some little confusion; some excitement, and some distance; then a lack of a cool, careful notice of *all* that happened. See that he did not notice particularly whether deceased was angry, touched his pocket; threatened or attempted violence first. If he did not know what led to it, so much the better. Very likely he did not. If he did know it, learn through one whom you should set to find out, the worst he is to say, and be ready, and see that *you do not make* the missing link of the people's case by over cross-examination.

In the case I have in mind, a third party witnessed the death, and measured the ground, and was an excellent support of defendant's theory. We will call his name Chapin. "Mr. Chapin, you are a farmer?" "Yes, for thirty years." "And saw the parties to the Christler affray?" (don't call it murder). "Yes, I come up just as the young man was dying." (All lean forward intently. This is a supreme moment, and you know what is coming, but need not appear to). "What was said, if anything, by either of the parties?" "I would not like to repeat it. It was very wicked." "Repeat it," says the court. "I was about to offer him the consolations of religion, when he turned from me with scorn. I told him he would soon go before his God to be judged, and wished to pray for him. To my astonishment he turned, and with terrible and shocking oaths he cursed me and the defendant together." "And you left him?" "Yes, sir." "That is all."

An excellent way — just as witness was leaving the stand — as if by chance, this question was put: "Did you observe the ground and the location where Mr. Christler speaks of seeing the shooting?" "Yes, I own the land, and know all about it." "And what have you to say of how well he could see from that location?" "Why, it is impossible; unless he could stand up in a wagon, or look through the hill, for I tried it myself, with my hired man standing in the same position. I couldn't believe when I heard the story in the Justice Court." This, with the hired man's story, left the jury a right to believe that deceased came to his death from a natural quarrel, cause unknown, except as detailed by defendant, which was that deceased had first threatened, and placed his hand to his hip pocket, in a threatening attitude. Counsel for defense, with wise discretion, rested, and the jury acquitted his client, on a *reasonable doubt* theory, well placed with the wicked words, hip pocket, and larger size of deceased over defendant.

TEN TURNING POINTS.

1. When a counsel gives away three little points of no value, and thereby gains the court's good will, the jury's confidence, and his client's verdict.

2. When a counsel forgets he is (or should be) a gentleman, and prefers to lose a friend to perpetrate a joke, and lose a client's case by his silliness.

3. When a counsel remembers gray hairs, timid children, or women unaccustomed to court houses, and treats them with clear kindness in place of abuse,

which is the weapon of a bully, and always is offensive to decency.

4. When a counsel excludes two ex-policemen, one deputy sheriff, and a justice from a jury in a criminal case, if he is for defendant, and retains them for plaintiff.

5. When a jury both laughs and cries with counsel, so heartily that there is no mistake of their united sympathies, they are his, unless a stronger touch of nature removes the impression, for few can be laughed at and recover handsomely.

6. When an advocate is tripped in a strange court by an overbearing opponent, and returns the compliment in a handsome chastisement, that is known to be just and deservedly delivered.

7. When a story, apt and conclusive, destroys the theory or reason of an opponent by a plain point that no one can cover, or put down with argument, it is effective, for a picture is an argument, and a story is an unpainted portrait.

8. When the people's witnesses make the juries *doubt*, and the evidence points equally to guilt or innocence, with a just judge gently leaning towards mercy.

9. When the looks, acts, friends, surroundings of a prisoner point to a life of past rectitude, and a heart not steeped in crime, and his story was given with confidence, and vividly put to the jury, with a character for integrity, and he shown to be in honest employment.

10. When counsel spends more time in trying sparring and technicalities, or in trying lawyers than in reaching the core of the controversy, then he is los-

ing with the jury, when by strict attention to the main issue, enforced by logic, power, illustrations, and *absolute clearness*, with evidence left off at telling sentences he is turning his tact to winning his law suit.

TEN CROSS-EXAMINING RULES.

Never expect to prove your case by the other side's witnesses. But treat what you get with coolness till the closing.

Never appear to have too strong a case, or boast of it in advance. The race may not be to the swift but to the valiant.

Never get angry, and say rude things to intimidate. A good steady look, long and untiring is instructive.

Never sit down and seem sleepy. Throw a bad witness into a habit of a great many yeses to your questions till ready to say it "snowed" in July, if need be.

Never trust a case on *one* question, nor drive a bad man in a corner so hard as to let his honor depend on truth or lies, for *he will lie on oath who lies without it.*

Never use a drag net and repeat bad evidence repeatedly in a jury's hearing. It may intensify it. The jury will commit it to memory.

Never be too anxious for an answer. A case often turns on identification, and after witness is drawn into admission of a possible mistake (first by a possible uncertainty), then he soon admits a reasonable doubt.

Never depend on trial day for examination; a thorough inquiry into the motive of witnesses may reveal weak points. Stand while examining, and commit the subject to memory so as to be interesting. Interest even fascinates witnesses besides a semi-applause at a happy turn is heard by the jury.

Never use strange language or harsh tones. Be as persuasive as possible, and wait for the anger of witness first. But if he be a bully, show his real character fearlessly, and show yourself master.

Never ask at the start for something that may make the case stronger for the other side. Such is very unwise.

Never hold a bad witness longer than you can get a good laugh on his meanness, or lay a foundation to impeach his assertions. Be brief. Be wary. Be ready. Be at your best. Be full of the subject. Master your witness by adroitness. Be sparing of this branch always.

FINE WORK.

In machinery and building, decorations and ornaments, jewelry and painting, music and acting, writing and teaching, and all excellent works or improvements, time, skill, labor and genius, are employed to reach the highest art in the undertaking. Children are sent abroad, graduates are placed under careful training, and endless sums are expended to perfect the handiwork or increase the skill to the highest finish, and yet we find people selecting as counsel, and advocates, men of small experience, and less actual training in means of practical knowledge.

If the study of Turner's paintings, and Wagner's music, is of benefit to students, why are not the arts of distinguished speakers of equal benefit to lawyers? Truly, paintings are not all copies. They may have similar shades, trees and landscapes, that make them resemble each other as mist resembles rain, but a study of colors need not be a copy of design. To a lawyer, words, sentences, points and skillful turns of evidence, must be beneficial. When Seward followed up the pettifoggers till he beat down their bluffing with Supreme Court verdicts, and won the name of "*no small* potatoes after all," he set a shining example of real courage. No one cheered him to begin; all cheered his closing career. When he brought in a section of picket fence to confront a lying witness, he showed he was a genius in cross-examination, and had studied his subject, and knew the distance between pickets, and observed what happened around him.

When Hendricks carries a map up among the twelve jurymen, it is the art of explanation. He is seeking the honor of victory more than the honor of oratory.

When Daniel Dickinson and John Graham crowded their speeches with eloquent Scripture quotations, and filled them with examples of similar trials, and how they resulted, they knew the effect of homely illustrations. Brady knew so well that he had the jury with him in the Sickles case, by a single pathetic turn in his argument to the court, that he willingly waived further summing up. Carpenter invariably quit with a victory, or ended on a salient point in which he gained an advantage. Crittenden culled the flowers of ancient rhetoric, and Marshall moved a jury with beautiful imagery, Storrs presents a most beautiful array of rhetorical pictures, fluent in speech, and animated in manner. Dexter is clear, ringing and forcible, from long use of expressive phrases. The sentences of Beach are rhythmical and sublime. Porter is a genius of long experience, Curtis both a born and cultivated orator; Shaffer an encyclopediæ of fine arts, in practice, read full and ripened in eloquence. Tremain mastered Cicero and Demosthenes, as Cicero did the ancient authors of oratory. Stanton had a fund of rare ready practice for fine work. Matthews is a fountain of knowledge in court practice. Ryan knew the power of language, and adopted it. And so, men of all States, cities and countries, all who loved to excel, *have made it a study.*

Men who have succeeded as advocates had at their tongue's end in memory, and in reaching distance, the right art and fine work to use at the right time, and make it tell in the cases they were advocating.

CHAPTER VIII.

SUCCESS AT THE BAR.

" It is success that colors all in life;
Success makes fools admired, makes villians honest;
All the proud virtues of this vaunting world
Fawns on success and power, how'er acquired."
—THOMPSON.

Chauncey Shaffer, of New York, thinks that success at the bar is not alone in the genius or birth-place of the advocate, but more often in his opportunity. Of course, he insists upon industry and intense application, but gifts are born in a man as speed is born in a race horse, neither can be cultivated without a native germ as a foundation. Mr. Shaffer believes that our great lawyers are mostly self-made; that the quality of integrity and industry often comes from early life, where one lays the foundation in self-denial, and intense application, which becomes written on the heart and engraved upon the bones, and is enduring.

He believes in standing alone and avoiding counsel, as much as possible, to acquire a toughness and independence of character. In his famous Elevated Railway cases, when he contended single handed with David Dudley Field and other great lights, he thinks the force of being alone gave him a fairer chance to win his $30,000 verdict for a single accident. He also believes that country lawyers, who rise to some eminence and go with their frugal habits to large cities, generally succeed from industry and eloquence. Of course, men like Judge Dillon, late of St. Louis, who acquired fame as an author, and *is*, in fact, an excellent lawyer, could easily take rank in New York with governors of States and generals of armies, or leaders in law in large cities. And it is also true that a brilliant lawyer in an inland city is brilliant in any city in the same sense that authors and advocates are not all in cities. But the chances for fame are two to one in cities with metropolitan papers to publish their efforts.

William H. Seward, as a young man in Auburn, was slim in stature, timid in manner, and early took the name of "Small potatoes Seward." This name was so basely humiliating and so little deserved, that young Seward bent his energies, day and night, to overcome it. It was given him by pettifoggers who in early years could laugh down a boy lawyer much more easily than in our day.

Seward worked on and on, with courage and industry, and soon won all his cases in higher courts, and after farmers had paid a few large bills of taxed costs in appeal cases, and lost their law suits with pettifoggers, it came to be reported something like this: "That Seward isn't no small potatoes after all." This pleased the young man, and he continued, always avoiding help if possible, so as to stand alone in his victories. He grew eminent, first, in court as a reasoner, second, in public, as a speaker, and at last became a statesman of wonderfully acute intellect. Doubtless he was born with large gifts, and the very hardship which inferiors forced upon him, helped to develope his character and intensify his greatness. He believed that John Van Buren, of New York, " Prince John," was the greatest of all criminal advocates. In the famous conspiracy case of 1859, where forty men were tried at Detroit for a conspiracy to burn the Michigan Central Depot, Gov. Seward defended and made the best and most powerful argument on his side of the case. It was intended that Van Buren should be employed, but he engaged Mr. Seward. Many marks of his genius appear in his conduct of the trial, and his eloquence was of a convincing and persuasive character. One witness swore to having crawled through a fence and listened to the story of some farmers — enemies of the road. Seward was precise about the *place* in the fence, *how many* pickets were off, etc., and showed but *one* which would not allow of more room than a cat's body would require to pass through. He did not kill his case by cross-examination, but brought a section of the fence before the jury, and they saw how wickedly the witness had sworn to a falsehood.

It is said that William A. Beach has acquired his fame largely as an advocate before juries, and made his practice by so completely overpowering his enemies that they always hired him after one solid defeat, in which he was the opposing counsel.

Chief Justice Waite made his fame as a lawyer by an iron sided fight, and an almost always signal victory. General Butler has come to fame in much the same way. Stanley Matthews has succeeded by large knowledge and immense determination, besides he is very eloquent. Many succeed by law arguments alone, like Judge Comstock, of Syracuse, or graphic illustrations and innate genius, like Gov. Dillingham, of Vermont, or the brilliant Matt Carpenter. But John Van Arman declares that location has much to do with success, especially the kind of practice followed. He believes that many are poor when they begin and drift into a bad line of criminal defenses. Some adopt a wrong specialty. He is a railroad attorney, having been one of the best criminal advocates ever settled in Chicago. Mr. Van Arman does not think railroad law has a tendency to advance a man legally or politically, but hampers him before juries, makes him appear to lose cases often, and never be very popular. He is a keen judge of human nature, and wins hard cases by tact and courage. In a recent coal case he spent three days underground, in coal and dust and disagreeable work, to estimate and explain fully to the jury. In the great Michigan Central Conspiracy Case he prepared the facts with masterly ability.

Judge Ryan's rise at the bar was from his mastery of words and their meaning, rules and their application. He neglected no case, but made it as clear and strong as if his reputation all depended on a single effort.

Senator McDonald, of Indianapolis, believes young men do best and succeed best in a city. Gov. Hendricks thinks a start first in the country is better, that it is like setting a light in a dark place, where it shows for something, while if placed by bright headlights, that the beginner finds in a city, the little light is lost sight of and obscured.

I could give numberless steps by which men have risen to fame, but the plan of personal self-reliance of the gifted Senator Seward is as worthy for a model as one need remember. Should the laugh turn first on the inexperienced, make it a rule to win times enough to compel attention and reverence. There is no one element like a series of consistent victories to advance any man in life in any profession. Skill and results tell the story.

CHAPTER IX.

TAKING WRONG POSITIONS.

The theory of a case often wins or defeats it. If counsel proceeds without a theory he has a strange path to follow, while with ripe judgment he could be an experienced traveler, knowing all the fine points of observation readily, and without surprise. It is better first to adopt a safe position, and not assume all, or risk all at once.

A full clear statement, with a Blucher's trusty 10,000 in reserve, just ready to bring up at the right moment, makes one feel like saying: "He that handleth a matter wisely shall find good."

But if one has taken a position he must not swap horses in crossing a stream, and upset his theory to the ruin of all prospects. Many a murder case denied outright could have been well defended by the "hip-pocket" argument: "He was about to fire on me," or, "I had reason to fear bodily harm," the attacked being the judge in all such cases—when a better reason must be shown than a denial of any part of the tragedy.

In the Romero case, lately vividly reported in *Las Vegas Optic*, by E. W. Freeman, an eye-witness to the circumstance, the prisoner was only nineteen, of good habits and character, with a mother, sister, and plenty of friends, and even friendly with the murdered man. It was shown that he had on his person, when captured, some supposed money and clothing of the victim, and had fled the country at the very date of the murder on a race-horse, "Silver-tail," belonging to the deceased, and acted somewhat guilty.

Counsel were appointed, and he was defended on the theory of *not guilty, and no knowledge*. He was convicted by a powerful array of circumstances, related to the jury with graphic force and telling effect by T. B. Catron and Col. Breedan, of Santa Fe; and after conviction he confessed facts, which, if known in season, would have saved him.

It seemed that he had kept company with a Mexican girl of rare beauty, and that a half-breed Indian was smitten by the same charmer. On the day of the killing, or the night before, so the confession goes, the Indian called, and was let in late to the murdered man's ranche, and remained sleeping by the fire till day-break.

Early in the morning Romero went to milk the goats, and the Indian and victim commenced shooting at a mark. When Romero finished, and came to the cabin, or adobe, with his milk pails, and saw his friend dead and bleeding, he confronted the Indian, who at once threatened great vengeance, and said that he would report that Romero had killed his employer! This so shocked and frightened Romero that he fled the country on horseback.

His fleeing denoted guilt, while the Indian gave evidence of an *alibi*, and showed he was ten miles distant when the tragedy happened (by quite likely to be perjured testimony). The Indian was cleared, and married the Mexican. Romero was hung, protesting his innocence to the last. A better theory would have been an early confession to a knowledge *after the fact*, and a denial of the killing. Here is a case of one presumed to have become suddenly vile, when one of the grandest old Roman maxims says: "No man becomes suddenly evil."

Nothing in law quite equals experience. *He is a wise man that has known many men and seen many cities.*

TRIFLES THAT TELL.

Costs that follow a verdict on the merits are freely paid to the victor. But costs begged at a court on every little motion or petty proceeding are worse than street begging; they may fill a pocket book with pennies that would be replaced with dollars gained from a good name and generous dealing.

How little and low one must feel who stoops to profit by the error of a brother or "snap" judgment, attained with absence of witnesses. I have never known a *mean* practitioner to secure many clients, or win many verdicts. It belittles one so much that the air is filled with hatred to him, and what he may say, even if witty, will be lost on the bar, as it should be.

Suppose counsel could gain two demurrers, and three motions a year, or thirty dollars in small practice, that is but a small part of a year's earnings, and make him three to six enemies and strong haters, either one of which would do him double the injury he had caused the other, by a bad name and a character for meanness — meanness is the only word that expresses it—and should be syllabled out from Maine to Kansas with emphasis in the ears of all stingy lawyers.

There is no profession that will stand less lack of integrity unrebuked, or petty advantage with impunity, than the legal fraternity. We all realize how dependent we are upon honor and fairness; how much may be lost by a single promise unkept; how much will be gained by the good will of others, and how pleasant it is to dwell in unity.

Leaders of the bar have never been captious exacting for petty gains in practice, or beggars of small fees from their fellow lawyers. Rather has it been the rule of the best advocates to cherish a fraternal feeling on all matters that were not prejudicial to their client's cases, to make money from suitors, and not lawyers; to live upon legitimate practice, and not as one clutching with greedy fingers the miserly pittance of some petty advantge that never reaches the merits of controversy. Littleness is evidence of small and narrow minds. It leads to hatred during life, and as one, once forcibly put it, there will always be men anxious to put gravel stones instead of flowers in the grave of men who have injured so many people in their lifetime.

By contrast, what a host of friends the good draw around them. What characters for honor! What talents conceded! What counsel fees paid! What good words are spoken, and business chances are turned over to men of large hearts and noble natures!

SPECIAL VERDICTS.

Puzzling questions, is the term well applied to special verdicts, and in some cases they prove to be too much for the jury to answer. The thing to be avoided is too many of them, and such as tie a double bow knot and draw the ends through.

More than one wise counsel has seen the verdict half made up in the eyes of a jury, and tried to hedge by a lot of questions to muddle the jury. It is fortunate for suitors that good counsel are sparing of this double-edged sabre, if, as in a recent railroad case, the wrong answer follows, the fault is with the advocate. It seems that A. & Co., brought suit for a car load of beans, shipped to Toledo when the Union Depot was flooded with an ice gorge, and water rapidly rising. The beans were badly damaged, and three hundred dollars worth destroyed. Under a charge of the court the company were liable for the lost beans, and if they found from the evidence that the company were guilty of carelessness in sending the cars into the depot while the floods were rising, they were liable to the full value of the load, regardless of salvage. Counsel seeing the probability of a disagreement, or small verdict, sent a special question to the jury as to the carelessness of the company. The jury agreed readily on a verdict of three hundred dollars, and as readily that the company was *guilty of carelessness* in backing in the car at their own risk in the face of fair warning. The special question controlled the general verdict, and gave plaintiff a verdict for over *three times* the original finding, and against the counsel asking the extra verdict.

In a recent libel case the plaintiff was charged with certain acts that indicated a guilty knowledge of a serious offense, the ground of the action. Plaintiff's counsel was so determined to face the jury on the issue, that he put a special question to them as to whether they found from the evidence that plaintiff was really guilty of, or knowing to the offense charged in the libel, and the jury answered, "Yes," to the great disgust of his counsel.

In another case a large number of questions were ruled as ambiguous, and not given to the jury for answer, and the appellate court decided it a wise discretion of the trial judge to exclude them as contrary to the statute allowing special verdicts.

These hints are given to show that counsel can go too far in over-trying their cases, as well as to fall below their whole duty by occasional acts of omission.

GENIUS AND INTEGRITY.

The quality that wins more clients than eloquence is integrity. It counts in court, before court and throughout the range of counsel's clientage. Integrity without genius is better than genius without integrity, for many a genius is lacking in method and practical usefulness.

Who does not know of leaders in their college classes that made excellent bar-keepers or tally clerks and nothing more; who does not know of stupid boys at school all the forenoon of their lives, and yet became giants in manhood? The middling talents of men are far more prosperous with energy and integrity, than the brilliant achievements that last but an hour and are forgotten.

Young men of energy and lacking in genius, have much to hope for in a profession, largely learned in books and business. Young men of genius have much to fear from indolent reliance on gifts and natural endowments. Men who point to Henry as an example of a born lawyer without the slow growth of experience, have a model that a vivid historian — Wirt — made a God of from a couple of short speeches, whose name is a notable exception, and proves nothing that will do to pattern after in actual practice.

Lawyers who aim at perfection will never take Henry as a standard. Clients, with the general public, distrust the legal profession. Before a case of importance is given to an attorney, careful inquiry will be made of his standing and integrity. The worst of recommends is, " He is *smart*, but *shaky*, etc., you must look out for him, look out for him." Look out for a confidential adviser! Why that is just the kind of counsel to be avoided, and a reputation of this character is one that may bring occasional good fees, but never bring a permanent practice of high value.

Men who become counsel of railways or corporations who organize banks and build up characters that carry weight and influence with their undertakings, are men of known integrity, whose word and promise and slightest obligation will never be questioned. Such men in a court room carry conscience and skill like unerring instruments tested and proved to be reliable. Confidence is so rare, of such slow growth, that a long life of rectitude is a fortune to its possessor. As a lawyer, it is his monument of past action, his friends point to it, and his enemies respect it. He is a strong man in any community who has stood with character unchallenged for a quarter of a century, and that is about the age of a ripe counselor's zenith in practice.

CHAPTER X.

LAWYERS AS LEADERS.

The leaders in a general assemblage of men, suddenly summoned together to decide almost any question of public interest, will be composed largely of lawyers. The Parliament of Europe, the Congress and Senate of the United States, and each of the several State governments of the nation, draw their rules and wisdom in general from legal advisors. This is true of banks, corporations and companies of large monied interests.

Where careless contracts might easily involve their houses in ruin, or sensible advise could steer their course so safely that accidents need never impair the capital, or losses invade their private fortunes, considering the large sums spent in litigation, the time, anxiety and prospects of defeat for want of safe counsel, how strange it seems that more reliance is not placed on men whose business calls their attention to legislative enactments and the precedents of court decisions.

With the vast responsibility before them, with the daily prospect of being questioned on State, municipal and business affairs, with the thought that on the answer given may depend the success of him who counsels wisely, is it unreasonable to ask trial lawyers to be ready and well read on the affairs of the world? Would you ask a description of frontier life or far away customs, speak with one who has tasted the hardships of the former, and witnessed workings of the latter.

Lawyers are often chosen for age and presumed wisdom whose learning is inapt and meaningless as the limited observation of their plodding lives would mould and make it. Doctors, on the other hand, are more wisely selected from some known specialty wherein they excel and cure their patients. Lawyers ought to be well read in matters outside of their profession. Read in history, romance, Scripture and human nature. History will be dense with examples of righted wrongs through courts and laws and regulations. The pages of history are full of ripe experiences of heroic lives and eloquent appeals for liberty written all over in italics of long suffering men finally triumphant.

Romances are drawn from mysteries in courts, over wills or marriages, about characters that live and have their being very often in the commonest affairs of business. The moral of the author, if he be one of worthy fame, will add interest to tradition, and weave in the rarest touches of pathetic incident and ingenious releases. The lesson of "put yourself in his place," intensified by Reade, the character pictures of Dickens, and historical sketches of Irving and Cooper, are all full of wisdom and beauty; to neglect them is to omit such a record of heart histories that no ripe scholar can afford to ignore, even if saved for a fund of illustration. It may be no wiser to speak of a matter as true in history, than of something that happened yesterday, but the sanction of age adds authority to enforce attention.

The study of the Scriptures has ever been a means of strength in criminal advocacy. Webster, Ryan, Carpenter, Crittenden, Voorhees, Graham and Van Buren all reasoned through Scripture characters, and so full is the confidence of a jury in the truthfulness of Bible sayings, that they lodge in the mind and refuse to be removed by argument, while hundreds believe that the Proverbs of Solomon are the sanctifications of common sense.

But what lawyers most need is directness of purpose. Genius is never so much lacking as application. The most brilliant of the bar often take to drink and grow lower and lower year by year, till they end in the mad-house, the alms-house or the gutter, and lawyers more than others need to control their appetites. Excessive drink is the temptation before a speech to make it fervid, and it generally makes it flat or silly; and the temptation after the speech to make up for the waste or over-exertion, when rest is the real thing lacking. I often think that race horses are far better cared for after a contest, than lawyers after an exhaustive argument. But judgment dictates that quiet and rest is better than any form of stimulants.

The ambition of all lawyers is to speak well, and to such, the words of Fowler should be engraved upon their memory, "The best teachers of humanity are the lives of great men," to which may be well added, the best teachers of good speaking, are the lives and sayings of good speakers interwoven with intense practice.

Henry Clay attributed his success in speaking to his early practice of committing speeches, and debating. Webster was a great student of oratory, and O'Connell believed that a good speech is a good thing, but the verdict is *the* thing. Gladstone is the only man in Parliament who speaks always in *italics*, and he is full of maxims.

While the best of teachers may fail with a dull student, one born with eloquent tendencies, with heaven's great gift of genius, and a heart full of the subject, will need no rhetoric in words, but earnestness; and probably no quality can better aid a lawyer in his road to victory than is expressed in the simplest sentences. The statement of an event told in the tone and words as it happened, in a well modulated delivery, will best describe even the most terrible tragedy. The events in the Bible are all given in this manner.

No amount of economy on a meager income will ever bring riches. It is the proportion of money spent to money earned that regulates a fortune, so that to be rich in information, to be wise in knowledge of books one must be industrious, be he ever so careful, and still if unwise, how can he impart wise counsel? The field is a large one, the work exacting. A trial on patience, integrity and vital energy, bringing early silver of locks and furrows of care in its busy energy, where the wheels of life run rapidly, and some day the engine stops from lack of propelling power. But of all men lawyers live long, and see much of life's mixtures.

As success in racing requires training, so progress at the bar is marked by aptness in references selected in clearness of principles, and reasons given, and fullness of the subject at hand, so that industry is beyond all natural requirements in the conduct of difficult cases. "I never realized what labor was," said Shaffer, "until they attempted to baffle me in the poisoning case." "When I had been three days under ground, and measured every vein, and studied it like a miner, I knew I was right in my position," said Van Arman, of his Ohio coal case.

And what other rule can be given that will increase one's practice and income? This is it, and the last one: *Kindness. The success of a man in business depends upon the number that he can make himself agreeable to.* His customers come out of their way to deal with him. His integrity being presumed, and honesty unquestioned, and industry conceded, even then he may be a bear in appearance or actions. If he is, he is sure to be avoided.

Much in law comes to the courteous and deserving. No man knows when he passes a little shop with a key hung out as a sign, that he may ever need to call there, but the first broken lock reminds him of its location. No one knows that all around him may be men and women of peaceful habits, utterly unknown to courts and lawsuits, whose friends may be deeply involved in trouble, and the sunny smile or kindly tone accompanied by other essentials, may have left an impression deep and lasting on one who shall send the lawyer his best client, all through some act of kindness.

If we knew much depended on good will in law business, we would all practice courtesy. Often in his earliest cases will counsel be tempted into severe language. He may be overfull of prejudice from his own client's story. Most likely he has had the enemy pictured as a brute, and the opposing counsel seems a wretch to contend with such rights as his client seems to possesss, but time will change this materially. It will be better by and by to avoid personal offense, even to defendant. The bone of contention has doubtless been magnified. The opponent has many equities that can be fairly conceded, and far wiser is he who oils the ruffled feathers by kind words, and makes an early settlement possible.

With a wise enthusiasm and honest purpose, and a thorough skill and ripe knowledge of facts and principles, kindness will win all hearts and many verdicts. And in a calling so high, great and noble ; so honored by the lives of statesmen and orators of the past: honored by being the body of followers whose laws govern humanity ; honored by having framed great constitutions, systems of government, and national settlements that has saved the lives of whole nations, and systems of finance, trade protection and international commerce ; with all of them to remind us, and inspire us, how small, and low, and mean, seems a little quarrel, and how great and grand are wisdom, honesty and nobility! To acquire which, we must be diligent and genial with purity of purpose and charity in practice, so that when death, the great reconciler, is come—to divide us—it is never our *tenderness*, but our *severity* that we repent of. Let us talk, act, and live, and do *our duty*, but forgive our enemies in whispers, where the " soft answer turneth away wrath, and grievious words stir up anger."

WEALTHY LAWYERS.

The practice of law is not always remunerative. Many an advocate turns before he reaches success to other and more profitable employment. The cost of books, offices and travel, the delay of trials and worry in weary waiting comes to most men as a discouragement.

Men wait for a lawyer's success, as they do for an actor's celebrity. They dislike to advance much on the great unknown. This is a terrible blunder of men who need legal talent. If one is apt, keen and alert in his profession, and has but little practice, he is the very one who will spend days over a question that older attorneys would be unable to devote a good hour's study to investigate. The cheapest talent is the medium priced and rather younger classed lawyers; men who have reputations to win, and need to be dilligent.

As new houses put out many goods at small profits, and old ones rest on their reputation, so lawyers are full of rare service at low pay when they start in practice.

I have seldom known very rich lawyers to be *very* anxious to try knotty cases. They prefer ease in practice. A man worth many millions that has tried all classes says: " Give me a poor lawyer, not too poor to be needy, but give me one who wants reputation and will earn it." Give me young talent like new buggies, fresh horses and new houses; the forenoon chance is always the best. When one is rich and able to rest, why should he kill himself with over work and hard cases? The young are the burden bearers of business generally, and no less in law than in merchandise. It is reserved for the poor men to do the fine work, study and invent machinery, improve on the old methods and take the long steps forward, and no one need fear that poverty will forever keep him under in practice.

It is a mistake to regret a humble birth, or envy the rich practitioner. It takes no genius or tact to be born rich, but, as Ingersoll well says, "the honor of the thing is in improving on the common stock — doing, and being, a little better than our ancestors." It is not what one's position may have been, or what his parents may have been, or how he attained his rank at the bar, but *what he is*, and how well he can maintain his position, that *tells* in practice. The genius that counts his fingers till he learns the rules more clearly, is none the less a genius. The boy lawyer with brains and grit who struggles with his superiors and succeeds, is more deserving than the senior of name, character and standing. Time evens such things nicely in the long run, and rich, gray haired men need never be envied by the young and ambitious, for few lawyers are wealthy under fifty who make their money in practice.

CHAPTER XI.

BELIEF IN YOUR CASE.

The jury will soon know if you have a doubtful case. To be sure about it, let them know early that you, at least, are confident in your positions. This may be expressed in calmness, in not growing petulant over little defects, in kind and courteous behavior, in a manner of reserve force that denotes courage, and an unshaken belief in evidence as it passes in the hearing of the jury.

Any nervous or petulant anxiety will leak out in the sight of the jury, who watch counsel as they would a couple of athletes in an arena — especially if the case has any interest in it, which all good cases are sure to excite, more or less, during the early stages of the trial.

The true course is to assume and maintain serene confidence throughout, by an impressive statement of facts and law, if need be, and a strict adherence to your positions. Should the court disagree with you, insist upon an exception. Keep up the exceptions on all important rulings to the latest moment. The best judges may err, and a large number of exceptions can be sifted down for the purpose of review. Five will be ample for a higher court, but twenty may be good to fall back upon in selecting.

A friend was badly ruled out of court recently, and quietly said: "It's a short road, and beaten track to Lansing; I shall be able to get there in term time." And he did, and returned with a complete victory. The coolness reassured his client, who instantly decided to aid in a final review and hearing, where mistakes, if made, are legalized.

Belief in a case should extend through the trial and court of last resort. There is no reason why counsel who once look up the law, and determine that they are well grounded in their belief, should surrender on a single defeat in any case. The clear grit plan will lead to a firm, silent, but persistent contest to the bitter end. Belief in victory, helps to win it. "Thrice is he armed, who hath his quarrel just." There is no evidence like a *good case*.

ONE OPINION.

The world has but one opinion of a man at a time. With the very wide influence of the press, every bad thing is sure to be noted and extended. If a lawyer loses too many cases, or runs too much in a single rut, adopts a special line of practice, gives too much time to politics, charges too high fees, is inclined to sporting or fastness, public opinion will soon take his measure, and for years after will hold it in memory.

In a very busy world, where every man is full of his own affairs, there is too little time to weigh character. A single reporter of a single paper may set on foot a story of a great man's victory that makes his reputation for a quarter of a century, simply for the reason that no other reporter for another paper is likely to contradict the statement, it being printed — and one man's opinion only — it weighs against a score of years in character building.

Some men will outlive injury to character. Theodore Tilton is an example. Some will struggle, but remain scarred by it, like Conkling, who rallies like a true Roman; others will surmount it, like Arthur. The force of circumstances aided each in the ending of his trouble.

The American people love idols. They have some pet in every community, city and State. They succeed for a season, go out like a candle burned down and discarded. This is peculiarly American. The higher a man goes, the more liberally they reward him; the lower he sinks, the harder they hate him.

When Grant took the sword of Lee, and received the surrender of an army, he was applauded and treated as a conqueror and king. His trip around the world was a continued ovation; his meeting with the Queen, who walked down twenty-eight steps, and held out both hands to show him welcome; his arm-in-arm walk with Prince Bismarck; his passing under the Giant Arch at Jerusalem, and return by the Golden Gate, and later through Old Mexico, — would seem to be honor enough for a monarch to enjoy. But how soon were the scenes shifted at the Chicago Convention! The world had but one place for Grant. They had made him a military hero, and were determined that was enough for one man, and it was the highest honor he can achieve while living—once removed beyond the possibility of rivalry, and he will be praised with great freedom.

Lawyers have this to remember: If they seek Congress they are looked upon as Congressmen, and their legal reputation changes. If they seek criminal practice (next thing to Congress), they will be known as criminal lawyers. If they are fair, open, generous, that reputation will cling to them. There is no class so much the architects of their own fortunes as lawyers.

INTEREST IN SPEAKING.

Every advocate has his means of enforcing attention. Some are intense, some graphic, others ironical, and many attractive aside from the general argument. Few men ever sustain at any length, a long line of eloquent periods. In a speech of many hours, but a few moments in all will approach true eloquence. But with a subject of public interest, much of the speeches made to an audience is the story of the matter in question. So the story of a case is always its chief interest. If a subject is dry and void of sentiment, deep earnestness in attending to its details is all that counsel can add to his ordinary duty. No matter how dry it is, there is one party (your client) deeply interested in the issue, and you are bound to share his intensity. Stories, illustrations, examples and good humored treatment of others will awaken an interest, and hold attention when you most need listeners. The heart of an advocate must be warm, and beat responsive to the music of good jokes and apt answers of witnesses, for of all things pleasing in a court room, none is more relished than a joke from a witness on his examiner.

BRIEFS.

From the moment a case comes to the office, to the collection of a judgment, *interest*, and constant interest, must be paid to its details; make it your own, is an excellent way to manage anothers dispute. Cut it as short as possible without sacrifice, but keep it in mind, and file away with every case a clear statement of parties, their address, and the residence of witnesses, as well as reference to their part of the testimony, and the leading cases relied upon for trial day. This will prevent confusion, and enable another to be called in and try it in your absence intelligently. To this end a BRIEF, is of all things, essential at the earliest stage of all retainers. Make at once a clear *brief*, and file it away for immediate reference. Cases come on oftener at random than by any note of warning. See to it that you are ready and waiting for trial, and lacking in nothing on your part to make it a victory. Many a lawyer has lost his suit, that by a little care could have been gained easily. The best tried cases are those handled by young enthusiastic lawyers, full of their facts, and deeply read up on the law of the subject. It is not safe even to rely upon memory, a clearly written brief of points in a good bold hand, is the surest way to success on trial days.

This preparation leaves you room for other thinking. It paves the road that leads to the jury. How can counsel hope to explain matters all muddled in his own brain, to a dozen men with minds untrained on such subjects? It is one of the chief things of all to remember in practice, that clearness is itself full of interest. Be lucid, graphic, intense, attentive and alive to the interest of clients, and you must succeed.

GREELEY'S "BIG TREE."

Horace Greeley, while on a trip to California in 1857, visited the Mariposa Valley and the Big Tree region to describe the mammoth cedars through the *Tribune*. He had measured one about a hundred feet around when the guide begged him to wait, and said he had found a larger one. "Never mind, never mind," said the ready witted Horace, "they *won't believe this when they see it in the Tribune*. Where they are all unreasonable, I'd rather mention a medium tree."

Horace would have made a good lawyer. There is more than one story told in court by witnesses not believed, simply because they measure *too big a tree*. The mind will carry about so much and no more. The average advocate proves too much in many cases; and witnesses tell unreasonable stories.

To believe that one man in an assault case would injure another without cause, is not in accord with human reason. To claim that one is wholly right, and the other is all wrong in a quarrel, is not the right sized tree for an average jury. Men are, in many respects, like Charles Reade's hero. They put themselves in the place of another quite often.

The best reasoners are mindful of human weakness, and reach conclusions only after a fair investigation.

So that the sage saying of the wise journalist is apt in trials. Don't measure too big a tree. They won't believe it if you get it in evidence.

Trained judgment alone would dictate this caution. Mr. Greeley was a master of human reason. He took in the future at the same glance that others looked at the present. It was to him not to-day only, but the great second thought of to-morrow that governed. Accuracy in judgment, to be able to read the will and average opinion of men, is a rare gift in advocacy. Juries in the box are only men, neither greater nor brighter nor truer than an equal number selected and spoken to outside of a court trial. The common sense of twelve men is about the average sense of the community. The chief difference being that they hear the evidence. But take the story of a mean witness that no one would credit if read in the papers, and a jury will apply nearly the same rule to his evidence. Witnesses are never wholly believed on both sides, for in most cases there are flat contradictions. The most reasonable and likely statements are most readily credited as truthful.

CHAPTER XII.

CANDOR AND DIGNITY.

Parlor talk is more taking than loud tones and vehement manner. Not that earnestness can be replaced by soft tones altogether, but modulation being the music of all oratory, it requires low tones to reason, strong ones to denounce, and words full of feeling to move the sympathies. The tones that capture the judgment and overcome prejudice are full of kindness and music. Human nature is more easily coaxed than driven to act against the will, and politeness opens many a door that scurrility would have locked and bolted.

I remember an occasion of a man calling at an office where there was a director's meeting, with closed doors, and, after rapping, he said gently through the letter-box opening: "*Bitte*, *Herr French!* may I speak just a moment with you? It's *very* important." The two words, "*Please*, *Mr.*," before French brought the door open instantly, while he might have pounded an hour, and no one noticed him.

Kindness is a Yale key that unlocks the strong combination of many a heart-door closed to harshness. If one would influence another with reason, he should couch his part in modest words that reach the finest impulses.

I remember a salesman of cheese-safes who was very successful. He would point to a few good things, and rest patiently for the offer to take effect, and never attempt to argue the objections raised by answers other than simply pointing to the good things of his article for sale, and finding their position not so serious as to need combatting with argument, he succeeded in his sales admirably.

Lessons of this kind are found apt and suggestive to a lawyer, who meets opposition at every step of a court contest or settlement. Better by far to listen patiently, and even take a little abuse, if you have the closing, than enter into a wrangle and quarrel all through on little things that never reach the core of the controversy.

In a famous case in New York, where Judge Beach prosecuted, a lawyer from the interior objected so much to evidence for incompetency, that all were becoming tired of his intolerable bother and delay. Finally, the court reprimanded his captious style of practice, and Judge Beach raised in his chair, and with a tone I shall never forget, said: "I *thank* your Honor!" The effect was more than a dozen sharp answers. He had borne it long enough for the enemy to come in reach of his gun, and killed the whole wrangle with a single shot.

There is no more stinging reply than a look of contempt, and an action to match, especially if the saying or interruption is contemptible. So much of outside feeling enters into a jury's finding, and so much of reading between the lines goes on during trials, that the Guiteau style of firing off a stale reply, or impertinent (and attempted) witty remark, is fast losing caste in good practice.

Good trial lawyers start without jockeying, and win without breaking. The keenest observers of a race soon sympathize with the honest, even trotters, and dislike one that breaks up and gets unsteady; and so in trials, the man selected in important cases is not chosen for sharpness or petty wit, or a trick to play with a jury, but for some sterling quality of skill and adroitness or eloquence that is likely to reach the real merits of the contest, and, if possible, cut the knot for the court or jury.

It is bad enough that people must go to law to obtain their rights of dispute. But counsel who will badger them with vile names, and their lawyers with meaningless nonsense, deserve to be beaten as an example.

Candor, absolute honor and fair dealing, are not only essential to success in practice, but they carry with them character and clientage, and unite the disputants, while they elevate the standard and dignity of the profession. We can all remember the boys who declaimed " funny pieces " at school, but the most impressive speeches were of words fitly spoken, and full of sense and wisdom, delivered with dignity and candor.

FREQUENT OBJECTIONS.

The smoother and more direct way of admitting evidence, the better for court, counsel and jury. One who raises captious questions, and worries the patience of all by a running line of "We object," "We object," without good solid grounds for the objection, is losing his case as fast as possible.

The course of a court trial is more or less tedious as counsel see fit to make it. No wonder that juries are sickened by unprofitable quibbles. Objecting calls off the mind from vital issues, confuses witnesses and prolongs testimony. All this is noted. Opposite counsel are irritated, and take advantage of the time in naively hinting to the jury that something they would show is headed off, least it may hurt the objector. More is said in the argument, worse words are used, and a worse effect produced, than could be made if the real facts were admitted.

Then we have three serious effects to overcome in argument: A court's displeasure, a counsel's hints, and a jury's prejudice. They have heard the offer to show; they assume it is truthful; they know it must be bad, or it would not have been questioned. Then when we think of that love of fairness which juries must have carried all through, and that comes to remind them how each side has been heard and well treated, we can only wonder at the sharp practice style of attempted interruptions. There is but one opinion about lawyers, fair or unfair, in trials. They cannot retain their self-respect by unfairness, nor their clientage by tediousness. The wearing-out process is long out of date, and the sooner the issue is determined, the better for counsel and client.

TALKING TOO MUCH.

"Pleasant words are sweet to the soul."

Aaron Burr made a rule of thirty minutes speeches. That is a little too short for most men to conclude their stating portions of an argument. But Burr al- was commenced in the middle and cut both ways, with vivid intensity he reached the vital issue and held it like a quivering victim in his toils, till he mastered the issue and convinced his hearers.

Most advocates start too far away, and end long after the end is out of sight and out of hearing. Once well told is told enough. One good reason need not be worn thread-bare by over-handling, and when a counsel goes off into science, metaphysics and gene- ralities over minor matters, he dulls the edge of reason and tires his jury.

There is such a strong disposition to cut across lots in business, and juries are so well informed, and should be so fully convinced by the testimony, that speeches are lost if made tiresome. Men have a right to look for apt words. "A word spoken in due sea- son, how good it is." "He that hath knowledge, spareth his words." One had better say too much than too little, but just the right thing will be neither extreme.

Careful attention will show the stopping point, and place the closing period where the end should be, be- fore the sharp point is over-worded. Endless talkers are sure to lose their grip. It is the man who talks little and in pithy sentences that wins suits and settles differences. Constantly objecting, or frequent side cuts of interruption, may require some lively sparring to get even, but the telling speeches are the short, sharp, clear cut stinging ones that pierce to the heart like a swift arrow and execute the will of the advocate. Witness the address of McReynold's in the Stevens' Insurance suit, where talent, character and eloquence were arrayed in force against a country lawyer, who, with a *period* seldom equalled in an any language, told more in ten minutes, than hours of round about reasoning could accomplish. Judge Curtis, whose opinion is second only to Beach's in America — and in this case shared in by the latter — says of this Reynold closing * : "It is a gem in English literature, sublime in sentiment, eloquent in heart thoughts, grand in its simple simplicity. Who could resist such strength of reason, combined with his power of vivid pathos." Here is part of it:

"Even now, by your silence and interest in this case, I hear you say stop, delay not longer, let us begin the work of justice! Stop till we right this wrong at once! Stop till we restore these orphan children to their own, to that character they will love to honor — a character as pure as they believed it on that last sad night, the night before the night of death! Stop till we give a verdict and a vindication!"

Judge Beach was more especially pleased with the passage of the accident just before the one quoted, which he pronounces *rare*.

"I can see her now, as plain as yesterday. It is evening. It is twilight. The snow is falling fast and slippery, whitening the little white walk to the cistern. She is confused; she has company. She seizes the pail, hurries to the cistern, catches up the hook, leans over the curbing, Slips! Falls! the water covers her! No one hears her! She is drowned! It is an accident." (See Modern Jury Trials.)

CHAPTER XIII.

ON HIS MERITS.

The success of a doctor may be aided by good nursing, and nature's efforts to revive the patient. In eight cases out of ten, except in seasons of epidemic, rest and a natural vitality will withstand ordinary diseases. This fact gives doctors a great reputation, but such is not true of lawyers, whose clients once in trouble, generally stay in for a good season, and no reputation can be made in law, save on the merits of the lawyers.

Some may dream that wealthy relatives will do it; some that influential friends can elevate one to power and position—and they may for a brief season—but the lawyer has one road, and one only: *he must win for himself*, and be as much independent of relatives, friends and riches, as if rowing a boat race; mettle, and mettle alone, must count in him if he conquers. Cheers help a speaker, but no amount of cheers win a law suit. Wealth helps one socially, but not in a law suit, before a jury, to any great extent.

There may be instances of purchased positions, but they are clerical or secondary places; there may be corporation counsel appointments, where wealth turns the scale, and secures the place for a favorite; but corporations are none to ready to rely on other than actual merit in legal matters. So that at the outset a strange feeling must come over a young student in his early practice; that he must make his own way in practice, and to preferment, unaided by anybody.

There is one source of encouragement in this thought to the worthy, and that is the fact that he will own his honor when he earns it. It may stimulate his energy in character building, which of all things is the best capital in practice. It may urge him to braver work, and nerve him to endurance, to reflect that in the legal arena he is struggling alone, for a name of winning cases, and earning fame, that with the lookers on, are the friends and relatives who will cheer his first victory, but he is the racer, who must out run others to secure it, and probably it does cheer him, for few are so careless of a good name as not to desire, and wish to deserve one, for this reason, if for no other, the legal profession opens a broad arena of competition. There is no storekeeper, dealer or merchant who meets an equal competition with the lawyer.

His way is beset with tricks and accidents. His client may be honest, and may be knavish. He may be wise, and is more likely to be foolish. He may be discreet, but has more likely given away his case in some left handed letter, or admission where opposite counsel will say " we have the best of witnesses — a confessing defendant," and mean it. But while the law never requires of one to do impossible things, it has said in a wise maxim that " reason is the soul of law," and all one really needs is earnest endeavor and common sense to reach the true basis of practice.

The rare chance may not come in the beginning. It may come later. Most good lawyers mature well along in life, with gray hairs and increased confidence; with cases won and large experiences; with friendships made that turn into line quickly when one is known to be successful. Such is the whim of human nature that once on the wave of popular favor, every one who knows you is pleased to be friendly and joyous at your victories.

Who did not know that Garfield was great, and would exceed Grant's popularity in Chicago? Who was more willing to call Grant great while away over the water, standing at the foot of the high stone steps, as Queen Victoria came down and held out both hands to greet him? Who did not thrill with pride as he marched arm in arm with Bismarck? and later rode through Jerusalem in triumph? rounded the Globe and landed at the golden gate of his native shores; called out vast crowds to greet him, and was the lion of two Continents?

Such is life, and such is victory. Success makes friends, and defeat makes enemies. The world will bow in season, or growl in season. Let one slip like Colfax — once one of the greatest of senators — how soon were his enemies ready to belittle his honesty? See Conkling, one of the most brilliant of statesmen, and whom millions believed the leader of all stalwarts, how soon he was maligned by slanders?

But the glory of the lawyer is his strength. His knowledge and acumen must be forever respected. It is his lasting capital. Fires never burn it; slanders cannot kill it. Distance, time or rivalry cannot destroy a man's legal capital actually acquired and frequently tested. This is the merit of the whole matter. What one owns in knowledge *is his*, is valuable, is lasting.

SHARP PRACTICE.

The worst thing that can ever happen to a young lawyer, is to believe that he is smarter than the average. If he gets that notion before others learn it, and commences to play the low tricks of taking snap judgments, he is known to be on the high roads to infamy by all good advocates.

A thousand and one cases occur in practice that make counsel rely on each other for courtesies, and extensions, that appeal to sense and reason, and can better be granted than denied, and never should be treated with captious dealing or little advantages that are always unprofessional. Absence from home, sickness, or engaged elsewhere, have often been used by some to make costs to clients, and bring discredit to his counsel by a long wrangle to reinstate himself in the lost opportunity. An advantage so gained would be but faded laurels to deck the brow of an advocate's good name, which, after all, is better than great riches.

It does seem silly and senseless to practice such arts and deceits, for they are not arts in business, when the readiest means of making friends is fairness. There is no art like the system of fair play. As soon should one strike a child or a woman, or a man when down and disabled, as to take mean advantage in a counsel's absence.

This fairness, is of course, limited, and must be governed by firmness, else some indolent attorney will be ready to use it as a means of undue extension. The border line of where courtesy ends, and right asserts itself, is generally well marked and easily followed. A high-minded lawyer will win his cases on their merits, and can easily be selected from one who trifles with confidence, and this leads to the fact that is vital in practice: A clear knowledge of the character of one's fellow lawyers. Many a man would be better trusted, if better known, and a few would never be trusted so well after their conduct was proven. It is safe to overcome evil with good, and assume that none are so bad that could not fall lower, and he is a *hard* man that would injure another wilfully.

The worst of all things about sharp practice is the bad name that follows its author. No one can be mean with his neighbors, and hold their respect or confidence. Sooner or later they will be detected and branded as tricksters or sharpers, and who can recover from the title of a traitor? The most contemptible dealing in life is that of *left-handed, underhanded advantages.*

TURNING VERDICTS.

During a slander trial in an eastern city, which practically involved the character and chastity of a beautiful young lady, the plaintiff became very much affected by the issue, and made this appeal to her counsel: "O! sir, may God and the saints protect you! You hold my good name in your keeping! Do your best for my sake! Talk to the jury, if their sister or their child had been used as I have, how they would feel toward the one who caused it! Plead with them! Don't sit down till they see my wrong as you do!" This, said counsel, so nerved me that I brought out in argument an imaginary interview, which at once secured the interest and good will of the jury, and a verdict of heavy damages. Her suggestion, he adds, was the most taking of all things to be said in her behalf.

In a railroad case with seven witnesses to one, he used these taking paragraphs:

Gentlemen: — The case of this obscure man is before you. You have seen him battling against all the power of a great corporation. The defendant is one of a confederacy of corporate monopolies that is gradually if not rapidly stealing the lands and franchises of the American people. Before the day when England oppressed the people of India, through the East India Company, great corporate powers as sanctioned by law, were not understood to be vested in individuals comprising or constituting corporations, and certainly never expressed. The history of legislation in Great Britain and the United States, demonstrates clearly that the powers and privileges of corporate bodies have grown until they overshadow and oppose the rights of the people. In this country alone they have permeated into the Executive Mansion; have poured the leprosy of corruption into legislative enactments, and administered the law from the bench.

Take the single example of the State of Texas. It has an area of six to seven times the size of New York, comprising 144,000 more square miles than the Empire of France before the fatal day of Sedan. On its broad plains roam millions of cattle; and the beef of Texas is eaten to-day in London, and on the banks of the Ganges. Along its water courses, and in its mountain gorges are mineral deposits as rich as those that fascinated the gaze of Cæsar or Pizzarro. It has a wealth of live oak timber capable of constructing the modern vessels of the world. Still this great commonwealth is given over to the spoiler. Its people deprived of its lands, and its labor taxed to pay tribute to railroads and corporations, the worst of all the monopolies of the land.

Gentlemen, it is true that we have but *one* witness against this mighty plaintiff and its *seven* champions. But my client is hopeful, for *he is right*. He has dropped the anchor of his fate in your consciences, and patiently abides the issue with unfaltering confidence.

READING LAW.

A great teacher of Shakespeare kept telling his students they must read, and read, and read, to know the great author; and one said, "What shall I read, Professor?" "Read," said the teacher, "read every thing; anything; all reading helps to understand Shakespeare." This is a hint to a lawyer; read much, read often, read constantly. Master the details of law and its surroundings. It will all help; it will be a fountain to draw from, and a wealth of learning is always useful. The time will come when you can use it. Fuller's success in the great Rubber Patent cases of New York, was from his accurate knowledge of the theme. Webster saved stories ten and fifteen years before he found a place for them in argument. He drew from Walter Scott, in his Bunker Hill monument speech, from the same author in another fine picture, and seldom addressed the senate without borrowed figures of beautiful imagery. Everett in his "thrice welcome to General Lafayette," has three excellent Bible sayings, and every speaker of national note is a borrower or a gleaner of others thoughts and sayings.

Good things said are carried away and help to make a speaker's character. Sooner or later if one is ripe, and full, and fluent in good thoughts, whether culled from the classics or the doings of daily life, he will be marked and remembered, as Robert Collier is, for his research and ripeness in scholarship. No one can learn too much, no one can know too much, no one can be rounded, and full as a fountain of life thoughts, without reading and travel.

The standard text books are, of course, the foundation. These should be read, and their salient rules and principles written out by the student and large portions committed. Principles should be memorized and repeated often by recitations to each other like a grammar lesson. It is not what we read, but what we write out and make our own, that is useful.

Next in order are Special Works, now so common and so useful, where one man spends years in bringing the essence of fifty volumes into one. Such reading is invaluable. It is a brief on their subjects treated.

These are the standard works of advance practice. I need not name them; to read them is to enjoy the latest court contests.

There is another class of law books that are mere dictionaries of reference — the reports and digests of the different State and Supreme Court decisions. No one is expected to read them all. No one could. Life is not long enough if he desired to. With these a chance acquaintance, an introduction, at least, is useful.

It is with books as with associates. Some are good companions; some good friends; others will do to cultivate, and may become friends in due season. Many a gem lies hidden away in a book that has for years been slighted and neglected. But, as a rule, if one reads the legal journals, weekly and monthly, he will find the useful legal literature well defined and suitably advertised.

The legal profession is the learned profession, and seeing that the doctors faithfully report all amputations, tumors and strange achievements and successes, I have often wondered why more attention has not been paid to the use and benefit, the experience of different lawyers would be to each other in trial practice.

CIRCUMSTANTIAL EVIDENCE.

Many strange cases of circumstantial evidence are reported, and more has been written against capital punishment on this account than all others combined. Here is an instance of strange circumstances ending strangely:

In 1775 there lived near London one Marble who owed a miller £600. Marble was known to leave home with the money to pay the debt, and after a week's absence, foul play was presumed and diligent search instituted. About the same time the miller lost a dog by poisoning, but suspicioned no one, and assumed it was an accident.

The authorities called on the miller, who had seen Marble receive the £600 from bank, and asked where Marble had gone to. The miller replied that he had left by the back way intending to call on a hunter, buy some game and return. That it was in the evening when he left as stated.

Great excitement prevailed. Men had seen Marble enter, but no one ever heard of his leaving the mill. Some suggested that the £600 made him a prey to robbers. But suspicion soon fell on the miller. He was searched willingly. When they reached the cellar they found fresh earth, which he said was where his dead dog was buried. Digging, they found, not the dog, but the body of Marble!

The miller stoutly protested his innocence, but the hunter suddenly remembered that he heard blows in the mill when one man said: "We'll settle all our scores here." Doctors said the blow on the skull killed Marble. The miller grew excited and protested his innocence, but was convicted and beheaded, and the people thought the law had been vindicated.

One day, three years later, a gentleman shot a hunter by accident, and heard him scream. Twelve hours later he was found dead, and in his hand, with paper stained in blood, was written a confession that he, Gordon, the hunter, had killed Marble for his money, and buried him where he knew the dog had been buried, having first removed the dog, which he had also killed to prevent alarm at the mill where he had been stealing meal. The miller's name was fully vindicated. He was innocent.

HIS FIRST CASE.

There is a rosy halo of imagination surrounding a young lawyer's ideal of professional success. He imagines, to begin with, that his first case will turn the tide of his whole future existence. He has pictured to himself a widow's son accused of a dreadful crime but little less than murder; of a network of circumstances which his keen insight will unravel, and his eloquence shall hold up to the jury in a bashful, trembling, pathetic, original and eloquent style which sways the minds of men like willows in the wind. And then, when, by rising in their seats, they utter the welcome words, "Not guilty," he imagines that he will lead the widow through the crowded throng amid the hushed silence of an admiring people, who will be ever ready thereafter to seek him out in times of legal danger.

But what a blunder this must be! But one such can in a million ever happen. In most cases, if, by a series of little losses, and a long line of labor (five years, at least), a lawyer learns, by the bitter school of experience, that people who go to law are cautious in hiring new lawyers, and more cautious of suits after the first one, he has learned to bear rebuffs with patience, he has made a good beginning.

Imaginary cases seldom happen. Imaginary success is doubtful in any business. It needs contact with reality to rub the dust from a boy's dreams of greatness.

This case that I am to speak of is not one of the ordinary occurrences in practice, but more nearly lifelike than a boy-picture; and I may say here, that *I believe as they were told me*, the central facts are as true as Scripture. I use his words:

"About the middle of June, 186-, in a little office on G—— Street, some sixty days after admission to the bar, and while burning with the youthful fires of enthusiasm, I had written some friends in the interior that I would gladly serve them in any capacity, especially if they ever got into trouble. Why I wrote it I never knew. Hardly had the letters time to reach their destination when a telegram reached me from Q——, saying, "Come first train — case ahead."

"I don't remember much that happened that afternoon. I paced up and down the office, taking down first one book, then another; glancing at Greenleaf on Evidence, Chitty on Pleading, Green's Practice; looking over the law books, and finally I thought best to examine the forms of trespass, trover and attachment, thinking, of course, that a store must be closed or a swindler prosecuted. But nothing seemed to satisfy me.

"I took the night train, and slept most of the way, reaching the scene of action early in the morning. I had thoroughly resolved, before leaving, to "take as little baggage and as much wit as possible," for I have always considered this a standard maxim in all cases. I was, therefore, not burdened with a valise, and, taking a hurried breakfast, I started for my friend who had sent the telegram, and met him half-way to the village; he lived in the suburbs. He was not long in showing me the situation, and together we soon planned the campaign.

"The cause of action was murder, and, strange to say, little was yet known of the circumstances. On the night previous, while the quiet villagers were about retiring, between the hours of nine and ten in the evening, a shrill scream was heard from the banks of the river Rasin, some eighty rods from Main Street. The scream was quickly followed by a sound resembling that of a heavy wagon drawn over a high bridge. As near as could be remembered, the words uttered in the last agony of death were, "Don't kill me! Oh, Cal, don't kill me!" Or, "Oh, Cal, you'll kill me!" The words were shrill, and dreadfully tragic, of mingled praying, pleading and entreating—enough to melt the heart of adamant. But no help was given.

"Let us see the river," was my first salutation; and already I trembled at the tragedy.

Taking a little row-boat we paddled leisurely to the opposite bank to the hut lately occupied by Cal Waterman, who worked in a mill near by, and who had not yet finished his breakfast. I had previously learned of a joint insurance on the life of Waterman and his wife, the murdered woman, and determined to make the most of it. And here I may say that the agent who insured them was the means of my connection with the story.

"Will you remain here, and let me meet him unawares?" I said, as we neared the lonely cottage.

Walking slowly up to the doorway, I met a young man of nearly twenty-six years of age. Strong, well built, with black eyes, dark features, an ugly chin, and an arm like a giant's.

"Good morning, Mr. Waterman: that is your name, I believe."

Why did he turn pale at a common salutation?

"Good morning," came back rather gruffly.

"I live in Chicago, and have come to your city to take proofs in the loss of your wife (the insurance I refer to,") looking him steadily in the face, while his eyes went everywhere.

"Yes, yes," was his only reply in words, but language is not all words; "any means by which one person communicates his ideas to another," is a better definition.

"You had an insurance, I think, Mr. Waterman, that in case either you or your wife died the other received the whole amount?"

"Yes, that's the plan," said he. "Five thousand dollars."

"And you know we have to prove the loss?" I continued.

"Yes, I suppose so."

"Well, Mr. Waterman, we are troubled most at not finding the body; can you relate to me some of the particulars of the accident?"

To him I treated it all as an accident; this pleased him, and I followed up the advantage.

"Let us go over to where it happened." Over we went. "Now tell me the story in detail."

He started off in a rambling, irregular way, but said enough to give me a key to the mystery.

"I will meet you at the office of Justice Thomas at two, and reduce the statement to writing in the form of an affidavit, which will complete the proofs, if you will be there," I remarked, and he assented.

Seeing the justice, and summoning all the witnesses who heard the sounds, and knew of the search for the body, I was ready at the hour for the proofs to be perfected. Quite a little assemblage convened at the magistrate's office to hear the news of the tragedy; for a stranger in a village bent on an errand of such interest created no little excitement.

The story of Waterman was short and sullen. He had not worked that day, and at about eight in the evening had taken his wife in a row-boat for a ride. They passed up some five times, and floated down with the current till a little after nine, when the boat struck a log in an eddy and upset both in the water. He had swam to the shore, some four rods to the right, and, hearing the noise, one of the neighbors called to know what was the matter, when he told him his wife had fallen overboard. The man said, "Where is she?" Waterman replied, "It's no use to look for her now; it's dark, and the river is very high; it will go down in the morning."

"Is that all, Mr. Waterman?" I asked, as he concluded.

"Yes, that's all I remember."

"You say you left home at eight in the evening?"

"Yes."

"Did you not know that the river was high, and were you not afraid of it?" "Oh, no, I am not afraid of water."

"A good swimmer, are you?" "Yes."

"How far can you swim?" "A half mile."

"Can you dive without strangling?" "Oh, yes, five times in succession."

"And you went up and down about an hour and a half, altogether?" "Yes."

"And the eddy is very near to the bank on the left, is it not?" "Yes, about twenty feet off, I should think."

"And where you landed was some four rods away?" "Yes, near that."

"You started directly for the shore when you fell in, did you not?" "Yes."

"How long did you stand in one place on the shore before Mr. L—— came along?" "About fifteen minutes."

"Your wife fell out last, did she?" "No, I fell out last, when the boat tipped over."

"Did your wife call for help?" "Yes."

"And you stood on the bank and looked on?" "No, I couldn't see much."

"Could you see when you found the boat, what was in the bottom?" "Yes, a heel of a slipper was in the bottom."

"Were the oars shipped in their places?" "Yes, I think they were."

"And you went directly home from there?" "Yes."

"And rose early next morning?" "No, not till half-past seven."

"How long had you been married?" "About three months."

"How much insurance did you have?" "Seven thousand dollars."

"All in one company?" "Yes."

"And you are a good swimmer, and heard your wife beg for God's sake to save her, and yet you left her to die, and left her in the water without alarming the village, and went home and slept till seven and after, and this is all you have to say in proof of your claim to the insurance?" "No, I have got the papers," handing out the policies.

"That will do; stand down."

The balance of the story is short. Witnesses were sworn to show that none to good a feeling existed between the newly married pair. Evidence conclusive was shown of the boat's never having been tipped over at all. The heel of the slipper, wrenched off, denoted foul play. The struggle and screams were evidence of more than collision with a saw log. The strong man had deserted a drowning woman only when she was dead.

That was the belief all over the court room; else, why did he sleep like a log when his wife was lost in the water? Why stand like a brute and hear no appeal to rescue—he, the swimmer, the diver, the mill hand whose life for years had made him accustomed to water! Would a man treat a dog in this way?

This was a kind of a little speech that cropped out unawares. I was boiling over with revenge. But the justice looked wise as he said: "The *Corpus Delicti* has not been full enough for a warrant for murder. We must first find the body."

Before we separated, each witness had signed the testimony, which I rolled up carefully, and started for the city.

I had killed the squirrel — my object was to defeat the payment of the insurance. It was defeated. But the little speech was too warm for the furtherance of justice. Waterman departed, where, I know not. The body of his wife was found, ten days later, eight or nine miles below, with marks of violence upon it. The slipper heel fitted exactly. And now, as I look back on my first case, I can see with sorrow how I "killed the squirrel," but frightened away the larger game.

The result of the victory brought business, and courage, in the sense of the indians' theory, that the spirit of every enemy slain in battle enters into our spirit to make us stronger indians, while defeat takes the spirit all out of the defeated."

LIKES AND DISLIKES.

A jury of twelve men is usually composed of one-fourth to one-half farmers, an equal one-fourth of business men, one-fourth of tradesmen, and the last quarter men of "elegant leisure." This is a city estimate. In country courts supervisors prevail. In United States court juries are very largely from leading farmers of their district.

Of the first class farmers in general there is more than an average of hard common sense — an excellent element on any jury. No class of men believe more in even handed justice. They are seldom approached with bribe offers. They are naturally honest and careful. They reckon slowly, but surely. They are economical and tender-hearted, and if they understand the rights of parties, they are generally sure enough of agreeing on a correct verdict.

The chief thing in dealing with farmers is to be straightforward and fair minded. They care less about fine words, and more of upright positions. To attempt to be captious, or tricky, or unjust with farmers, is certain to prejudice your rights, and more than likely make lasting impressions.

Farmers that attend in high courts are leaders at home. They are proud of opinions. They form a general judgment from slight circumstances. One juryman said in a recent slander case, where a man was charged with speaking evil of a woman to her husband: "Well, what of it? Hasn't she covered up his property to the tune of $20,000, for a half dozen years?" "Yes," said another, "and I know him well. He is a great man to allow his wife to sue for slander when she was short $60 on a church fund not long since, and *he* is the man that bought five bags of wheat of me, and all I ever got was the empty bags back. Damages! Damages to such a family! Not this year!" Instantly the theme changed, and six cents was the verdict.

This illustrates the prejudice of farmers. Had it been a jury of tradesmen, several of whom had failed in their own business, their sympathy would have been awakened for the miller who fell short of payment only five bags of wheat to a farmer.

The mechanics of a jury panel are more inclined to figures and science — a demonstration of the case by rules and exact reasons. Their habits are not so general or off-hand as either merchants or farmers. Trained to think through careful practice, they dissect things with skill and accuracy. A mechanic once convinced is a firm and stubborn juror; especially a machinist. Their measurement must be certain, and once made gives great faith to a good workman. A man that can build in separate blocks and pieces a city hall of stone and iron, or one who can construct an engine, must have self confidence in a large degree.

Then, too, men about town who own property and sit upon juries, are men of great general information. They are talkers. They tell stories, laugh down positions opposed to their theories, and have such an air of star actors that they often over-persuade others less brilliant in affairs. Talkers, great talkers, men of stubborn habits, are dangerous, if once biased in a trial, for either party. Men picked up from the retired class are not all stubborn; but the clever men are so easily selected by pleasant faces, that little need be said on the subject.

A single glance over the panel will reveal the *hard* men, and these are moved only by reason, logic or deep prejudice. They are all selfish, and show it in their faces. By the same look the good natured will be discovered, to whom a pointed story is the best argument. The steady church going class, with high foreheads and florid faces, are generally emotional, and relish the sayings of wise men and eloquent passages. So young men are sure to be influenced by emotion. Where the blood is warm, and free, and active, a merciful mind and tender affections are easily kindled; while the *hard* men despise appeals to sympathy.

There are three things that all jurymen like, and three that they equally dislike. These are: First, terseness, clearness of statement and evidence; second, even handed justice; third, all placed before them with an earnest, accurate and interesting delivery. The three dislikes are: First, higgling over trifles; second, petty advantages; and, third, dullness and rasping harsh language. A fourth dislike may be added, the practice called by jurors "throwing dirt." This may not be elegant, but it tells the whole story. Human nature revolts at indecency in practice. Some lawyers esteem it a high art to repeat and intensify words spoken in anger, that are better never mentioned again in like language. It is an excuse, perhaps, to the originator that he was angry, but to one who repeats it willingly no fine-minded person can excuse.

On a panel of jurymen will be found many noble men, many superior reasoners, many hungry hearers and diligent readers. Feed them, and not insult them. Never explain too much. Let all jokes explain themselves. Leave off all reasoning at a ripe point, and avoid over argument, but stop not too soon. And this reminds me that short and plain sentences are best and most relished by a jury. Much as they like eloquence or wit, if the subject of the suit is blind and obscure, they mark you as not a good lawyer.

In a recent slander trial the court charged the jury that if they found the words uttered were the same as those charged and set forth in plaintiff's declaration, and that they were false, and intentionally false, and tended to injure, and had, in fact, injured the reputation of plaintiff, then she was entitled to damages. "At least, gentlemen, under such a state of facts, you should find for plaintiff a verdict for six cents damages."

What a charge! The jury actually supposed they were instructed to find just six cents, for the last end of the sentence was all they could carry. I think they were told that they could add to the verdict punitory damages if they believed the slander was willful. But what a poverty of language in a court to call over such an avalanche of large and obscure phrases!

Such a charge was enough to kill any verdict. No wonder juries disagree under such instruction. Clearness, fairness, smoothness, interest and terseness are the telling points in practice.

LETTERS AS WITNESSES.

"Every man should kiss the lips that giveth the right answer."

The fear of a rigid cross-examination prevents many persons from telling the whole truth to counsel. But no fear need ever follow truth telling — that case is weak indeed which rests on falsehoods — if any are seeking to *learn tricks in practice*, this is no work of instruction.

"Better a good name and loving favor than silver and gold."

Witnesses that come to court with a memorandum, a book account and written voucher referred to in the nick of time, as if by accident, will so fortify their testimony that he becomes a power in turning doubtful settlements or half-made contracts. Witnesses never attach weight enough to their own story, if true, and they know its true. Why cringe and quail, or hesitate? Is not the word of one man equal to a thousand; if the circumstances outside of his testimony are all believed by the thousand? Can a man deny a fixed date like a holiday? Can a man deny his own letters, and his book entries? Surely days and dates are *notches on the stick,* as the old-time tally boys termed them, that tell their own story.

A diary kept at the time and referred to, provided it is a real, genuine article, is almost certain to render a witness invulnerable. Few men can recall the events, payments and dealings of a single busy month in business. But most men could glance at an item entered at the time, and turning from it, swear to the certainty that the item is true.

Five years of my life I kept a diary. I have them yet — red, blue, black and maroon covered — five little soiled and blurred books. Some items in ink, some in pencil; some tell where I worked, others where I spent money; others of a meagre income twenty-six years ago — yet all are true — true as boyhood's thoughts are sure to be. I could take each book at random, turn to any page, and soon recall the year, and day, and all I earned or spent that day, *with greater certainty* than of any event or any day of a single year ago.

Witnesses are aided by events — helped by memoranda, rendered absolutely solid by letters from the party to be charged. Of all the witnesses on earth, *letter* witnesses, well used, are the most believed and convincing. They come with the sanctity of coolness. They are like promissory notes and Bible records — hard to dispute from their sacredness and solemnity.

CHAPTER XIV.

JUSTICE CASES.

Early mention has been made of Dickinson's start in practice as a barefooted lawyer in a bar-room justice court trial, and Waite's integrity in the Maumee Valley in similar cases; of Shaffer's battle with Van Arman, of Seward's country cases near Auburn, and a volume more might be written of Lincoln's luck in pioneer practice. But the purpose of this item is to illustrate the turn of justice cases.

Justice court practice is never to be despised by one who would know the law in all its different phases. In fact, it is generally believed that more real work is given to the square inch in this division of trial practice than even the Supreme Court cases. The sums involved are, of course, limited to one or three hundred dollars, and yet justice cases constitute about one-half in number of any county's court business, either by original or appeal cases. Their number is very considerable, and of much interest to the community.

The law has wisely simplified the pleadings, and almost all declarations are oral, with ample room for an amendment. Should one assume to file written declarations he will be held to greater certainty, and therefore they are not in common use with western courts and lawyers. With issue joined but few cases are won for defendant without a jury, and the struggle at once becomes interesting. There are two methods of procedure open to the advocate — one to try his case fully with a jury, and the other to rely on an appeal. If there is a sure defense, the jury method is safest.

But suppose it is a disputed building bill — a case where defendant's set-off exceeds plaintiff's demand? Then, by all means, *sue separately*, and let each party litigate his own action in his own way. If A. has a claim of $50, and B. $200, the chances of recovery beyond the $50 would be better in a separate action. To illustrate: Baer & Son sued Backus for their commission in selling a lot for $1,150, and recovered $25, which was duly appealed. Then Backus sued Baer for breach of a contract to sell him the lot for $950, the stipulated price, and after giving in evidence the contracts on the letter-head of Baer & Son, signed by the firm name, dated six months previous, and showing he was compelled to purchase at an advance of $200 without the aid of Baer & Son, recovered $200. This case was appealed, and by chance both came on for trial by jury at same day in the circuit.

So far, it was clear that if they either had a cause of action it was better to separate them. So it further appears the larger case is called first. The contract and some evidence offered to make a *prima facie* case, is put before the jury, when suddenly the defendants deny their partnership, and insist that the elder Baer is relieved by absence from the State at the date of the written memoranda, and even when the commission suit was brought never knew of it, and was not bound by it, having dissolved with the son six months before.

Ingenuous as this appears, it was met by a sevenfold answer: (1) that for four years defendants had been partners, and never gave notice of dissolution; (2) that they had leased their office as partners, and the young man had remained in it; (3) they used the same signs and letter-heads; (4) they sued as partners; (5) they appealed the cross-suit as such; (6) the young man swore to partnership in presence of three witnesses; (7) he signed the firm name, and continued to, for a year after the alleged dissolution. It was then urged that in seven ways they left themselves held out as partners; in short, it was *forgery* in signing papers, *perjury* in swearing to it, or *partnership* in having authority to act for the firm within the scope of the partnership. Judgment passed for $200, and the smaller suit was discontinued, the real merits reached by separate suits.

I have chosen this case as instructive, and will add one more to enforce the lesson: A. and G. were partners, settled up and dissolved before the war. After the war G. became tenant of A., and suit was brought for rent, which resulted in its collection — some $200. G. was very angry, and sued out before a German justice, who allowed G. to read his bill of particulars in evidence, to the great disgust of defendant's counsel. Judgment passed for $217. The case was remanded by *certiorari*, and affirmed! there having been no evidence shown for A, and the justice's return was carefully drawn to match all assumed errors.

A. was greatly annoyed, and in danger of losing a snug sum unlawfully. His counsel sued the other side of the account, $228, and applied to the Appellate Court to stay proceedings, in a strong showing of A.'s ability to pay, if he justly ought to, and G.'s inability. The stay was granted. The last suit resulted in an interesting trial. The old books had been pasted full of soldier pictures and ballads nearly covering the items of partnership settlements, but finally showed the last balance. The jury found for A. $228, and thus relieved him of a double payment by determined efforts of counsel.

I think the foregoing incidents known to have happened, together with the humorous experience in the next item, will explain and enforce the lesson that there is some art in justice practice, and he who would win his case must not forget that great men like Seward and Waite were never ashamed of their victories in the lower courts — the poor man's hope for justice.

WESTERN JUSTICE. *

In 1881 a wealthy farmer named Brocksmit, with his son William, a youth of eighteen, went to New Mexico from Cedar Rapids, Iowa, to engage in cattle farming. A well stocked ranch of 300 acres was purchased near Sante Fe, and the father subsequently returned to Iowa, leaving William in charge. William was educated, refined and intelligent, and soon became very popular in society, attending balls and socials,

---

* Case before referred to, but not sufficiently to illustrate the *fine work* fully.

dressed in the height of fashion, was exceedingly prepossessing in appearance, and a universal favorite in the region for miles around.

Early in January, 1882, he was found dead in the doorway of his house, with three bullet holes in his head, the indications pointing to a brutal murder. A reward of $500 was offered for the arrest of the murderer, and three weeks later Damoin Romero was arrested, with $60 in cash, a sealskin cap and a horse blanket belonging to young Brocksmit in his possession. Romero was a former friend of Brocksmit's, and one year older; rather fine looking, of good family, and excellent character.

The two lived together and were very intimate, attended the same balls, exchanged clothing—or rather William often lent Romero his clothes to appear well at parties, mainly to improve his friend's appearance and increase his chances in winning a fair Spanish maiden whom Romero went with, and who was also attached to a half-breed Indian, a strong rival of Romero. Brocksmit was murdered on Wednesday, and his body was discovered on Sunday evening by Mr. Shaffer, the former owner of the ranch, with whom both he and Romero boarded. Brocksmit had evidently been standing in the front doorway, as indicated by fresh blood stains on the carpet just inside the door, but the body was dragged inside and left till discovered.

Suspicion was not alone confined to Romero, whose possession of property belonging to William was a matter quite general in their daily business. He often wore William's clothing, and was more like a brother than a possible murderer. He had no bad habits such as drinking, swearing or quarreling, was harmless in appearance, with nothing to indicate a nature so debased as the crime seemed to require. He was below medium height, slender, jet black hair, clear black eyes that looked steadily at one, and had a large, broad forehead. There was no apparent motive for him to commit such a crime, and he had never quarreled with Brocksmit as far as was known.

Romero's story which he told at the trial sounds plausible, and an extract is herewith given: "I am innocent of the murder. Brocksmit was killed by an Indian by the name of Rael, who was taken from the Comanches, and raised by a Mexican family. I was in the yard milking the cows, and this Indian and William were out in front of the house shooting at a mark. I went through the kitchen with the milk, and the Indian said, 'Now you want to go with me.' I asked why? He said, 'You will have to.' I asked him again, and he said, 'You have killed the man,' pointing to William. I was so frightened I dropped the milk pail on the floor, walked out with him and found 'Silver Tail' and the Indian's horse tied to a wagon. We untied them, and walked down for a mile. Then the Indian took a lot of money out and gave me $60. I think William had nearly $300 when the Indian killed him. The night before the killing, the Indian came, and William was asleep. He knocked, and wanted to stay all night. William awoke and said, 'let him in,' which I did, and he slept by the fire, and next morning went away. He came back at night. I went after the cows, and when I returned Brocksmit and the Indian were shooting at a mark. After the Indian killed William he took the money, except $9 in silver. I was so frightened when I found he was dead that I did not know what to do. I liked him. I was teaching him Spanish, and he teaching me English, so each could talk plainer to the other. He often lent me his clothes to visit Senorita Padilla. The Indian was jealous of me."

Justice Dacey released the Indian, who proved by three Mexicans that he was seen several miles away at the time of the killing. (Time not being very definitely fixed, seems to render his *alibi* none too substantial.) There are grave doubts now about the genuineness of the Indian's *alibi*. He has recently married the fair Senorita Padilla, and indications point to his possessing considerable wealth at present, a condition heretofore unknown of him. Romero was tried, convicted and sentenced to be hanged February 2, 1883. His case was appealed, but the sentence was confirmed. His mother and sisters visited him in prison, kissed his hands, cheeks and eyes most tenderly. Never could a parting scene on any stage equal their emotion. He bore up bravely, and to each told the same story of his innocence. To the Catholic Father Corsini he firmly denied all guilt. He slept soundly, took his meals regularly, and never showed any sign of changing his statement. No man ever faced the gallow more bravely. Even in the touching scene with his little sisters he was brave and tender, and as the mother and children took their last embrace, the picture of one going to death and disgrace for another's crime, if his story is to be believed, was a sad, sad ending of a young man's friendship; for Romero loved Brocksmit as few men ever love each other.

Seeing there was another with a double motive— the Indian, who goes unwhipped of justice, I am convinced that Romero was incapable of the brutal act, lacked a motive, and should have been held to await results or acquitted.

It only illustrates the anxiety of a people to get a speedy revenge.

The danger of capital punishment, when certainty of guilt is lacking, and how circumstances may embarrass one and lead to appearances of guilt. "No man becomes suddenly vile," is one of the old, old Roman maxims, believed for ages, and seems to have been forgotten in Romero's defense, else overcome by the prosecution and outside pressure.

From the description of the prisoner, his habits, life, looks, relatives and story of the murder, he should have been held as a witness to convict the Indian, the real guilty party, by all means. Remember, I do not favor loose criminal laws. Punishment should be certain, that society may be safe. If it appeared that he knew of the murder, which he must have known, it was his duty to speak out, and not conceal it. But the more was required. He lacked hardness of heart, intent, the essence of all crimes; may have been ignorant of the law that compels one to expose high crimes and return stolen property. Many people have been careless and concealed crimes that were not guilty of the act. The hanging law should never do worse than the prisoner. In Romero's case it was worse than a "life for a life." The Indian's treachery and jealousy did that deed, and the Indiana law, leaving it to the jury to say "hanging or imprisonment," would correct the danger of hanging the innocent.

It required no great gift to win such a suit. A full opening statement well followed by circumstances, *admitting all but the killing*, would have insured victory.

A NEW YORK JUSTICE STORY.

Judge C—— tells a good story of a young Irish justice in New York, whose qualifications for the office were well suited to his class of customers, being as ignorant of law as he was well versed in prize fights and prison discipline. It happened that the judge had a client sued before the new justice, as indorser to a $160 note, secured by the clearest kind of fraud. The judge was loth to take the case, and expressing many doubts of his likelihood of winning, walked down to the crowded little court room with his German client to meet the Hibernian plaintiff before his honor. The note was offered, and examination commenced, when the judge began to question as to fraud in its execution. He was cut short by his honor, who refused to hear any argument.

"But, your honor," said the judge, "let me read you the statute of our State, with which your honor is familiar as the settled law of New York."

"I don't want to hear any statute lah!" said the court indignantly. "I'll try this case on the rights of it, lah or no lah!"

"But, your honor," said the judge, "let me read you a decision of our Court of Appeals. The words seem made for this case."

"And how cud thot be," interrupted the court, "when this case had not been tried at oll yet?" (Applause in the court room). The court looked pleased at his last victory.

"But one word, and I am done, your honor," said the judge. "I see your honor is no novice in law. I have heard of your honor's learning in the popular run in the campaign just over in which your honor distanced all competition. (Applause). I know something of your honor's skill as a marksman, and coming from the wealthy and educated classes of Ireland, your honor must have read thoroughly the British law which is similar to our own—"

"I want nothing of your British lah," interrupted the bewildered court.

"But I had not completed my sentence," continued the judge. "I was about to carry your honor back to your early college days, and give you that Latin quotation from the Roman law that your honor surely remembers." (Here the judge recited a few sentences of Cicero, while the court looked wise.) "I would not cite this law to every court, much less to courts of this nature, but I well know to whom I am talking, and could as well be understood and appreciated by a man of your honor's rare learning as by the highest court in our Empire State — a seat upon whose bench I hope your honor may yet adorn."

"Repate that lah agin," said the court. It was repeated. The court drew himself up with great dignity, and said:

"I was agin ye on the statute lah, ye mind; I was agin ye on the Appeals lah; I was strong agin ye on the

British lah — I want no British lah; but, do ye mind, I'm *wid ye on the Roman lah*. (Turning to plaintiff.) Go way wid yer note and burn it, it was made by fraud."

Strange to say, his honor became noted as a learned judge, and respected as one who was *wise* in the law.

CIRCUIT PRACTICE.

Circuit Court cases are, in the main, of about five kinds: (1.) Appeals from Probate and Commissioners or Justice Courts. The most important of these are contested will cases. As the question of competency to make a will, or undue influence in its executoin, are matters of fact for a jury to determine, and evidence may be given of it by lay witnesses, as well as professional experts, the chief issue is: who can show the clearest proof, and who best present it in this branch of practice. And it is well to say in passing that in the trial of circuit cases about *twenty* questions of fact will arise to one question of law, and the one who best masters his *facts* will generally win on the merits.

Courts all like to reach the core of a controversy, and will do so if they can at the earliest instance. It will then be assumed that early on receiving a case into his office, every good lawyer will set down in black and white the points relied upon, the witnesses, the address of each, and what is to be shown by them. Judge Curtis goes a step further, and has their testimony written out, and signed, and sworn to, if need be, for a greater certainty.

Assuming these precautions are observed — and all of them, save the last, should be rigidly adhered to —

the next step is equal attention to the law of the case, in its order to be posted. What a decision holds to be the law of a given subject, if ready and in reach, may be the turning point of the issue.

A simple list of witnesses, without knowing what can be proved by them, is only a half brief on any question. It must be like writing — as intelligent to another as to its author. Who knows who will try the issue? Who knows but sickness, absence or accident may throw it in the hands of an utter stranger? Then bear in mind this important item: " Be ye also ready," in fact, and law, and evidence.

Names of witnesses' residence, and their evidence; names of authority where found, and its essence, taken down early in every case, filed with the case, or written on the file cover inside, will pay a thousand-fold for time consumed. It will prevent confusion when the case comes suddenly for trial, often without a moment's warning.

Read Ten Trial Rules often, and see the necessity of visiting the scene of the circumstance. There are little things that form a background to cases that set out the picture with far greater clearness; and if I repeat this word often it is intentional, for no word equals it in any case. Clearness of fact, clearness of law, clearness of statement, clearness of argument, and clearness of the issue can never be over-estimated. It must not be tedious. Good lawyers know by intuition when to stop proving, and reading, and speaking.

The issue in a will case is not *what ought to have been done*, but whether what was done was the testator's will, unclouded by incompetency, and uninfluenced by interested heirs and advisers.

The issue in a civil damage case is, "where one of two *innocent* parties must suffer a loss from the carelessness of a third person, *the party who enabled the loss to occur must bear it.*" This is a general rule in torts and accident cases, where by careless driving, or imperfect bridges and machinery, some one was injured, the guilty should bear the loss.

He who continued to use a defective boiler, knowing it to be so, was forced to pay damages. He who allowed a rotten clothes reel to stand in his yard was forced by a new tenant (to whom all things were warranted to be set in good order), recently to pay for an injury from the falling reel. He who enabled the loss to occur had to bear it.

Very much depends on *tact* in railroad accident cases that are liable to require skill in management. The runner who was badly injured by falling out of a car door, as a train suddenly halted at the Grand Trunk Junction, recovered a heavy verdict through the adroitness of Ben. Butler, who insisted that the man was inside the door, and not at all guilty of negligence. And although the victim moaned aloud, "I'm to blame! I'm to blame! If I'd kept inside, this never would have happened!" Even this was called *delirium!* and a pathetic appeal made by repeating it at the very opening of the argument. Taking the "bull by the horns" and disarming the enemy.

This leads to the great question of contributory negligence, that the best of counsel must guard well to avoid showing. There is no recovery where it is shown, and it is vital to the issue. Still courts allow the jury to say, for it is their province, who was the guilty party in the line of negligence.

If there is any conflict — even a *scintilla* of evidence that gives the case to a jury to decide, narrow as a wire though the facts in dispute may be, a jury will construe them as equity dictates. The evidence will furnish the foundation, the law will apply it to principles, but the jury will judge the merits of the injury, and fix the blame of it on him who should bear it.

The issue in accounts or debts, or business paper, depends so much on the candor of witnesses, that thoroughness is the only true motto to prepare by.

So with the trials of slander and libel cases, that fill so many days of city court business, they turn on the foundation facts from which they arose. Much will rest on candor; much on character, and not very much on unknown law of libel. These are sensational or paper cases, that consume time and pay poorly.

Under breach of contracts of various kinds, considerable money is yearly recovered. It is not only right but righteous to compel men to live up to their contracts, and counsel who appear for plaintiff have an easy road to enforce such matters as right and equity should enforce in a court of justice.

The trial of grain gambling cases, collisions, endorsements, sureties on bonds, and land contracts, with occasional breach of promise and malpractice cases, will fill a good space on every circuit docket, but the rules governing each are best explained in special works on the subject.

It is enough to know that the law of a trial is like other trials, but the *facts* of every trial may vary, and are likely to differ materially. That is why a brief of facts and law is essential. That is why evidence must be studied, and witnesses made to reveal the truth without concealment, and with candor and circumstances.

There will arise arson cases, right of way cases, corporation contracts and paving matters, lines to determine, titles to establish, estates to settle, and election contests.

Mysterious are the ways of men in business! They often spend a hundred dollars to settle a quarter hundred dispute. But the true lawyer need not advise bad law suits. The true rule is the case early mentioned in this volume of Chief Justice Waite's career: To find the real merits in the office, regardless of what clients want them to be, and advise accordingly, allowing no client to be judge in your own office, but make that office and your judgment the Supreme Court of all cases before any burden is brought on clients unwisely.

CHAPTER XV.

CRIMINAL COURT CASES.

TWO STRANGE DEFENSES.

Larceny, burglary, arson, assault with intent to kill, robbery, forgery, embezzlement and murder, are the chief offenses tried in criminal courts. The first is so common that the proof of property and the taking requires but a few moments, and generally results in a speedy determination. The works on criminal practice treat extensively of the essentials to be shown, and hint at the defenses. The felonious taking of another's goods is always confined to the depraved, and character is one of the best defenses for the early offenders; failure of identity, with steady employment and lack of motive, go a great way to disprove it, and few good men or women suffer under this charge, if properly defended. That the police should single out one, it is not always conclusive of guilty knowledge or intention.

Burglary, a crime next to murder, will also bear the marks of a hardened nature. Burglars are either caught near the act, in the act, or with marks of the crime upon their persons. Character should be of weight, for no good man would ever become so depraved, and instances must be rare of this crime being committed by early offenders. As the Almighty never mistakes in putting up a human face, so a jury should be able to judge some by appearances, and counsel with a real burglar to defend, has his hands full in preparing.

Arson may be different. Too many over insurances are collected by men who burn buildings with mercenary intent, and never dream of the dreadful consequences. Rich men, or comparatively well off, have committed arson and embezzlement. Indeed, so common has become the latter offense, that few can not remember some one well up in society who defaulted and condoned it, or left for a neighboring nation. I recall an instance successfully defended, where one worked twenty-one months traveling for a tobacco house, and was short $2,200, who changed the books to conceal it, failed to report as collected, worked at $600 a year and expenses, hoping to have an increase in July and again in January, whose wife had been told that he was an excellent salesman, and should be rewarded; that it mattered less what his expenses were if sales were in proportion. Well, January came, and no increase. The salesman made a statement, slipped it under the store door, and fled to Canada. It clearly showed the embezzlement. He wrote to the house to meet him, and he would settle. He was told by one of the firm to come back and work it out, and consented. Once in the States he was arrested. Covered all over with guilt, to all appearances, how can one so guilty be defended?

Lawyers do get such cases. Let us see:

"How did this shortage arise?" "By advertising, and treating, and spending too much for the house."

"Why did you conceal it?" "To retain my position," he answers.

"Did you not fear detection?" "No, I was paying up old debts with new collections, like a retail merchant buying on credit."

"Did they know of your high expenses?" "Yes, they threatened me once, and wanted to limit it to $4 a day. They turned me off partly, and my wife interceded."

"Ah, she knew of it?" "Yes, all about it."

One witness and two circumstances may not show an *intent* after all.

So, with these facts before the jury, a good character, an excellent wife — a fine witness — a splendid and full statement, all consistent as stated; a memorandum book with thirty paid up and crossed off embezzled items, it was urged to the jury:

That there was no intent, the essence of the offense established—going to Canada was not embezzlement.

The statement was not of itself an offense. The memorandum showed, if anything — anxiety to pay. The wife's statement showed he had hope of high wages. He was holding on, and hoping to pay all and be even.

The time for a raise was a time of disaster. He was overtaken by a storm, and hung on the life-boat of one reason which should clear him; *anxiety to maintain his little home, and increase the firm's business.* Not for finery, or fine houses, or horses, but on a limited salary, night and day, he roamed the States to build up a revenue for his cigar firm. Going through 400 saloons at their bidding, treating, as directed "not to be too stingy," who knows but the firm had received its value? Who knows but for twenty years their revenue would be increased by the expenditure, had he not, after all, *exceeded* his authority, and used too much of that money out of which he had permission to pay expenses and his paltry salary?

Sure enough, this line of thought cleared him.

The very best defense in forgery cases, is implied authority to sign. That is, if through some dealing, it can be implied. The next best is not guilty and good character. This is not a case of *alibi* defense. It must be boldly met, and mastered in the office first, then in the court room. And in this connection, it may be said all cases should be first won in the office, then in the court room. It is the only safe rule, the only reliance to reach a victory.

The defense of murder and manslaughter cases, judged by results, is more often successful than almost any other. I remember many an instance, where on first reading of a brutal homicide, it seemed sure conviction to the perpetrator, and as surely ended in an acquittal. Of course there were circumstances of an outraged home, or a quarrel, a plea of self-defense, or an immediate cause that gave room for doubt, that before seemed a certainty.

Take the Barnard-Curtis homicide of Lapeer. The accused was supposed to be in love with a seventy year old minister, more adoration than love about it. She was fair, rich, and under forty. But such was her desire to attend his service, that she followed him from place to place to attend his meetings. He seems to have been annoyed, and his wife also, by her attentions. It is mid-winter in Lapeer. An evening service has commenced. The snow is deep; the village houses dimly lighted. Mrs. Barnard enters church late. Her face is marked and scratched; her hair disarranged, and she is in a deep blush of confusion. A few moments more and messengers arrive to call Elder Curtis to the house, there to find his wife burned to a blister nearly all over the body. Her long gray hair burned off her head; her face blackened; her arms charred; her body in a horrible condition, and she in dreadful agony. A notary takes her dying declaration. It is, in effect, that she was reading by the stand by lamplight, and was not able to attend evening service. That Mrs. Barnard called, and threw a standcloth over her, poured oil all over it — during which Mrs. Curtis clawed and scratched and contended with her murderer. That the hot flames soon smothered her. But she was sure Sarah Barnard had tried to kill her.

Mrs. Barnard's whereabouts were traced. She claimed to have been lost on the way to church, but not to have been near Mrs. Curtis. Her face marks and deranged hair were said to come from a fall; she slipped down on the way, and was excited from being lost. This was her story. The poor victim died suddenly, proclaiming in dying breath, Mrs. Barnard has killed me!

This seems a clearly made out murder case. Let us see. Rich people employ counsel. Judges grant a change of venue. Experts, under the artful management of J. B. Moore, of Lapeer, and G. V. N. Lothrop, of Detroit, explain that of thirteen exploded lamps, eleven broke, looked and appeared like the Curtis lamp left burning on the stand that evening. It was an explosion they say, and a confusion. But what of the scratches on Mrs. Barnard? Oh, as she says, marks of a fall on the crust, and confusion from losing her way in a strange village. But what of the dying words of Mrs. Curtis? That is accounted for, says Dr. Pratt, by a *vivid dream,* so common to old people. She was, doubtless, very jealous, doubtless knew of Mrs. Barnard's being in Lapeer, fell asleep, dreamed, half awake suddenly clutched the stand cloth, jarred the lamp; it exploded and set her on fire, and, in the confusion, it seemed to her that her enemy had been there in reality. Two arguments on this theory led a jury to say not guilty. But they *may have been mistaken.*

If there is one lesson clear in this chapter, it seems to be that in all criminal cases nothing is impossible to one who has fertility of resources, adroitness and tact to apply them, and eloquence enough to enforce the theory successfully. Remember, *every case must have a theory*; every defense must seem reasonable, and every lawyer must be ingenious to be lucky in criminal practice.

GIVE A LITTLE.

I have watched the progress of great advocates when trifles arose like clogs in their pathway; how they yielded, and gave way some trifling thing to get a better one, and never noticed a strong man to be very captious over minor matters.

If a man has merit in his action he can not afford to smother it with husks and shavings, or obscure it with the dust of petty differences. When one is hunting for deer he can pass by quails and pheasants, in the hope of better game with the same ammunition. But many a lawyer spends his force on everything alike, in one long dead monotony; as if he must win every point or stand defeated.

Racers are never so silly. They lose a score often for interest, or gain their end at the home stretch amid applause and surprise together.

I have seen a lawyer spend a half-hour of his speech in abusing witnesses that a hint of his mistaken story would have reconciled with reason. It is far better to give way a little, and gain by it, than to adhere too closely and divide a jury on trifles. The truth is, in many cases parties testify with doubtful intensity, and counsel should be guarded not to allow his client's belief to form the foundation of his demand. Belief is one thing, evidence quite another thing. Often we believe fraud has been committed in assignment and chattel mortgage cases; seldom are we able to show it by evidence, sworn to from actual knowledge.

Suspicions are common in belief, but are never evidence, and they are the usual foundation on which fraud cases are based and prosecuted.

Facts that cannot be proven should be dropped. Matters of no bearing should be treated accordingly. Cases are not won in abuse of counsel, or abuse of witnesses, or often on *extreme* positions. The average mind prefers some sense and reason in argument. To reach a jury one need not be too very certain of every point, and thereby lose all, if anything. Far better to give a little; to go a step in the direction of an adversary, and he may go so far in return.

After every case some things will come to light which met in the true spirit of manliness earlier, may have saved hundreds in expenses, and may have settled the whole matter.

I was never more touched by the sense of fairness then in listening to Judge V., in Leavenworth, at the hearing of a divorce case where both parties had shown far too much bitterness. After hearing all patiently, the judge remarked:

"Have you always lived this way?" "No, sir," said the wife mildly, "only since he neglected me for other women."

"Did you not love this man when you married him?" "Certainly. I would love him yet, if he used me decently."

"Come nearer, sir," said the court, addressing the defendant, "How long has this trouble lasted?" "Only for a year or so, your honor."

"Did you not love this woman when you married her?" "Yes, your honor."

By this time both were in tears, and the court added: "I am afraid you have been magnifying your differences. I advise you to make up at once. If you will, I'll help you."

"So, you think (turning to the wife), that you could live happily together?" "Yes, your honor."

A few more words, and man and wife went out arm in arm from the effect of a little touch of nature in the court's kind words. Had lawyers always done as much, many quarrels could have been peaceably settled.

COURAGE IN COURT.

True courage is not boastful. Determined men are silent and full of deeds, with few words. To threaten, is to betray weakness. Real strength is better shown in deeds — something done, something executed. "Report what has happened, and never talk of what is likely to happen," was a rule of the *Tribune* under Greeley's management. Simple courage can be shown by even refusing to quarrel, or even show anger over little matters, and reserving one's strength for better uses. "If I only had courage," said a student, "but when I stand up in court, I tremble." Then *go where you are afraid to go, and go there often.*

Courage comes in three ways, first, by confidence in your positions, second, by thorough familiarity with law and evidence to sustain them, and last, by frequent experiences in like matters. Swimmers learn and gain by practice; singers by drill, and speakers by similar means in a like manner.

"When I first walked down the aisle of a great church," said a leader of society, "I felt that if I could fall through the floor, it would be a relief to me; now I never think of it, and I made up my mind," he continued, "that I would go till I overcome my bashfulness."

There is little more needed than an aptness, a will, courage and frequent trials to ripen one in practice. Learning early is the right course. Neither too forward nor too slow, but with a resolute stand to keep in line, and not be beaten out of one's course by his own fault, is the true resolution. There is no reason why one lawyer should yield all rights to another. There is no rule why one with right on his side (which is always a majority), should quail before a multitude. If he does so, he does it at his peril, and will find himself weakening, where he should be gaining courage and clientage. Clients like to be well represented. They hate to be talked out of court, or bluffed out of a verdict by lack of proper resentment of counsel. If a lawyer is defeated after a hard fight and an artful and courageous action, he loses little by defeat, and gains much by his adroitness; but a heartless and half heedless defense, is never respected even by an adversary. Every lawyer must make his rank by deserving acts of practice that shows his worthiness. Counsel are *timed* like racers — they are judged by their record. Too many losses, too many petty quarrels, too many little acts of inefficiency, even one such act, endangers the confidence in ability, and prevents promotion.

Soldiers are promoted for valor, citizens are elevated for their uprightness and ability, with a reasonable art of showing it, and lawyers are not sought out in dingy back offices, dressed and surrounded by negligence, unless they have mental courage and caliber to win court victories. Why is the rare painting singled out from the others, except for some bold outlines and striking features that others have failed to equal. He that would win, must pay the price of advancement — courage, patience, clearness and a will to hold on faithfully to the end.

A SOLDIER'S VERDICT.

Col. Charles Spencer, of Brooklyn, tells of his experience with the late Edwin James, in a soldier's claim for $1,800, money loaned to a friend after the war, and in the story is a rare point of practice — a hint on cross-examination, which the *Brooklyn Eagle* gives as follows:

Defendant's counsel, Mr. James: — "You loaned him $1,800?" "I did sir."

"When, sir?" "In 1866."

"Where did you get it?" "I earned it, sir," he replied, meekly.

"When did you earn it?" "During the war, sir," (meekly).

"What was your occupation during the war?" "Fighting, sir," (modestly).

Up to this time the case had been doubtful, but the preponderance of evidence was easily seen for the soldier.

Col. Spencer went to the jury with great force on the career of the soldier: "Who guarded our liberties, helped to save one nation for one people, risked his life," etc., and grew touchingly eloquent, and gained a full verdict.

"That war speech did it," said attorney James, "and you discovered it all through my cross-examination."

"Yes," said Spencer," and you failed to discern that my client was a *Confederate* soldier! or you could have changed the verdict."

It don't need a double four-horse team to draw a sure conclusion as to the effect of this cross-examination, and the shrewd replies of Spencer's client, who, with his counsel, knew where to stop,— the key to many a signal victory.

WHEN TO STOP.

Aaron Burr and Abraham Lincoln both knew when to stop talking to a jury. Burr spoke generally only thirty minutes; Mr. Lincoln's best efforts were delivered in about twenty minutes. Patrick Henry was of the same terse style of speakers, and Tom Marshall not far behind in sharply cut sentences. These men all knew when to stop.

Horace Greeley, Wilber F. Story and Whitelaw Reid, are of this happy style of writers whose words end up a period with a ring and tingle to be remembered. Spurgeon, Collier and Buckley have a share in the gift of brevity, but few ministers, and fewer lawyers, begin to know the right ending to an argument.

Many lack insight. Some lack confidence, and others prove on beyond the merits, and attempt to prove their side, then disprove the other side for greater certainty. They generally create uncertainty. No amount of instruction can teach what should come by intuition. If an advocate can't take the hint by the eyes of his jury, he will not be likely to profit by a law lecture. The fact is, this work is less intended for instruction, and more for suggestions and examples of good practice drawn from the efforts of many counsel.

It will be noticed by a speaker of any note, that he states interestingly, argues logically, and closes with warmth and energy. The clear, deliberate start, the forcible and determined body, and eloquent ending of an address, pleases most people best; and *when to stop*, is instantly after the three things named are accomplished. It is not necessary to play a repeat ten or twelve times to be impressive. The music of a band or an opera is not looked for in a court room argument. "I could listen to that man all night," said a hearer of Wendell Phillips; but will he not be all the better listener again by getting a little less than the full measure?

Lawyers who expect to increase their business, will have time enough for practice in speaking; but to practice on an audience, or more especially on a poor patient jury, is a sad error in judgment.

As in the story of Col. Spencer's soldier verdict, a broad hint is given on over trying cases or too much cross-examination, so the rule applies to too many witnesses. Two of a kind, six on character, and a kind of men to be believed, is better than a cloud of unreliables. Quit with a victory; begin and end with good evidence; chink in with medium one's if they are needed, but never depend on counting witnesses to secure a preponderance of evidence. It shows a weakness to tell a story over too often; even a good telling dulls the pith of it. Some one will vary and change the shading, till it falls short of interest and loses its corners. The round cornered periods and sentences never take like a vigorous, sharp ending.

Think, for a moment, of the vast crowd of poor speakers that tire a court and weary a jury with endless speeches, burying their evidence under words, covering their points three deep under periods of great length and great transparency. While one should guard against stopping one second short of saying the right thing, and *always* proving his own case completely by his own witnesses, he cannot be too careful to end his evidence and close his argument with a climax that is telling and convincing. There is no rule so safe in testimony and argument, as to *quit with a victory.*

REMEMBER LITTLE THINGS.

It is well to remember not only that kindness begets kindness, but that "vainly is the net set in sight of the bird;" so that kindness must be a growth of our being, an every day practice. Chief Justice Waite never passed an old acquaintance, juryman, witness, or party to a case, without a cordial recognition. His nature was one long day of even dealing, and considerate deportment to others, high and low alike.

A friend says of Matt Carpenter: " I was with him in an important ship canal case, when hundreds of thousands depended on the issue. He had turned away caller after caller of distinguished senators and visitors ; he had declined all company, when the secretary announced, ' Mr. Carpenter, the little colored girl waits to see you.' Instantly the pen dropped, and the senator had her come in, and said in a kind voice, 'well Liza, did you get the place?' 'No, Massa Carpenter; that place was all full.' It was to be janitress of a committee room; the senator added, 'wait a moment, and I'll go with you, Liza;' and out into the evening to the committee room, went the great supreme court lawyer, and soon secured the situation, saying: 'these men callers can come again, but it would break the little girl's heart to turn her away rudely.' The next day he won the canal case, but the joy at finding a place for little Liza was as great to the advocate as his greater victory."

The incident touched me; acts like these give all orators a better hearing before a jury; it is not enough to be great once, true greatness is always great.

I was in a United States court, when a distinguished counsel returned from a long trip to Europe. His return to the bar was cordially greeted; first he paid his respects to the court, and then turning towards the bar he met the old janitor on his way with an ice pitcher, whom he greeted with equal politeness, and so on through the bar, but nothing marked the gentleman more than the natural ease with which he remembered the colored janitor.

In most cases lawyers have to win the respect of parties and witnesses, and when one gets the name of sharpness, he draws that much less from his witness, and is that much more discounted by the jury. As "modulation is the music of oratory," so tact is the weapon of an examiner. Men of fairness, men of candor and reputation are not long in getting the facts of a controversy in issue; therefore, it is all essential to be manly, to overcome the dread of testifying, to lead a witness to truth telling in natural language.

To gain the confidence of everyone, and deserve it, requires a life of uprightness. To such a lawyer, half of his cases are easy victories. His words are weighty. Suppose such a man asks a witness, "may you not be a little mistaken?" the answer will be, "Yes, possibly." "May not the plaintiff have been just a little to blame?" "Yes, he may have." "And you may be just a little prejudiced?" "Yes." "May he not have spoken harshly?" "Yes." "May he not have looked just a little angry, or disappointed; or attempted to show his manhood; then his courage; then his anger; then he did brace up?" "Yes, sir." "Just as you or any brave man would do, did he?" "Yes, sir." "And was ready to strike (or shoot) if forced to?" "Yes, of course he was." After these yeses begin to be repeated, the judge would get "yes" to matters of importance. If one can listen a few days to the average run of court arguments, he will soon see how poor and awkward, how dull and monotonous most of them sound to outsiders. It is the province of counsel to present facts in a winning way, and in language persuasive. If he sang in a choir, he would practice; if he lectured, he would write and commit every paragraph; if he dreamed of fame as a painter, he would study fine art diligently; and this is but *one man's opinion*, but firmly believed in, that any advocate can be greatly aided by a thorough study of fine speeches, arts, and samples of rare work by others, and one that also believes many cases have been won by pleasant and pungent arguments, where the facts pointed to the other side without this rarest of all gifts, earnest eloquence.

"He that is wise, is wise for himself," is a saying that ought to be framed, and hung up in every law office in the land. If he is wise for himself, he will neglect not to secure prompt settlements, and thereby lasting friendship with clients. That man who owes his counsel an X, or double eagle, or half hundred, some amount too small to be sued for, will go elsewhere, and pay his money so long as the debt case can slide along uncancelled; and more clients change lawyers for lack of prompt settlements than any other cause, but the losing of cases. Of course lack of success always leads to change of counsel. But a lawyer is to blame who has failed to tell the real prospects of success and failure at the beginning; he that is wise will take a long look ahead, and provide a permanent life work by reasonable charges, honest advice and sturdy integrity. These all make friends, and friends make practice.

I have heard attorneys say, "All the business I ever got came first from strangers; my friends never helped me any." Poor fellow, he had never "grappled any friend to him with hooks of steel," or his story would be different. "He that would have friends, must show himself friendly," is too true to need one word of comment. The wisdom of the ages by the wit of one, need never be distrusted. "Better a good name and loving favor, than great riches, makes another of the rare rules of law practice." One who would have "reason impelled by passion, sustained by learning, and adored by fancy," should gather maxims and rules, and commit passages until his mind becomes a fountain of fine thoughts and rare sayings, that come like an authority, for quotations always sound like authorities.

CHAPTER XVI.

ORDER OF TRIALS.

The first step after a counsel is retained, as attorney of record, is to determine how the parties will bring on the matter for trial or hearing. In the States where a code practice prevails, with but two actions, *ex delicto* and *ex contractu,* to entitle the cause on legal paper, *set up the facts fully*, and have plaintiff swear to them is all. This important act should be carefully done; at least, a pencil draft to be made by a competent lawyer. This, with answer or demurrer, forms an issue.

In common law practice States suits are begun by attachment, declaration, *capias*, replevin and summons, which are generally on printed forms and easily filled, except the first which requires the greatest care. Attention to details in either form will prevent confusion, and often a non-suit or demurrer, that greatly annoys a beginner in practice. Indeed, an experienced counsel of fixed reputation is injured by defeat on preliminary questions, and beginners are sorely mortified and recover slowly from early falls of this nature.

The things most to be noted are: *Names* of parties. There is no excuse for not knowing the full name of a plaintiff, and yet a $7,000 verdict was recently obtained, and that, too, after a lengthy trial, without noticing the error. An amendment cured the misnomer.

It may be well here to state that, under the now universally broad and liberal rules of amendment, the court has power, at any time before judgment, to amend any *process*, *pleading* or *proceeding* for the furtherance of justice.

As little is gained by dilatory pleas that at most lead merely to better pleadings, no time need be given here to that branch of unpopular practice. Suffice it to say, that sooner or later cases must come to trial on their merits, and the sooner so reached the better: except where one defends in criminal cases with a bitter prejudice, and then *time* is a feature to adhere to.

Suppose then a general issue, or not guilty, is pleaded, and the day is set for trial, are you ready? Let us see: Have you read your jury list? If not, some may be clients of your learned brother, others may belong by kindred or special relationship. This study of the panel is a rare point in practice. Two bad jurors may destroy the best argument. I know of one who raised a verdict many thousand dollars in a railroad condemnation case. Too much stress cannot be laid on a wise selection of a jury; not in the sense to get biased men in your favor, but fair, even handed, upright men. A verdict of twelve good men should satisfy almost any reasonable client.

With a jury sworn, are you ready? Well, you must be. But if some thorough work has been neglected in securing competent testimony and attending to bringing witnesses into court, you are still lacking. These details of practice can no more be neglected than colors in painting. The very best lawyers are most *thorough* in details. Judge Curtis is a master of this branch. Spending *three months* in the Buford case to prepare his facts and authorities, very much of the time with witnesses and people of the county, he knew the testimony by heart before an expert was sworn. This case was unusual, but is a reward for a lifetime. Like Patrick Henry's Parsons Case, it is immortal. So terse and touching is the address, that two friends read it alternately for twenty miles riding in a buggy to each other. It was born of great labor. All great efforts in court are born of intense labor. Van Dyke's speech in the Conspiracy Case, required weeks in process of preparing. So, too, was Seward's powerful appeal in the same contest, and Van Arman put the power of his young ambition for a half year in the same trial, and it made him a leader with western lawyers.

But I had not finished with the order of trials. All the eloquence, and art and personal skill avail little without *evidence!* Evidence is *the* great cellar wall, corner stone, body and arch of all cases. Argument is the keystone, only you must have the arch to fit it. Therefore besides the first step — selecting a good case to go to court with ; the second step, getting it well at issue ; the third step, choosing a good jury ; the fourth step, having your facts well sustained by evidence, or the fifth step, having formed and mastered your theory, you are reasonably certain, if your heart is in your case, of a good argument. True earnestness scorns all rules of rhetoric or logic. It speaks right on, like Mark Anthony, and will "put a tongue in every wound of Cæsar," to stir a jury up to duty. Study the arts of trial lawyers, like the painter studies his colors. Combine them, as he does, in harmony. Use them, as Anthony did, to attract, please, convince, excite and sway an audience to the side of right and justice.

A STRANGE SUCCESS.

During the early part of the war, in one of the Five Point regions of New York, a young Irish boy was arrested for larceny, tried, convicted, sent to Randall's Island Reformatory. While there, his brightness attracted the superintendent's attention, and he was apprenticed to a New Jersey farmer until of age, and removed from confinement.

In his new capacity he soon became useful, and gathered up his little savings. He called often on his poverty-stricken mother and sister, and soon gained a place for the latter, and a better home for the former. It was conditioned in his articles that he should receive four months schooling each year, two suits of clothes and $100 when of age, and he was permitted to do little odd jobs besides.

At eighteen he showed such a proficiency in scholarship as to desire to be a teacher, and bought his time of the farmer for the $100 and the extra clothing, and engaged as a district school teacher, meanwhile continuing to help his mother and sister, whom he removed from New York to Elizabethtown, New Jersey.

He succeeded well as a teacher, and studied law at odd hours; was admitted when of age, and commenced practice with great earnestness. Succeeding beyond his expectations, at the age of twenty-eight he had a practice worth four thousand a-year, when the Governor of the State appointed him District Judge at $2,000 salary, an office which requires less than half of his attention, so that he still continues practice, and is counsel for a railroad company, with fair prospects of future promotion, many believing he will yet be Governor of New Jersey!

Through all his prosperity he has never attempted to conceal his origin, but often in his eloquent addresses will crop out some pathetic allusion to his early life that makes him none the less respected for the burdens he has borne.

Is there any parallel picture in history? Starting from the lowest, fresh from the doors of crime, struggling over the double obstacles of character and poverty, he has conquered adversity by his own unaided efforts, and stands as a brilliant light of the New Jersey bar, and an honored advocate.

SHORT SAYINGS.

From Bible and best authors, Shakespeare and my scrap book:

Unstable as water, thou shalt not excel.

Quit yourselves like men.

Let him that girdeth on his harness boast not as he that putteth it off.

All that a man hath will he give for his life.

A word spoken in due season how good is it?

A word fitly spoken is like apples of gold in pictures of silver.

Faithful are wounds of a friend, but the kisses of an enemy are deceitful.

Iron sharpeneth iron, so a man sharpeneth the countenance of his friend.

The race is not to the swift, nor the battle to the strong, but time and chance happeneth to them all.

Love is strong as death.

Jealousy is cruel as the grave.

To give unto them beauty for ashes. The oil of joy for mourning; the garment of praise for the spirit of heaviness.

Consider the lilies of the field how they grow; they toil not, neither do they spin.

Out of the abundance of the heart the mouth speaketh.

The law is good, if a man use it lawfully.

The love of money is the root of all evil.

* * * * * *

Speech was given to man to disguise his thoughts.

The greatest happiness for the greatest number is the foundation of morals and legislation.

He that wrestles with us strengthens our nerves and sharpens our skill.

The cold neutrality of an impartial judge.

There is, however, a limit at which forbearance ceases to be a virtue.

He best can point them who can tell them most.

Praise undeserved is scandal in disguise, at every word a reputation dies.

For fools rush in where angels fear to tread.

To err is human, to forgive divine.

Great wits are sure to madness near allied.

None but the brave deserve the fair.

Dear beauteous death—the jewel of the just.—*Vaughan.*

" So dear to heaven is saintly chasity, that when a soul is sincerely so, a thousand liveried angels lackey her.

Driving far off each thing of sin and guilt."—*Milton.*

Of one who loved not wisely, but too well.

Trifles light as air are to the jealous confirmations strong as proofs of Holy Writ.

A good name in man or woman is the immediate jewel of their souls.

The robbed that smiles, steals something from the thief.

How sharper than a serpent's tooth is it to have a thankless child.

What a man's enemies say about him ought not to be taken as evidence.

We must be as courteous to a man as to a picture, which we are willing to give the advantage of a good light.

Critics are men who have failed in literature and art.

The secret of success in life, is for a man to be ready for his opportunity when it comes.

Massena was not himself until the battle began to go against him.

Fame is the perfume of heroic deeds.

Oh! Icy-hearted counsellors! if thou hopest for mercy in heaven, show mercy upon earth! worse than bloody hands is a hardened heart!

Keep with the good, and you will be one of them.

The ancients were inspired in races by dipping a torch in burning oil, and running with it in hand; the torches of the winners never went out.

There is no fiercer hell than failure in a great attempt.

Of all the agonies of life, the worst is that we have been deceived where we placed all the trust of love.

In character, in manner, in style, in all things, the supreme *excellence* is *simplicity.*

I am in earnest and I will not excuse, I will not retract an inch, I will be heard.

Popular opinion is the greatest lie in the world.— *Carlyle.*

Words only live when worthy to be said.

What a piece of work is man! How noble in reason; how infinite in faculties; in form and moving how express and admirable; in action how like an angel; in apprehension how like a God!

TO PREVENT DIVORCES.

The following beautiful and touching lines are from the closing portion of a discarded wife's letter to her angry husband, and such was the effect produced upon him by them that he returned to her and reformed. For beauty of expression and poetic imagery, these lines are unsurpassed by anything in the English language:

"May the gates of honor, plenty and happiness be ever open to thee and thine: may no sorrow disturb thy days nor grief distract thy nights; may the pillow of peace kiss thy cheeks, and the pleasures of imagination attend thy dreams; and, when length of years shall make thee tired of earth's joys, and the curtain of death gently closes around the last sleep of thy mortal existence, may the angels of Heaven attend thy couch, and take care that the expiring lamp of life receives no rude blast to hasten its extinction."

He that layeth his hand upon a woman, save in the way of kindness, is a wretch whom 'twere base flattery to call a *coward!*

SHORT LEGAL MAXIMS.

Speech is the index of the mind.
The law blushes when children correct their parents. — *Coke*.
Vainly does he who offends against the law seek the help of law.— *Coke*.
No one ought to depart out of a court of chancery without a remedy.— *Year Book*.
No one is bound to do an impossibility.
A wise judge ought always to regard equity.
No one is presumed to trifle at the point of death.
All things are presumed against a wrong-doer.
Argument drawn from authority is strongest in law.
Every one is to be believed in his own art.
Deceit and fraud shall excuse and benefit no man.
Reason is the soul of the law; when it ceases, so does law.— *Coke*.
Let every one employ himself in what he knows.
He that adheres to the letter adheres to the book.

Many men know many things, no man knows everything.—*Coke*.

Words spoken vanish; words written remain.

There is no obligation to perform impossible things.

The agreement of parties makes the law of their contract.

We have the best witness, a *confessing* defendant.

Few men have ever repented of silence.

The block of granite which was an obstacle in the pathway of the weak, becomes a stepping-stone in the pathway of the strong.

As the shadows in the early morning, is friendship with the wicked; it dwindles hour by hour. But friendship with the good increases like the evening shadows till the sun of life sets.

The hand that rocks the cradle is the hand that rules the world.

This is the country where hope is the tailor of every ragged boy.

Who never walks save where he sees men's tracks makes no discoveries.

Cowards die many times before their time.

The valiant never taste of death but once.—*Shakespeare*.

Let what every Roman thinks of his country be written on his brow.

CHAPTER XVII.

THE BOOTH SEDUCTION CASE

TRIED IN MILWAUKEE, JULY, 1859.

This trial was considered a test of skill between the distinguished rival advocates, Ryan and Carpenter, of Wisconsin, wherein each did his best to secure a signal victory.

The case abounds in highly rhetorical passages, and was conducted with that master skill and signal ability with which both counsel were amply endowed.

Mr. Carpenter divided his defense into four branches, and eloquently argued on each. Mr. Ryan answered Mr. Carpenter in fact and law, and launched into a bold and independent position in his own vindictive style of oratory, while Mr. Palmer, who assisted Mr. Carpenter, was exceedingly skillful in cross-examination, and half won the case by adroitly showing no act was accomplished to constitute a legally defined crime.

The report is out of print, and the case is exceedingly rare and valuable. The nature of the circumstances, and even the law cited would be in language too delicate to repeat at length, but the story is easily read in the chaste and ingenious statements of counsel.

The case is one of the most celebrated in the Northwest, and attracted vast crowds of listeners and much newspaper comment in Wisconsin, where the defendant was a man of great influence.

As the law cited was largely from the British decisions, and has become thoroughly known through the State reports — besides being a little aside from this line of reports — it is not given in this connection.

Mr. Carpenter spoke four hours, and Mr. Ryan eight, each using about half his time in reading to the court on separate branches of the case.

Mr. Carpenter said in closing:

"I suppose no one will question the proposition laid down in this instruction, but I have put it in the form of an instruction, that it may come to you in that form with the authority of law from the bench. That it may stand before you as a fixed light in your path while you deliberate upon the argument of the counsel who will close the discussion of this case; whose special duty it will be to sum up on behalf of the prosecution. He is a strong man, and he comes to the task with that feeling which no lawyer who has long been enlisted in a cause can put out of his heart — least of all Mr. Ryan. He will come to you with a strong conviction himself, and with those earnest feelings and that desire for success which he can no more divorce himself from than he can change any attribute of his mind and heart. I expect he will speak learnedly and eloquently, as he goes through the case. He will examine this testimony in detail with piercing acumen, and point out the inconsistencies of our witnesses. I expect this. I expect him to analyze our proof with all his severity; see him do what I have often seen him and other great lawyers do — when there are no facts to stand upon — soar upward into the regions of poetry and imagination; and appeal to the deep feelings of your nature; when he feels and trembles at the weakness of his proof upon seduction — he will soar away above the testimony and deal in glittering generalities, and wonderful flights of speculation. He can do it well, and *he will do it.* He will put Booth through such a course of sprouts on morality and virtue as no human being in this world was ever taken through before. He will torture him, and crucify him, and bring the blood to his cheek, and dismiss it to his heart at his sarcasm and his scorching sentences. He smiles and shakes his head at me. He can not help doing it. [Laughter.] But I have to remind you that the instructions of the court will come after his remarks, to call you back again to the region of the testimony, and explain to you the duty you will have to perform, remaining fixed and firm in your minds after his eloquence is over, and you have retired to your solemn determination in the jury room.

* * * * * *

"Now, gentlemen, I will leave this case with you, hoping that you will banish from your hearts all prejudice; all mere feeling; resist the enchantment of eloquence; and look only upon the law and the testimony. I have confidence that twelve men sitting here, with your look of fairness and intelligence, cannot be bewildered by the gentleman with all *his* power. That you will consider the facts alone: interpreting them by the law as given to you from the bench, upon which this defendant is to be tried and a verdict rendered of conviction or acquittal — speaking only the conclusions of truth. That you will not allow yourselves to be switched off the track of evidence by any exaggerated denunciations of vice and licentiousness; or an appeal to you to rebuke sin generally. You will examine carefully into this particular transaction — and this alone. It is a solemn duty on your part, to throw out of your minds all prejudice, bias and passion, and search for facts as they appear in the light of truth. One of you who are now jurors judging this man, may come here asking justice at the hands of another jury. You are liable, at any time of your lives, to be involved in such trouble. Innocence may be yours, yet it may not always shelter you from arrest and prosecution. Although it may sustain your conscience, it does not always prevent indictments, arrests, prosecutions and trials, and any one of you, although innocent as the heart of man can be, may, in a month from this day, stand here charged with such a crime as is now urged against this defendant. It is the great lesson from the Great Teacher that I am now trying to enforce upon you: "With what judgment ye judge, ye shall be judged; and with what measure ye mete, it shall be measured to you again."

I do not believe that the counsel can more sincerely or honestly regret this transaction than I do, or denounce immorality and vice generally with one single word with which you and I would not cheerfully agree, but we come here to administer criminal justice among men, fallen as they are, degraded by passions, and often led astray by the prompting of our erring nature, and to hold us up to the severe standard of law as it will, perhaps, be administered in the good time coming — to make men responsible to the severest rule for the slightest offense; to deprive a man of his life and liberty for the least possible insult to a woman, would be a gross outrage upon our common nature. Your oath does not bind you to enforce justice as if you lived in that fortunate age when the law in all its perfection will be executed, and man with regenerated nature observe, or suffer for the violation of all its requirements: "When the wolf also shall dwell with the lamb, and the leopard shall lie down with the kid, and the calf and the young lion and the fatling together, and a little child shall lead them."

The theory of the counsel will probably apply, but it never can be enforced till that time. You are to administer justice calmly and with charity. There is something in the heart of every man when he comes out in the sun and looks at vice, that is apt to startle him, and lead him into great extravagance, yet all men, under certain circumstances, may at least be tempted. I do not say that every man will fall, but we know that all men may be tempted, and you are to remember that it is your duty to try man as he is. You are not to be led away and lost in any extravagant denunciation of crime and immorality in general, but to investigate this one particular offense, and say in the same quiet and calm manner in which you would settle any other question that might be brought before you in the discharge of your duty as jurors. You may entertain as much indignation as you please against vice and licentiousness generally, but do not pour it all out in this case. Give us only our share; remember that we claim no exemption from the ordinary condition of humanity — remember that none of us stand " by the course of strict justice," but because mercy is mingled with justice — remember that we all look for redemption from the frailties and infirmities of this state, and for admission into the circles of immortal blessedness, to the intercessions of a Savior of infirmities *and passions.*

JUDGE RYAN'S CLOSING ARGUMENT.

Gentlemen of the jury: — A great deal of explanation has taken place both in the progress and summing up of this trial, as to the nature of this crime. I must say that I do not think that the first counsel who summed up here for the defense made light of it. I do not recollect that his associate shared in the light tone with which the first counsel spoke of this crime and its commission. I am not to dwell at length upon it again, gentlemen, but I say it is a crime in our day and generation of a grave nature, and the time is coming, and coming fast, when it will be graver. The sanctity of woman's person, the holiness of woman's chastity, are among human objects, next to life alone, the gravest subject of legal protection. What are we, or what have we, if we have no reverence for the person,— faith in the chastity of woman. Take chastity from her, and turn her out to run riot with the passion as men do, and where is society? Where the organization of the world? Lose faith in the paternity of children, lose faith in consanguinity, and you have no marriage, no paternity, no family — and what is society but the combination of familes? Man in the sense of sex is but a better brute, but unlike other brutes has faith in the chastity of his female. And, gentlemen, God meant that we should have it. God gave us that faith. I remarked yesterday that He had not given to us the same chastity that we might understand and comprehend the chastity of woman. But if God did not give us that, He gave us innate faith in hers. It is not because of the sex of our mother, our wife, our sister, our daughter; it is because we have an instinct of nature that woman is of a purer mould than man, and her chastity is a thing to be trusted in, as we trust in the providence of God. And when we speak lightly of it, as I must confess to the shame of us all who are apt to do it, it is because in mere vulgar riot of language we do injustice to our feelings and thoughts, or because we have degraded our own nature by lewd practices down almost to the level of the brute. What is the world worth without the chastity of woman? Or what is man worth who has not a high respect for the sex of woman, a strong faith in her chastity? Such a man is to be dreaded; distrusted as one in whom you can put no faith, for his character has fallen or is falling.

As has been said here by both counsel for the defense, there are four things necessary to establish in this crime, I will follow somewhat in their order.

First, the marriage of the defendant, which is not disputed; *second*, the previous chaste condition of the female; *third*, seduction, and *fourth*, illicit connection. I do not agree with the counsel that the seduction and the connection are so very materially apart in fact, as they seem to think; but I will take these things in the order in which they name them, and go through them with them.

We then come first, gentlemen, to the previous chastity of character of that little girl, Caroline Cook, who was here before us on the stand. The learned counsel who has summed up this cause said we had christened her a child during this trial for stage effect. Did the gentleman suppose that any stage effect we could use, would dupe you who saw the witness upon the stand twice, and toward whom your attention was particularly drawn. I called her a child without reflection, because she seemed to me a child; because, in all the proper attributes of childhood she appeared upon the stand, and was proved to be a child. And, gentlemen, when we brought that child upon the stand and showed her to you, and proved by her that on the 28th of February last, scarcely then more than fourteen years of age, she had had criminal connection with this defendant, when she swore to her own shame upon her simple oath; you heard the simple story of a simple child; a child you could see was not a witness telling a story. Upon the manner and nature of her testimony I shall comment hereafter. She was a witness who looked back upon her memory for all she said, and then plainly and truthfully told it. She stood cross-examination here under peculiar circumstances. She was a simple girl in the hands of an able lawyer, and she stood there surrounded with all the embarrassments of her position — the terrible embarrassments of a child at that age making such a disclosure, after the months of shame she must have borne since the first discovery, broken in spirit, conscious that every cold eye here was fixed staringly at her with somewhat of morbid curiosity. Under all these circumstances that child stood cross-examination as no bold practiced, determined, resolute woman, that they introduced here through the agency of Mr. Peter Turck, stood it. The gentleman cross-examined her long and severely, yet she never tripped; for no honest, truth-speaking witness need ever trip. It is when witnesses do what Peter Turck's witness did, what Sheridan once said another statesman did, draw on his imagination for his facts, that witnesses stumble, and trip, and break down. Do you suppose that that little child, of an age so young, and frail and childlike that every one was surprised at her appearance, could, by any possibility of things, have had a previous unchaste career? In the name of God, where can unchastity begin? Is a female child, a little innocent child, which sometimes disturbs its drapery, unchaste in the view of the counsel? Would they consider a child of three years old that drops its pantalets as unchaste? At what age, I ask, can unchastity begin, for God's sake. No, gentlemen, let man keep unchaste influence from the childhood of woman, and she will grow up chaste. Woman is never corrupted by woman. There is an outcast race of women who corrupt for profit, who corrupt as a trade, but not until they themselves have been corrupted by man — not until a long career of corruption has qualified them for the work. No woman becomes a prostitute or a lewd woman save through the influence of the affections God gave her towards man. We may safely say that whenever woman loses her virtue, she loses it from no innate lust, from no female influence, but she gives up chastity, virtue, reputation, character, everything, to her affection for some rascal of a man, who betrays her, through the weakness of love, to guilt. And was it conceivable that this little girl, found throughout all the evidence on both sides, a child amongst children, as was well observed by Mr. Corson, should, of her own nature, and at her tender years, have formed an unchaste character, and become an unchaste woman? You have all the malignity that could be brought to bear upon her poured out before you in the form of testimony.

How does their testimony agree? Gentlemen, we sometimes look for too much policy in villainy. We are apt to suppose that villainy is necessarily able. It is not so. Rascals are very often fools. In one sense every rascal is a fool, for honesty is the best policy. But often when men have become rascals, there is no sense in their rascality. They are often foolish in its practice. I think I can show you one rascal who has been a great fool in this cause. There is not a witness brought, or attempted to be brought here, who has not been visited again and again and over again by Mr. Peter Turck. Mark you, we find him out of that little neighborhood. He has been scouring the whole town. We find him on Michigan street, and in other places as we proceed in the investigation. The counsel may say that it is proper for an employed attorney — a man if you please — employed to do the dirty work of the case, to go and see the witnesses and find out what they know. I grant that. If it were my cause, however, I should prefer another man. I should not like the association. I would not bear it. I tell you now, I say it in the presence of this bar, and there is no lawyer here, although I see them from abroad, as well as from this city, who will deny what I say. Demagogues may tell you what they will, but lawyers are a great old race. Lawyers are a great and a good race, and the disgrace and shame which has been attached to the profession, has been brought upon it by those who intrude themselves into it without qualification, who hang around its outskirts — the shysters of the law. Give us the power to organize ourselves, let us have the power of expulsion, and I will guarantee to you that the bar of Milwaukee, with the power of expelling its unworthy members, would in six months be as pure as any church. But you, the people, give such a man as this the power to call himself a lawyer, in our defiance.

They say that seduction must be a lengthy process, going on a long while; there must be a great resistance, and a final involuntary surrender. The learned counsel quoted a passage from one of the most immoral pieces of poetry in the English language — Don Juan — about a lady who, "Saying she would ne'er consent, consented:" feigning denial in the act of consenting. I read that poetry a long while ago, when I knew no better. I do not study it now, and I would not like to quote it very extensively. But I recollect the history of that lady. My impression is that she was not the subject of seduction. She was a young and dashing lady, married to an old, imbecile man, who had the happiness of supporting her, but his other functions were vicariously discharged. [Laughter.] Her example will not serve in the seduction of a girl. There need be no long process. There must be some seduction, I admit. A man meets a woman, whether he speaks to her about statues or not, invites her as this girl was invited, and she, a woman of maturity, knowing the uses of sex, deliberately yields to him without persuasion. I do not think that is seduction. It is a mutual connection — a sort of Ramsbeck marriage. But the statute says that if a man promises to marry a girl, and under that promise knows her person, it is seduction. There need be no resistance. The promise makes it seduction. So if a married man seduce a woman; that cannot be under promise of marriage, if she knows he is married, as this girl knew of the defendant. There must be other means. How much, how little, is not important. Any adequate means is enough. I make this remark to the court, also. And these means are to be estimated by the age of the woman, her experience, knowledge of the world, and comprehension of what she is about; and somewhat by the relative age and position of the seducer.

He sits alone by that child in his parlor, and he kisses her. The clammy kiss of lust is upon her young mouth. The burning touch of lust is upon her person, and he wonders what sort of a statue she would make.

He tells her Mr. Lund pays girls much money for their statues made from the person, and he wonders what sort of a statue she would make. Gentlemen, you can fill up the gap of knowledge. You can remember what the child has forgotten; all the insensible approaches of lust, coming with the air of authority from the protecting hand of the man who stood as her guardian and father, the man who in the eye of the law stood in *loco parentis* over her. He was charged with a father's duty and protection, and with that authority, approach after approach of lust can be well imagined. The poor girl tells of the kiss, and the vile suggestion of the statue. You can imagine the fiery touch of his lustful kiss, and the desecrations of the sanctity of her person. You can imagine the intoxication of mind, the sly but burning manipulations of body. She cannot remember them, because she did not comprehend them; she was bewildered by them. But she was not there an hour and a half for nothing but a solitary kiss, and a lewd suggestion about her statue. She was to be invited to his bed, and he is not the man to lose his time when the opportunity was offered. He is enterprising and diligent in all things. He was diligent in seduction. What did he bring her there for? Why did he hide her in that back parlor from her mother, from the other children, from the servant girl, but to seduce her to his bed? We have the vile purpose — not denied here. No one has the gravity to deny the motive. He had her there to seduce her, and do you think he wasted his time? Do you think he spent those hours in reading or smoking, or doing nothing? No, whatever work he is at, he is diligent to accomplish it. In seduction, as in everything else, he is a good worker. He never idled away hour after hour. He made good use of it. He had a girl premature of body, but immature of mind, fourteen years of age. What did she do? In the language of the English authority, she yielded " a passive non-resistance — not an active consent." With her seduction could go no farther.

Is there no seduction in these relations in that position? I know that counsel, Mr. Palmer, and I know his associate well. I know that if these facts had happened to a child of either of them — just the facts as they admit them, this indictment never would have been found. If either Mr. Palmer's or Mr. Carpenter's child, of the same age and under the same circumstances, had returned home to tell this story, no indictment would have been found. There might afterwards have been found an indictment for *murder!* [Sensation.]

And there is that mark of deeper crime — I may comment upon it — the taking of the poor, humble, powerless man's daughter. Why not take the daughter of his equal, of a man who dared to act as a father should act — face the community with the guilt of blood upon his hands (to Mr. Palmer), as you would have done? I will go further. There sits the judge of the law, and there the executive of the law — they would have done it. I do not believe you can find ten men in this room who would not have done it just on that knowledge. Call it seduction, or not seduction. If that man had failed in his purpose, if he had merely invited my child or yours there, merely kissed her with the kiss of lust, merely suggested that damned model-artist practice to her, and the child had left the house, the man would have died! By heaven, the man would have been shot! If the child had come unspotted, save by the insult, there are few honest and hot-blooded men who would not have shot him for the attempt that failed. You may call that murder, if you will. It never yet was punished for murder. The lad who shot the seducer of his sister on the boat at Philadelphia, was as clearly guilty of legal murder as any man ever was, but no jury convicted him, though I believe he made no defense. I speak of that not to exaggerate what was done, but to show to every man's comprehension that it was seduction — to yours, to mine, to the judge's, to every man's. It was seduction at that age, in those relations. With all the gaps in the fading memory of that poor child, so outraged, we can see it is seduction, seduction beyond doubt. That there was more of it, we have none of us any doubt. There was more we all know. But without asking the jury to fill up any vacancies in the evidence, there was seduction enough.

The invocation was made to you by the learned counsel, Mr. Carpenter, to remember that your verdict of guilty here, would not merely damn the character of this defendant, damn his reputation, but in some measure, by reflection, injure the reputation, and destroy the happiness of his family. Gentlemen, it is the misfortune of innocence that guilt is almost never incurred that some part of the blow does not fall heavily upon the innocent. Every man who commits a crime has some wife, some child, some sister, some mother, some kin, some dependant, innocent, but ruined and broken-hearted in the punishment of of his guilt. That is not our fault. We prosecute guilt, not innocence. If innocence suffer, we all have sympathy for it. But if the reflected suffering of innocence is to acquit this defendant, it is to acquit every defendant indicted on a criminal charge. For there is no man so outcast, so removed from the heart of society, that some faithful, true woman's heart will not bleed at his misfortune; that some child will not be left fatherless, worse than fatherless, with an indelible stigma upon the father's name. But, gentlemen, I think in this case you are relieved from even that difficulty. It is immaterial for the character of this accused, whether you convict or not. The disclosures of this trial, his own defense, his own confession, fix his moral guilt as long as his name lasts. And whoever remembers his name hereafter, remembers the moral guilt of this tragedy forever. His guilty name goes with him forever, be your verdict what it may.

The first counsel pleaded hard to you to find a doubt in this case, and acquit upon that doubt. This court will tell you, and I will tell you, in broad language, it is the duty of every one coming as prosecutor, to tell the jury that, if they have a reasonable doubt of the defendant's guilt, they must acquit. We have no verdict of "not proven," as in the Scotch law. You cannot say that he is not proved guilty. You are to find him guilty or not guilty. In England they speak of adopting the Scotch verdicts of guilty, or not proven, or not guilty; but the verdict of not proven is not in our law. If you have a reasonable doubt, a rational doubt, on your minds, of his guilt, you are to find him not guilty.

I invoke you, not in the name of the father, my client in the civil suit, but in the name of the State, my client in this suit, before you do that, pause well and solemnly. Give back to society the child it has lost — the virtuous child that would have been a virtuous woman. Give back to the world one of the gems of society, a pure and virtuous virgin, to become in time a pure and virtuous matron. Restore to mankind unsullied one of the foundations of civilization — a pure and true and spotless woman. If you give back a polluted child, a deflowered virgin, I claim your verdict against the guilt that made her so.

"And the Lord sent Nathan unto David. And he came unto him and said unto him, There were two men in one city; the one rich, and the other poor. The rich had exceeding many flocks and herds; but the poor man had nothing, save one little ewe lamb which he had bought and nourished up; and it grew up together with him, and with his children; it did eat of his own meat, and drank of his own cup, and lay in his bosom, and was unto him as a daughter.

"And there came a traveler unto the rich man, and he spared to take of his own flock, and of his own herd, to dress for the wayfaring man that was come unto him; but took the poor man's lamb and dressed it for the man that was come to him.

"And David's anger was greatly kindled against the man: and he said to Nathan, as the Lord liveth, the man that hath done this thing shall surely die. And he shall restore the lamb four-fold, because he did this thing, and because he had no pity. And Nathan said to David," (Mr. Ryan pointed solemnly to the accused), "THOU ART THE MAN."

CHAPTER XVIII.

RIGHTS AND REMEDIES.

The following condensed summary of common rights and remedies cannot fail to be useful to students and laymen, if not to trial lawyers, who can see at a glance the essentials of each division. The separate divisions are all from standard text books abbreviated:

An *action* is the demand of a right by process of law, divided into:

Real actions, such as pertain to the recovery of real estate.

Personal, such as pertain to the recovery of goods and chattel.

Mixed, where recovery of real property and also goods and chattels are demanded.

MIXED AND REAL ACTIONS ARE:

Ejectment, for possession of land and damages.
Right of dower, for widow's right in property.

PERSONAL ACTIONS ARE:

Debt, where a party sues for the recovery of a liquidated amount due him, as on a judgment rendered elsewhere.

Covenant, where a party claims damages for a breach of covenant.

Detinue, where a party claims specific recovery of goods detained, as where a person promises in a note to pay the bearer so many bushels of wheat, oats, etc., and fails to perform.

Trespass, where party claims damages for injuries committed with violence.

Trespass on the case, where party claims damages for injuries which are *not direct*, but consequential; broad enough for slander, libel and trespass.

Trover, where one wrongfully converts the goods of another.

Replevin,to recover goods wrongfully detained from their owner or person lawfully entitled to possession.

Evidence required, is to *set up the facts and prove them.—Blackstone.*

ASSUMPSIT.

Founded on undertaking of defendant, not under seal. The averment is that he undertook and promised to pay, etc., the money lent, work done, goods furnished, or do the act named.

If there is a special contract still open, and of same subject-matter as common counts, and plaintiff fail on contract, he may recover on the other. Three rules govern assumpsit:

1. So long as the contract continues unfinished, plaintiff must declare specially, but when executed on his part, and nothing but payment remains, he may declare generally on common counts.

2. When contract partly performed is abandoned by consent, plaintiff may sue on common counts for amount done under special contract.

3. Where what has been done was under special contract, but no time fixed, and yet benefited defendant, and was accepted by him, even if plaintiff has not fully performed, he can recover for the worth and value done, not exceeding contract price, less any damage for failure to do all.

The plea in assumpsit is the general issue, and puts plaintiff to his proof of all material matters— time, place, debt, or implied promise. Defendant may plead in abatement, or prove payment, or misnomer, and may use a set-off, if he has one, but that is better saved for a separate cross suit.—*Kent.*

BILLS AND NOTES.

A note is a written promise to pay a fixed sum at a time named to the person or order designated, signed by the person contracting, and generally by endorsers. They are presumed to be founded on a valid consideration. The burden is on defendant to show otherwise.

Under general statutes, notes not denied under oath prove themselves. When sued upon, declaration must be special and the note offered in evidence. Generally, the signature and amount due are proven.

BILLS OF GOODS,

Over which many suits arise should be itemized. Claims for damaged goods not made within ten days after delivery, are not valid. Common counts are sufficient for declaration, and general issue for plea. It is best to have bills admitted, which an adroit attorney will do before trial, and before suit begins, if possible.

Protested notes to hold endorsers should be done by a bank notary. They know that three full days of grace are allowed, and notice to be good must not be mailed nor served before the end of the third bank day.—*Parsons on Bills and Notes.*

CONTRACTS.

A contract is an agreement between two or more competent persons for a sufficient consideration to do or not to do a given thing.

It is express, if put in express words, and implied, if something is done without a bargain when the law implies one.

The essentials are: Sufficient age and capacity of parties; freedom of will, and a free exercise of that will. Each must possess faculties to understand and comprehend their acts. The parties must be competent. The contract must be lawful. The consideration must be good or valuable. There must be a full *assent*, all minds meeting at once on the same thing. Once made in writing, parties are concluded by it. But surrounding circumstances may be shown. Latent ambiguity may be explained. Experts may testify as to terms in trades and scientific matters. Contracts to pay the debt of another, to sell land, to lease land over a year, to sell goods over fifty dollars in value —unless delivered —should be in writing, signed

and delivered, otherwise void under statute of frauds.
—*Parsons.*

DAMAGES

Are given as compensation to plaintiff for any injury caused by defendant or his servant. The damages should make whole the injured party, so far as can be, in money. They must be the result of the injury, and such as flow naturally from it. They must arise without fault of plaintiff. If from a railroad injury, he must, on crossing the track, "look and listen," and guard himself from accident. The least contributory negligence may excuse defendant. But where defendant used old and defective boilers and dangerous machinery, he was held liable. The general damages arise from breach of civil contracts, building, jobbing, etc., also from breach of promise; from seductions, from wounds and bruises in forced quarrels, from runaway teams, collisions, and the like. The greatest money damages come from injuries to passengers by rail. In an elevated railway case in New York $30,000 was recovered; $45,000 was collected from the Grand Trunk Road by Field, Lighter & Co.'s salesman. Policies of fire insurance are fruitful sources of suits, and in general great care and labor are used in showing plaintiff without fault, and defendant negligent. No class of law practice pays as well generally as these accident cases.

EJECTMENT AND EVIDENCE.

Plaintiff must show that he owned the legal title to the estate at the time of making and filing the declaration. That he had the right of possession, while defendant was in possession. The party is not permitted to dispute the title of whom he obtained. The strength of plaintiff's title, and not weakness of defense, is the issue.

EVIDENCE.

Faith in human testimony is sanctioned by experience. It is all the means by which an alleged matter is proved or denied.

Four rules govern the production of evidence:

1. It must correspond with the allegations and be confined to the point in issue.
2. The substance only need be proved.
3. The best evidence of which the case in its nature is susceptible, must be produced.
4. The burden of proof is upon the party holding the affirmative.

It is conclusive, if certain — as by statute of limitations. It is uncertain, when the conclusion does not necessarily follow. It is circumstantial, where it is inferred from facts satisfactorily proved. It is positive, when eye-witnesses are uncontradicted, or defendant confesses. It is hearsay, when one to be charged has admitted facts to be established. Matters of public interest, statutes, ancient possessions, dying declarations, admissions against the interest of party making them, and any admissions brought out in his presence and assented to by him, are admissible.

In criminal cases, admissions alone are not of late held sufficient without searching inquiry as to their good motive. Admissions acted upon are sufficient. Acts done that would warrant a presumption of assent are admissible. The real question in trials of fact is not whether it is possible that the testimony may be false, but whether there is sufficient probability of its truth shown by competent testimony as to remove reasonable doubts!

Oral evidence cannot replace written when an instrument can be produced in writing where it was once committed to paper. But lost and destroyed contracts may be proven by parol. So, such as have been left with the other party, who suppresses them after notice to produce, etc. All material writing should be produced if known to exist. Facts showing that writings were made and witnessed can be shown by parol. Admissions that the law does not allow denied, are all estoppel.—*Greenleaf.*

FRAUD

Is a trick by which one is drawn to do acts to his prejudice. It avoids all contracts. It is not to be presumed. It must be proven with great certainty. The burden is on the one who charges it. It is always a question of fact for a jury. Suspicions are not evidences of fraud. It must be as to material matters and effect the essence of the contract. If it is such that had it not been practiced the contract would not have been made, then it is material.

It must work an actual injury. The injured party must have *relied* upon it. As in case of false pretenses, it is not enough that the statement and pretenses were false; they must have been the means of deceiving the injured party — not *one* means, but *the* means.

Party defrauded must act at once, and not sleep on his rights. He must return property if cheated in a trade. Deed back, if deceived in land. Set his opponent where he found him at earliest opportunity. No man shall found a right upon his own wrong. Equity usually steps in, and does that which the law fails to do in matters of fraud.

GENERAL AGENCY.

An agent is one who is authorized to act for another. It is authority that he is employed by another, and does acts which are ratified. If limited, one must act within the scope of his authority. General agents will bind their principal so long as they have general authority, but not in matters of deeding property without express authority that may be recorded. The main rule is that he who acts by his agent acts by himself for that part only where he was employed.

He should disclose the name of his principal; that he acted in his behalf; the extent of his authority. The act of partners are frequently such as principal and agent. So, it becomes the duty of a firm at once upon dissolution to publish to the world generally, and send special notices to all who have actually dealt with their firm, of the change, else they are each and all holden for new debts contracted, as each partner is deemed agent for the rest in the line of their copartnership.

HOMICIDE.

The simple killing of a human being—justifiable when done by an officer in discharge of his duty, or where one resists him when arrested.

Excusable when one, in a lawful act, kills another by accident or in self-defense. Felonious if done with evil intent; manslaughter if killing is in a quarrel, in sudden heat of passion; murder if done with malice or deliberate purpose to kill, other than in self-defense or defense of one's helpless wife, child, father, mother, or prevent a strong man from killing a weak child or woman.

In manslaughter, the fatal stroke must be given before passions could cool, else it it is murder. Proof of great provocation must be shown to excuse the use of deadly weapons.

In trials of either of these offenses, death must first be established, and how it resulted, then who could have caused it, and if sufficient motive, malice may be implied, as if one intending to kill one person actually kills another, this would be murder. In self-defense the attacked may use his judgment; he alone is judge. *People v. Hurd.* The proof of deliberate murder is generally difficult; of manslaugher quite easy; of killing in self-defense generally still more easy. In all high crimes there is more concealment. Poisoning is the worst kind of murder, and very secretly accomplished.

FORGERY.

Forgery is often committed by an alleged color of authority. The unlawful making or uttering a writing, to the prejudice of another, must be shown to be unlawful. In larceny, the value, ownership and and taking by force from another, usually covers all questions, while in murder it may be required to trace motives for a year or more to find a malicious cause.

LIBEL AND SLANDER.

A *prima facie* case of *slander* or *libel* is simple. The latter is ridiculing by picture, writing or printing, made with intent to injure another, and if false and does injure another, even if copied from another paper, it is libel. So slander, if false, puts defendant upon his proof of excuse. These cases are simple for plaintiff and difficult for defendant. Perjury is difficult to prove. It needs two witnesses, that some one has been perjured by the false swearing in a judicial proceeding, on a material matter. The essentials of proof in rape is forcible carnal knowledge of a chaste person.

ROBBERY.

Robbery must show forcible taking of another's property, with intent to convert it; and goods must be proven actually in the robber's possession, and actually taken from the person of the other by superior strength, or putting in fear, so that owner could not safely retain them. To part with them lawfully may change the action to trover.

These principles are from Bishop, who lays down the general rules by which indictments are framed, as follows: It must allege what in law is essential to the punishment sought to be inflicted; must inform of time, place and offense; how committed, and extent of the crime; must refer to statute as violated; statute must be in force, etc.

If offense charged is "from a dwelling house," or "from a store in the day time," the proof must correspond in each essential part. Acts are measured by intent or result. The law does not concern itself with trifles. Where "breaking" is charged, opening a door is sufficient. Every man is responsible for what follows from his unlawful acts; but no action can be criminal where it is impossible for one to do otherwise. What a wife does of a criminal nature with her husband, is presumed to be directed by him.

INDORSEMENT.

An indorser makes these conditions: That all names before his are genuine. That the note or bill shall be paid when due; that if not, he will personally pay it. Delivery without indorsement is insufficient, if payable to order. The payee may stop negotiability of a special indorsement. The release of prior indorser discharges all subsequent indorsers.

Great care must be taken in protests; on them delicate legal questions arise, too numerous for this section.

LIQUIDATED.

Where damages are uncertain, and where settlements are presumed, where some valid consideration has passed and full receipts are given, the law will favor the settlements, as it is a well known maxim, "there must be an end of litigation."

If one hires for a fixed period, and serves only part, and is prevented, he can recover for whole period, provided he was unable to secure employment. Warranty of goods is implied, and damages arise if not as represented.

MISCELLANEOUS.

A father may have custody of a child in preference to any one else, except: If he be cruel, and not a competent person to care for a child; if the mother be living, and desires the custody of the child of tender years; if the father neglects to support the child. In these cases the court or probate judge may bind out the child to a suitable person who guarantees to support it.

It is not larceny to take ones own property where he may find it.. A husband cannot sell his wife's goods. In many States he cannot sell his own real property without her assent, and she can sell all of her property in his absence. The wife is agent for her husband. Principal and agent extends to all of her purchases of clothing, furniture, household goods and natural living expenses, and there is no power but by separation and notice to prevent her making contracts binding on her husband for her necessaries. So also a child can bind its father for usual wearing apparel and living expenses, so long as it remains with its parents, and is suited to his circumstances.

PARTNERSHIP.

A contract between two or more persons to combine skill and capital for a lawful purpose, the losses and profits of which shall be shared by each in certain proportions, is a partnership. It must be a common interest in stock of company. It must be a personal responsibility for the firm debts—a business marriage.

There must be community of profits; each member liable to the whole debt without reference to their private contracts. Partners are joint tenants and general agents of each other. If money be invested in company lands, they belong in common to all. If one buy firm lands with firm money, taking title in himself, he is the legal trustee of the title, but not the actual owner.

The act of each partner binds all within the scope of their business. Partners who steal from each other do not commit larceny as known in law—they being part owners, cannot steal from their own.

Partners may by acts, signs and dealings, be held out as such, and bound after dissolution. One may dissolve any moment, and be liable in damages for breach of contract. They may be dissolved by death of either partner, by bankruptcy, insanity, limitation or judicial decree. If they have made debts, each is liable till all is paid.—*3 Kent.*

REAL ACTIONS.

An action will arise for permanent improvement, made in good faith by a farmer in the way of clearing, and of a householder in buildings that can be removed without injury to premises, if built in the line of business, like engines, boilers and temporary buildings, connected with mills and bakerys. But in general, one must improve premises at his own peril. Where store counters can be taken without injury, or partitions removed without damage to premises, they are usually taken. Crops sown in peace, are to be reaped in peace. Growing grain, unless specified, goes with the farm, but cut timber, lumber, rails not in fence, wheat in the stack and detached property, goes as personalty. The principal real actions are trespass and ejectment, each treated of separately.

PERSONAL PROPERTY.

Right to property originally came from occupancy. The possessor can give no better title than he has. The descent and transfer of property are creatures of law, and not natural rights; but the right of children can take property in preference to strangers, is founded on the law of nature. Every person must so use his property as not to injure his neighbor. The term chattels covers all kinds of personal property.

Personal property is such as bonds, money, furniture, fixtures, grain, goods, tools, implements, etc., and passes title generally by delivery. It may be acquired by purchase, descent, gift, or by act of law; usually it is from purchase, where the buyer has full and absolute power to use, sell, burn or exchange it at pleasure, provided he has the absolute title to it. All parol gifts (those made without writing) pass title only on delivery, and even then they are presumed to be void if made to strangers without consideration. It is a good consideration for relatives to give valuables to each other, and such as near kinsmen. A valuable consideration is money or other property in exchange.

SALES.

A sale or "contract to transfer property from one to another, for a valuable consideration," requires competent parties, subject matter consideration. The thing sold must exist; must be identified and capable of delivery. The seller must have control and right to sell it, and by the sale he warrants the title.

Each party is bound to state to the other material facts that he knows the other to be ignorant of, and out of his observation. The seller may permit the buyer to cheat himself, *but must in no way aid in the cheating.* In sales at auction, any bid may be rejected before the hammer falls. The auctioneer has a lien on sale money for his fees.

STOPPAGE IN TRANSITU.

The seller may recall goods at any time before final delivery, if buyer becomes insolvent, or if fraud has been committed, especially if goods are bought after failure for purposes of fraud. So buyers may notify sellers of insolvency, and refuse to accept their goods; but once freely delivered, the sale cannot be rescinded; it is final, and each has his separate rights thereafter, the purchaser his goods, the seller his credit.

TENDER.

To support the plea of tender, one must show the precise sum offered and shown in lawful money — not check or draft. The money itself may tempt one to accept it. He must also show that he has since been ever ready and willing to pay the sum he claims to be owing plaintiff. It must be produced on demand, and once in sight without demand. With these requisites, all costs made after the tender are payable by plaintiff, he having supposed to be in law needlessly incurred.

TROVER.

For the wrongful conversion of personal property, goods, chattels or money; must be shown that plaintiff owned it; that it came to possession of defendant; that he converted it. An agent may maintain trover. Absolute control is a right to maintain this action. Selling, destroying and concealing is appropriating in the meaning of the statute. A count for trover is usually added to *trespass on the case.*

WILLS.

The law of actual residence governs the location of probating wills. But they may be admitted where one dies in a foreign state, and has property therein.

In regard to wills of real property, it is clear that the law of place where it is situated, is where the will must be generally probated, or copies of the will filed to perfect the chain of title. Usually wills are probated where the decedent resided.

A *prima facie* case is made by showing the actual signature; the capacity to comprehend the business in which he was engaged; the witnesses; only one need be sworn. Testator's mark is sufficient if unable to sign. He may revoke it by subsequent wills; he may keep it or file with probate court; he can always destroy it; his marriage and subsequent issue will change its validity.

Wills should be simple, direct, and clearly convey the estate, naming at least each heir, but one can dispose of all his property save the wife's dower interest, even if it deprives some of his bounty. He is in control of it, and may select the objects of his bequests without interference. Two witnesses are necessary. Certain words like, I give, grant, devise and bequeath, should be remembered, and a plain business like statement will usually do the disposing of the property best.

If made by threats, duress, undue flattery, over persuasion, not in sound mind, under undue influence, it may be set aside by a jury. Any means that destroys a free agency, is contrary to the spirit of the law governing the validity of wills.

CHAPTER XIX.

ORATORS AND ORATORY.

The intense aversion that all good lawyers have for affectation, is, in a measure, a hinderance to the study of oratory. Many fear that they may acquire a stilted habit of delivery. But surprising as it may sound, the one thing most neglected in law schools, is the subject of delivery, or the art of speaking in a tone and manner easily understood, by a court and jury.

The high pitched key of loud talkers, and inaudible voices of others, fall on the ear like the prattle of the street vendor, and never leave the listener room to comprehend the subject, if he cared to follow the reasoner. Men are not moved and converted by such repulsive utterances. The music of modulation is a great essential in speaking, as men never quarrel in the hearing of sweet sounds, so with pleasing speeches, they steal in on the senses, and capture the judgment. They compel attention. They win juries, command verdicts, and secure large retainers.

Such is the power of eloquent speech, that trained and modulated, with some apt words to utter, it will quell a mob, nerve an army, rouse an audience, move an assemblage, and often change the destiny of nations.

The same words spoken without a forcible and apt delivery, would be lost on the listener, or fall, as Gough puts it, "like stones in the mud, to sink and disappear forever."

No man ever believed more in the power of well chosen sentences, and their right delivery, than Webster, the greatest model of American advocates. He was often absorbed in the study of forcible sayings for days before his greatest speeches, and never made an important effort unprepared. He would commit to memory, and carry illustrations, ten and fifteen years before using them. He was indebted to Dryden for his "raising mortals to the skies, and drawing angels down." He owed much to Scott for his "sea of upturned faces;" much to the Scriptures for his sublimity, and many strong sentences to Shakespeare, but he owed most of all to his wonderful delivery. In reply to Hayne he drew on all his resources.

At the dedication of Bunker Hill Monument, the crowd pressed hard upon the speaker's platform. The police were powerless to restrain them. In vain the master of ceremonies urged them to be quiet. It was a supreme moment just before Mr. Webster was to be introduced as the orator. All were anxious to hear his earliest utterances, but confusion became intense. The chairman begged Mr. Webster to say a few words to restore order. The great man came forward in his majestic way, and said: "Gentlemen, you must fall back!" "Mr. Webster, it is impossible!" "It is impossible!" shouted many voices in unison. Raising his arm and his voice, as his burning eyes flashed over the excited multitude before him, he said with Websterian emphasis: "Gentlemen, NOTHING *is impossible to Americans at Bunker Hill!*" A great shout rang through the audience as they surged back like the waves of the ocean. This was what Webster would call something higher than eloquence — action, noble, sublime, God-like action.

Carlyle says: "Let him who would be moved to convince others, be first moved to convince himself," and adds: "The race of life has become intense; the runners are treading on each other's heels; woe be to him who stops to tie his shoestrings."

While we may abhor the mimic style of elocution as sometimes taught by ranting readers of worn out themes, a well delivered speech, or play, is a rare pleasure; and there is no greater luxury on earth, than that experienced by accomplished singers, speakers and actors before an appreciative audience.

To acquire that ease and pleasant delivery, and know its value, is a work of time and patience; but I prefer to speak of it through men of larger experience, whose apt words are quoted, instead of personal counsel. These masters of their science speak with unquestioned authority. It goes without saying that American statesmen, notably the late President Garfield, first acquired eminence by their oratory.

Cicero says: "Delivery has the sole and supreme power of oratory. Without it a speaker of the greatest mental power cannot be held in any esteem, while with it, one of moderate ability may surpass those of the greatest talent." Quintillion says: "Indifferent discourse well delivered, is better received by a popular audience, than a good discourse badly delivered. It is not so important what our thoughts are, as in what manner they are delivered, since those whom we address are moved only as they hear." Humboldt says: "The essence of language lies in the living utterance. It is only by the spoken word that the speaker breathes his soul into the souls of his hearers." Sargent S. Prentiss, of whom S. S. Cox says: "No man, south or north, ever left a finer reputation for eloquence," in a letter to his brother, dated Vicksburg, August 9, 1833, writes: " Let me particularly recommend to you to cultivate as much as possible your powers of elocution. This attainment is to every man of the utmost importance. It is no less than the power of using his other attainments, for what advantage is information unless one is allowed to convey it, and show the world one possesses it. Indeed, my observation of mankind has convinced me that success in life depends not upon the quantity of knowledge a man possesses, as upon the skill and facility with which he is able to bring it to bear upon the affairs in which he may be engaged.

"This is particularly true with great men. Their greatness consists less in the extent of their knowledge, than in the way in which they use it. There are hundreds, perhaps thousands, of men in the United States who exceed Henry Clay in information on all subjects, but his superiority consists in the power and adroitness with which he uses his information.

"I would again press, before any other acquisition, necessity of training. What young man, having merely a fondness for painting, and a corresponding desire to paint, would dare to take up brush and palette, and expect his first ignorant daubs to be accepted by the Academy? What young woman without training would dare to sing before a public audience of cultivated people? What merely sub-architect would expect to have his random plans accepted, even for a State capitol? Every one understands the necessity of thorough technical education in these arts; but when you come to elocution, the highest of all arts, there is a general impression that the mere desire to do something indicates the power to do it. Art in elocution is the purest appropriate expression of thought, therefore no man who desires to use his mind can afford to dispense with the knowledge of its simplest and most apparent laws. And there can be no great success without severe technical study."

Professor Wm. Matthews says: "Let men once learn and deeply feel that no man ever has been, or ever can be, a true orator without a long and severe apprenticeship to the art; that it not only demands constant, daily practice in speaking and reading, but a sedulous culture of the memory, the judgment, and the fancy — a ceaseless storing of the cells of the brain with the treasures of literature, history, and science for its use, and they will shrink from haranguing their fellow-men, except after a careful training and the most conscientious preparation."

Henry Ward Beecher says: "While progress has been made, and is making, in the training of men for public speaking, I think I might say that relative to the exertions that are put forth in other departments of education, this subject is behind all others. Training in this department is the great want of our day, for we are living in a land whose genius, whose history, whose institutions, whose people, demand oratory. I advocate, therefore, in its full extent, and for every reason of humanity, of patriotism, and of religion, a more thorough culture of oratory.

"*Now in regard to the training of the orator, it should be a part and parcel of the school.* The first work is to teach a man's body to serve his soul. So long as men are in the body they need the body; and one of the very first steps in oratory is that which trains the body to be the welcome and glad servant of the soul. Grace, posture, force of manner, the training of the eye that it may look at men, and pierce them, and smile upon them, and bring summer to them, and call down storms and winter upon them; the development of the hand, that it may wield the scepter or beckon with sweet persuasion; these themes belong to man. And, among other things, the voice—perhaps the most important of all, and the least cultured.

"How many men are there who can speak from day to day, one hour, two hours, three hours, without exhaustion and without hoarseness? But it is in the power of the vocal organs, and of the ordinary vocal organs, to do this. What multitudes of men there are who weary themselves out because they put their voice on a hard run at the top of its compass, and there is no relief to them, and none unfortunately to the audience. But the voice is like an orchestra. It ranges high up and can shriek betimes like the scream of an eagle; or it is low as the lion's tone; and at every intermediate point is some peculiar quality. It has in it the mother's whisper and the father's command. It has in it warning and alarm. It has in it sweetness. It is full of mirth and full of gayety. It glitters, though it is not seen with all its sparkling fancies. It ranges high, intermediate, or low, in obedience to the will, unconscious to him who uses it; and men listen through the long hour wondering that it is so short, and quite unaware that they have been bewitched out of their weariness by the charm of a voice, not artificial, but by assiduous training made to be his second nature. Such a voice answers to the soul, and it is its beating.

"'But,' it is said, 'does not the voice come by nature?' Yes; but is there anything that 'comes by nature' that stays as it comes if it is worthily handled? There is no one thing in man that he has in perfection till he has it by culture. We know that in respect to everything but the voice. Is not the ear trained to hearing? Is not the eye trained to seeing? Is a man because he has learned a trade, and was not born with it, less a man? Is the school of human training to be disdained when by it we are rendered more useful to our fellow-men?

"But it is said that this culture is artificial; that it is simply ornamentation. Ah! that is not because there has been so much of it, but because there has been so little of it. If a man were to begin, as he should, early: or if, beginning late, he were to address himself assiduously to it, then the graces of speech, the graces of oratory, would be to him what all learning must be before it is perfect, namely — spontaneous. If he were to be trained earlier, then his training would not be called the science of ostentation or acting. Not until human nature is other than it is will the function of the living voice, the greatest force on earth among men, cease."

It sounds so old, and is so true, to say of the first of orators that he spent years in severe training; that he endured torture, and regarded the art as a pleasant task, and a valuable science, and succeeded in overcoming deformity of voice and body, and won at last the crown of gold and lasting fame as a reward for his energy. It sounds so very strange to speak of Clay as an ardent follower of this Grecian master, and Marshall as another, and Prentiss as another, each almost their master's equal, but their brilliancy as orators rewarded their years of training. And to-day, in the presence of Booth, who brings all nations at his feet, by purity of voice and grace of action, there are men enough to ridicule attempts to cultivate the finer qualities of delivery.

Men are not wanting who see in the scholarly language and majestic delivery of Conkling — one with mind and body most wonderfully developed — what they please to term too much of the *imperial* for an American. But what if it be imperial, and is really finished? Is not the body a part of the Creator's stamp, and the soul within it simply living up to its possibilities?

Men are not at all of an equal mould. They are not even created equal. Some are weak, and others strong; some are large, and others little; some are students, and others idlers; some look over the stars to other worlds, and others see but a single hamlet and that imperfectly.

That an orator like Butler should employ the strong and logical, while one like Cox reasons through his wit, and another like Matthews commands men by his dignity and eloquence, and many more possess but a tithe of their acquirements and succeed, is only an argument by contrast, for Butler, Cox and Matthews, each employ their best forces, and forces not untrained or neglected.

I sometimes wish that I could paint the real picture of a trained orator like Beach, as I heard him in the Brinkley case; a likeness of his flashing eye, his commanding form, and features all ablaze with eloquent looks, and voice of wonderful melody; or tell of Choate's swift flights of fancy; of Everett's rhythmical sentences; of Matthews in his strongest power, or Storrs in some closing appeal; where the form surges and trembles with thoughts too fast for utterance, but these men must be seen to be appreciated, and heard to be understood.

In a country where so much is demanded of orators, where place and power often comes to the eloquent and gifted, enough is left for the highest order of oratory and the finest finished speeches; no one need despair of a lack of present opportunity, but all should be ready to embrace their opportunity when it offers, for "There is a tide in the affairs of men which taken at the flood leads on to fortune."

CHAPTER XX.

MISTAKEN IDENTITY.

Cases of mistaken identity are by no means rare in large cities, and many are reported every year. Strange coincidences, unhappy results, often follow in the heat of some startling tragedy or robbery, that cooler judgment would never believe possible.

The facts in the following romantic cases are absolutely vouched for, yet seem almost incredible. One of the latest of the strange cases is exceedingly instructive on circumstantial evidence, and the last one equally strong on mistaken identity.

THE AKERTON CASE

Is that of an English merchant who, in 1867, was stabbed on a busy street in broad daylight, in the presence of twenty witnesses, and the young offender escaped without arrest.

The best detective talent of London was employed, and the supposed murderer captured in Belgium and brought to London for trial. The crown was ably represented, and only a poor barrister assigned for the defense.

Great interest was manifested at the trial, which developed the fact that Mr. Pierson, the merchant, had discharged Lewis Akerton a few weeks before the killing, and at the time the clerk had said: "You will one day regret this injustice."

Witness after witness was sworn to the question of killing, and the identity of the accused, and the crown rested with great confidence, when defendant's counsel requested the court to allow the jury to retire with the crown counsel, himself and the court, under guard, to the judge's private room, which request was granted.

Standing in the middle of the room was a complete counterpart of the prisoner. He was of the same height, build, hair, eyes, features and complexion of Akerton. The closest scrutiny of the two men revealed no points of difference in face or form. The jury gazed from the prisoner to his double in bewilderment. No one spoke for several moments; then the prisoner's counsel requested that the jury retire while the two persons changed clothing in the presence of the officers, and return and confront the witnesses separately, which was done, and each firmly declared his certainty of belief that the unaccused equally with the accused, was the guilty party. They were unshaken by cross-questions. The prisoner's counsel then moved for his release on the ground of a reasonable doubt, and the court directed a verdict of "*not guilty*," which was received amid applause. It later transpired that the two men were *twin brothers*, and one was the real clerk discharged, *but which one no jury could find out.*

IDENTITY OF SIGNATURE.

In the Probate Court of Detroit at the hearing of the Jones Will Case, April, 1883, L. M. Gates of Kalamazoo, testified that the signature of L. M. Gates, Edmonston Otsego County, N. Y., was identical with his hand writing, except the residence stated. He was requested to write his name and above address, and the handwriting was identical with that on the will.

Hon. Chas. S. May then testified to the L. M. Gates signature of Edmonston, N. Y., who was an entirely different person, and no relation, in fact a total stranger to Gates of Kalamazoo. The identity of names and handwriting was here the most complete ever shown in a suit at law.

In the Cadet Whittaker Case the testimony was about equally divided on his handwriting of the self-threatening letter, and in the Morey — Garfield letter many believed at first in its genuineness, so that the Pacific States were deceived by it, and voted against Garfield.

In Maclean — Scripps Libel Case, tried in Superior Court of Detroit, April, 1883, a famous letter known as the Brenton letter called out the first expert talent of the nation on identity. It was charged that the Brenton letter was written by Prof. Maclean to Mrs. Joseph Wardle from Kingston to Tilsonburg, Ontario, and other letters, mailed near the same hour, written on similar paper, with similar ink, admitted to be genuine, were used to compare, and pronounced by two standard experts, Ames and Gaylord, of N. Y., to be identical with the Brenton letter. The various tests left their *opinion* the same. Four other witness, long connected with banks, gave similar opinions, while an equal number (or fourteen in all) of Dr. Maclean's personal acquaintances all denied that he was the author of the Brenton letter. But they based their opinions on the style of wording and uncouth wording of the letter, as a *partial* reason for their conclusions.

In this case certain words, like "Tilsonburg," and "Ontario," were almost absolutely identical. On covering all other words but these, Col. Atkinson staggered the best friends of the Doctor with an inquiry of which one was the genuine. And Otto Kirchner made an equally fine comparison with the jury when he said: "Suppose you, sir, should meet on the streets to-morrow a friend of your youth from over the ocean, from your fatherland, and he recognised you, and you spoke of the boyhood sports of long ago; of the friends he knew and you knew; of the scenes of childhood away among the green fields of Germany, and recalled the past, while you had not seen him for twenty or thirty years, and he was old and wrinkled, and gray and bent, you still saw in his eyes, and knew from his voice, and *something that no one could explain*, that it was the friend of your youth, would you doubt it, or need an expert to confirm his identity?" It is believed that this style of reasoning did much to gain the $20,000 verdict for libel in publishing the story of the Brenton letter and the husband's insanity caused by it, even after others had been deceived by it and the Canada papers had quoted it. But this case is still pending in the supreme court on error, and may be soon entirely changed.

THE LOCKWOOD ROBBERY CASE.

The following remarkable story of two strange trials is vouched for by Ex-Congressman J. H. McGowen, of Washington, D. C., and Judge John B. Shipman, of Coldwater, both of whom participated in the trials and furnish facts as a basis of this report. The case is stranger than fiction:

In the Autumn of 1868, two young men entered the house of Jeremiah Lockwood, a farmer residing seven miles south of Coldwater, Michigan, and robbed it of considerable money, clothing, jewelry and goods, in broad daylight.

The family were all from home. The burglars broke in by prying up a window opening into the pantry. They ransacked the bureau drawers and clothes-presses, gathering enough plunder to make two large bundles. One of them had tied about his person when he entered the house a large red scarf. This he spread upon the floor and laid broad-cloth coats, silk dresses, ladies furs, and other clothing upon it, until he had a large package. Tied at the four corners and slung over his shoulder, he was in marching order. The other found a large oil-cloth satchel which was bound around the bottom and at the ends with red leather. This he filled with similar plunder, when the two left the house by the back way passing out through a skirt of woods and into one of the most frequented high-ways in the county.

Thus conspicuously loaded these two rogues traveled to the north-west directly through one of the best settled neighborhoods in the county, until they reached

Batavia Center, a distance of eight miles. More than twenty people saw them as they tramped along the highway that bright Autumn day.

They met a farmer who was going to the cider mill with a load of apples. He stopped and talked with them, while they stood beside his wagon and ate apples. They chatted with a woman who was at work in her door-yard near the road.

The red bundle, and the red bound satchel, made them conspicuous, and they were apparently well-scanned by all who noticed them. When they reached Batavia it was nearly dark. They took supper there at the country tavern. After supper they threw dice on the counter at the bar to determine who should pay for the drinks.

They then arranged with the landlord to take them as far as Bronson station on the railroad. In payment for their supper and ride they gave their host a five dollar greenback. It had been torn and patched in a peculiar way, and had other marks upon it by which it was readily identified. At Bronson they got out of the wagon just where the highway crossed the railroad, and with their packs on their backs started west on the railroad track.

The larceny was committed on Saturday. On the Monday or Tuesday following, two young men were arrested at Sturgis who were supposed to be the criminals. Sturgis is the second station west of Bronson. The parties arrested were brought to Coldwater and put in jail, and a number of parties who had seen the thieves as they tramped through the county on the Saturday previous, came to town and identified the men arrested as the men whom they had seen. Among those who so identified them was the old landlord who had given them their suppers and driven them to Bronson.

An examination was had before a justice, and they were bound over for trial in the Circuit Court. They loudly protested their innocence, but the testimony was so strong against them that but little attention was paid to their story. Lockwood identified the bill that was paid to the hotel man, and a score of witnesses, including the landlord, identified the prisoners as the young men who carried the red bundle and the red bound satchel.

The prisoners were without money, and compelled to lie in jail a number of weeks before their trial came off. John W. Turner was appointed by the court to defend the prisoners. Twenty witnesses on the part of the people swore they had seen the actual thieves, and were ready to testify to the identity of the prisoners. Some time during the progress of the trial Mr. E. G. Parsons, of counsel, whispered to the prosecuting officer, and said: "I have just been in-
"formed that the old landlord has been looking at
"these boys since they were brought into the court
"room, and has made up his mind that he was mis-
"taken when he saw them before, and that they are
"not the boys who gave him that five dollar bill.
"What shall we do about it?" The prosecutor answered: "We must put him on the witness stand to identify the bill at least. After asking him the necessary questions about the bill, we will then ask him if he did not see the prisoners immediately after their

arrest, and if he did not then, while the transaction was fresh in his mind, identify them as the men who had taken supper at his house and whom he had driven to Bronson."

The landlord was called and examined. He readily identified the patched greenback. The question was then put: "Did you not, immediately after the arrest of these prisoners, go to the jail, at the request of the sheriff, and there identify them as the men who gave you the greenback?" He answered: "Yes I did." Then he went on hurriedly to say: "I don't believe it now. I have been looking at them since I sat here and I don't believe they are the men. However, I could tell if I could see the tallest one's hand." "What about his hand," was asked. "Well," said the old man, "the boys threw dice after supper that night at my house, and the tall one laid his hand on the counter right under the lamp, and I noticed a peculiar scar on the back of it. I am sure that I could recognize that hand again anywhere." The taller of the prisoners was known as "Slimmy." Mr. Turner at once said to him: "Slimmy, walk up there and show your hand." He got up with some reluctance, and much flushed. He put his right hand upon the rail in front of the witness. "Oh, no," said the old landlord, "it was the left one." He put up his left hand. The witness, after deliberately adjusting his spectacles, took the hand up by the forefinger, turned the back of it to the light, and exclaimed: "My God, that is the hand!" The hand was examined, and a V shaped scar found just back of the forefinger. It was, as the witness had said, a peculiar looking scar.

The welt, or edge, of the scar stood well above the surface of the hand, and was very red.

The only defense of the prisoners was the unsworn statement of the prisoners themselves. Of course, they were readily convicted. The jury had scarcely left their seats before they returned with a verdict of guilty. The late Judge Bacon, of Niles, presided. The prisoners were called up for sentence. When the tall one was asked the usual question why sentence should not be pronounced upon him, he declared that on the day of the purported larceny he was in Niles, a hundred miles from Lockwood's house. On being questioned further by the court, he said that on that day he went out from Niles to a neighboring village; that on his return he caught a span of runaway horses that belonged to a certain livery man in Niles, whom he named; that after securing the horses the stage overtook him, and he rode into town with the driver. He named several prominent gentlemen of Niles, whom he said he knew, and several of whom he declared he saw on that day. Judge Bacon told him he lived in Niles, and that he would make inquiries respecting these things, and if he found that they were true, he would grant him a new trial, or ask the governor to pardon him. "But," he said, "you have had a remarkably fair trial, and have been convicted on the testimony of a large number of very respectable witnesses. And now I should be more inclined to believe your statement were it not for the testimony of the landlord, relating to the scar on your hand." When the question was propounded to the other prisoner, he declared that on the day of the larceny he was in

South Bend, Indiana. Said his occupation was peddling jewelry; that he had registered on that day at the hotel, and spent the day in his ordinary business.

The sentence was three years for each of the prisoners in the State prison at Jackson. Some time after their imprisonment, Judge John B. Shipman, now a prominent lawyer at Coldwater, was employed in their behalf. He at once secured depositions on which Judge Bacon granted a new trial. They were brought back to Coldwater, and tried in May, 1869, where "Slimmy" in the presence of his counsel, the sheriff and prosecutor, made a statement substantially as follows: That his business in the prison was finishing furniture; that one day while engaged in the second story of the shop a new man brought some furniture into the room, whom he at once remembered as an old acquaintance who had always been said to resemble him (the speaker). It at once came into his mind that that was the man who had stolen Lockwood's goods. He said he took a piece of paper and wrote on it, "I am here because you stole those goods out of Lockwood's house south of Coldwater." This he placed where the man would see it when he returned to the room. When the prisoner read it, he knew at once that he was right. That evening when the prisoners were washing for supper, he got near the newcomer, and talked with him freely—the man admitting the larceny, and giving the details as to how it was accomplished.

The attendance of this man from Jackson as a witness in the case was secured. During the second trial he was placed directly behind the prisoners. The case was tried thoroughly, as in the first instance. All the witnesses were again brought in, and all, including the landlord, swore very positively to the fact of identity. But when Mr. Shipman came to make the defense he proved an *alibi* for both his clients so completely and conclusively, that the jury rendered the verdict of not guilty, without delay.

There was no doubt left in the minds of all who heard the trial, of the innocence of the accused. "Slimmy" was in Niles, as he had stated to the court. The books of the livery stable man, and the testimony of a number of witnesses proved this beyond a shadow of doubt. That the other man was in South Bend was equally clear. The hotel register showed his name recorded among the names of the other guests at the hotel. He was also identified by the landlord of the hotel and other parties living at South Bend.

Now comes the curious coincidences of this case. The men who broke into Lockwood's house, and stole his goods, were *both young men without beards*. One was a tall, slim man, with a V shaped scar on his left hand, back of the forefinger. The other was a short, thick-set man with red hair, and spoke with a brogue. The innocent men, whom we arrested, were both young men without beards. One was tall and slim, and had a similar scar on the back of his left hand. The other was short, thick-set, with red hair, and spoke with a brogue. The thieves went from Bronson west on Saturday evening. The innocent men were arrested at the second station west of Bronson on the Monday or Tuesday following.

It is of interest to know that both of the *actual* thieves were sent to prison for other crimes before the innocent men had been acquitted. One, as already stated, was sent to Jackson; the other was convicted of some felony, and sent to one of the prisons in Indiana. The innocent men were incarcerated in all about six months.

The keen skill and courage of the prosecution in daring to swear the landlord first is commendable. The humane language and bearing of the court was noble, and the final victory of Judge Shipman was a work of charity that entitles each actor in this strange case to lasting honor. Remarkable as the story sounds there is no question of its reality.

ONLY ONE WITNESS.

The effect of a witness's manner in turning the jury's verdict was well shown in an United States Circuit Court case, tried in Detroit a few years ago, where the plaintiff was a mining captain of powerful frame, entirely ignorant of book-learning and courts, but possessing a strong memory and impressive manner.

The claim was sixty-seven thousand dollars, in a long complicated account to be made almost solely on the plaintiff's testimony. William P. Wells, now Professor in the Law Department of the Michigan University, and a permanent advocate, conducted the plaintiff's case. With G. V. N. Lothrop, of counsel, Messrs. Alfred Russell and C. I. Walker, defended.

The witness was skilled in the details of the facts, a man of great coolness and courage in affairs, but timid in a court room. He rose to his feet when examined and related a graphic and consistent story of the entire dealings from beginning to end; the sums paid, the matters left in dispute, with marvellous accuracy. For two long days he was rigidly cross-examined, and every circumstance tallied with his truthful statement. So apt and original in manner, so thoroughly honest were his figures, that the jury hung upon his sentences like listening to music.

The long accounts of both parties were extremely puzzling to counsel, but the brave captain handled them all like a painting. Turning on light when needed, and bringing out the important features in bold relief, he won a most signal victory over what appeared to be a powerful array of opposing testimony; illustrating the fact that witnesses must be *weighed*, not *counted;* that the testimony of one man, if true, and the jury feel its truth, and he is shown to have had the best means of knowing the circumstances, may weigh against many; for *one man* with right on his side, is always a majority. It is not enough for a witness to know a fact testified to, but he should *know that he knows it, feel* that he knows it, and *believe* that he *believes* it.

CHAPTER XXI.

IN THE PROCESSION.

The true rule in starting is to start well; to take the right track and follow it. Once *in the procession* it is not a long march till some one will thin the ranks, and leave the pathway open. "The first step over, the rest is easy," says the Spanish proverb. So to join the procession is the earliest step in law business.

If one seeks his rank in low grades of practice, and joins the procession near the rear, he must expect small returns from a poor clientage; but if alert in action, and wise in his opening an office he will reach a place in season, and retain the advantage.

Established lawyers are not out looking for students and partners, or offering rewards for specialists. They only notice merit if thrown in their way by business relations, so that to start with a live firm in a bright city is a fair beginning, and to start well *alone* is still better.

It is not always an easy matter to get good positions; many a one waits too long and is discouraged. I know a friend that began low, very low. He merely had a clerical position, but in turn came the absence of his employer, and later came on a rich director in a wealthy lumber company. The boy secured a position through his keen insight into the company's affairs: became secretary, and at last received a $7,000 salary — a handsome position for a young man to attain. Another took charge of an office, cleaned the books and cases, watched the trials, looked up the law; made the office like his own; learned the business, and now holds a third interest from his excellent habits of industry. Once in the procession, the profits and promotion fall easily to all men alike. There is a sort of "Civil Service reform" in law offices that few classes of business can equal.

I have never known a bright, shrewd, active, ambitious and competent clerk, student or lawyer, to remain a whole month without something to do. But the chances *in the procession* are six to one, and with reason. Men go to trusted subordinates for bank cashiers and foremen. They look for tried skill in most professions, preferring not to train experts, but to take them already educated, and there is no place where skill is more rewarded than in the legal profession.

Men are helped most who most deserve promotion. Skill is shown by its workmanship. Edison, Brush and Appleby earned their fame by invention. The last worked years in poverty to perfect his Twine Binder Reaper that now reaps him a golden harvest. If the lawyer will show equal energy, study and patience, he will find his reward. And if some hint is found in the experience of the men here mentioned, then my pleasant task shall not have failed in pointing to their wisdom.

TRIAL ELOQUENCE.

The following closing words of eminent counsel exhibit both the genius and art of the advocates. Occasions may arise where the simple reading of a master's language in his last appeal for life or damages, may stimulate many a student to a higher aim in eloquence. There is a deep interest in a lawyer's farewell to his jury. Couched in apt and appropriate words, *like the tongues of dying men, they compel attention.* The greatest cases demand the greatest efforts, but all arguments of importance deserve some impressive words that call out the nobler feelings of men in their high privilege of passing judgment on their fellow-men:

HON. BENJ. HARRISON IN "COLD SPRING TRAGEDY."

I have at my house an old engraving that represents the first trial by a jury — an English picture. The twelve men are gathered in an open field. No house encloses them. It is a murder trial that is represented, but it is very unlike this murder trial. We see here the accused and her family gathered about her weeping and appealing to the jury for sympathy. Not so there. The jury have assembled upon the commission of the crime, and the body of the dead lies at their feet upon a bier. A weeping relative of the deceased bends over the dead form, and her locks drop upon his face as her tears fall in her agony of grief. Another relative of the dead man, stooping over the lifeless form, points with one hand to the criminal and with the other to the gaping wound by which the life tide went out. This was an old trial for murder. I only ask you now, as this group gather around you, to remember the dead that are buried away out of sight; to remember the hearth stone whose fire has gone out forever. I ask you to remember that orphan child who is wandering fatherless and motherless to-day. If any appeal shall be made to your sympathies, I ask you to think of the grief that has come upon another household. I ask you to think of that horrid scene at "Cold Springs," when the charred and blackened remains of that woman lay on the floor, and that man with his head all torn and his teeth bent out as if grinning in horrid mirth. I ask you also in her behalf, to consider these questions that have been presented to you carefully, honestly and deliberately. If she is guilty, speak the word, if not, then let her go free, and may the God of wisdom lead you to the right discharge of this duty that remains to you, and bring you to a right verdict.

HON. W. P. FISHBACK IN "COLD SPRING TRAGEDY."

The thugs of India were a sect who worshipped Kalee, their Goddess of murder. They murdered travelers as they claimed in obedience to the decree of their deity. They would disguise themselves as pilgrims and ingratiate themselves into favor with travelers, and when their victims were off their guard strangle them. It is said that while a portion of a band of thugs would be partaking of the hospitality of their intended victim within their tent, others of the party would be digging their graves, and that at a given signal the hosts would all be murdered by their guests. This approaches the enormity of the great guilt of these defendants. And yet even here the comparison is favorable to the thugs. They were hypocritical, it is true. They were avaricious, but the belief that they were doing the will of their deity made the act a superstitious one, and is certainly some palliation when we reflect that the thugs practiced their bloody creed where the light of Christianity had not reached them. But thirty years ago the Bible and the British army exterminated the sect.

But what have we here — here in Marion County, in Indianapolis, the capital and pride of a noble Christian State? Here under the very shadow of the church spires which on every corner point the sinner to his God, we have a murder which for its cold-blooded atrocity, its avarice and cruelty in its hypocricy, puts thugery to the blush.

While such has been the guilt of this prisoner; while she was so merciless to her victim, I here echo the humane teachings of the law when I ask you to deal with her in no spirit of vindictiveness. Deal with her mercifully, if you choose, but with that measure of justice also that bloody-minded men will pause and forsake their guilty purposes.

COL. INGERSOLL CLOSING IN THE STAR ROUTE CASE.

You have nothing to do with the supposed desire of any man, or supposed desire of any department (turning and addressing his remarks to the Attorney-General), or the supposed desire of any government, or supposed desire of any president, or supposed desire of the public. You have nothing to do with these things; you have to do only with the evidence. Here all power is powerless except your own. When asked to please the public, you should think of the lives you are asked to wreck, of the homes your verdict would darken, of the hearts it would desolate, of the cheeks it would wet with tears, of the characters it would destroy, of the wife it would worse than widow, and of the children it would worse than orphan. When asked to please the public think of those consequences. When asked to act from fear, hatred, malice or cowardice, think of those consequences. Whoever does right, clothes himself in a suit of armor which the arrows of prejudice cannot penetrate, but whoever does wrong is responsible for all the consequences to the last sigh, to the last tear. You are told by Mr. Merrick that you should have no sympathy, that you should be like icicles, that you should be Godlike. That is not my doctrine, the higher you get in the scale of being the grander the nobler, the tenderer you will become. Kindness is always an evidence of greatness. Malice is the property of a small soul, and whoever allows the feeling of brotherhood to die in his heart becomes a wild beast.

> "Not a king's crown nor the deputed sword,
> The marshal's truncheon nor the judge's robe,
> Became them with one-half so good a grace
> As mercy does."

And yet the only mercy we ask is the mercy of an honest verdict. I appeal to you for my client, Stephen

W. Dorsey, because the evidence shows that he is a man with an intellectual horizon and a mental sky — a man of genius, generous and honest. Yet this prosecution, this government, these attorneys, representing the majesty of the republic, representing the only real republic that ever existed, have asked you not only to violate the law of the land, but also the law of nature. They maligned nature, they have laughed at mercy, they have trampled on the holiest human ties, and even made light because a wife in this trial has sat by her husband's side.

There is a painting in the Louvre, a painting of desolation, of despair and love. It represents the "Night of the Crucifixion." The world is wrapped in shadow, the stars are dead, and yet in the darkness is seen a kneeling form. It is Mary Magdalen with loving lips and hands pressed against the bleeding feet of Christ.

The skies were never dark enough nor starless enough, the storm never fierce enough nor wild enough, the quick bolts of heaven were never livid enough, and the arrows of slander never flew thick enough to drive a noble woman from her husband's side, and so it is in all of human speech, the holiest word, " woman."

ARNOLD AND RYAN IN THE HUBBELL CASE.

In 1853, Levi Hubbell, Judge of the Circuit Court for Milwaukee County, was impeached by the Assembly for high crimes and misdemeanors in office. The charges were eleven in number. The preliminary proceedings occupied six days. Mr. Ryan made an opening argument on all the charges, occupying nearly the entire day. Mrs. Hubbell was at that time lying ill at the house of a friend near to the Capitol. Mr. Arnold made the closing argument for the defense, occupying an entire day, and concluded as follows:

"And, in yonder cottage, almost within the hearing of my voice, there is yet another who is waiting, with intense solicitude, the result of your deliberations. She waits, in unshaken confidence and devoted love, for the accused. She is in deed as well as in law the wife of her husband, and she would clasp that man to her breast, though her arm were in a flame of living fire till it burned to its very socket; her prayers are all around you — her hopes are all dependent on you. On bended knee, and with eye uplifted prayerfully to heaven, before you, she implores you: 'Oh! give me back the husband of my youth! I can surrender him to God — I can surrender him to my country — but Oh! spare the blow which, while it destroys him, dooms me to lean upon a broken reed, and to a life without a hope.' Fell blow, indeed, which would destroy the prospects of one so young and beautiful, which, in a moment, would

> Change the current of her sinless years,
> And turn her pure heart's purest blood to tears.

Her arms are outstretched to receive him, and their embrace will be warmer and purer, should the judgment of this court vindicate the honor and fame of her husband in the judgment of the world."

MR. RYAN'S CLOSING.

He said: "It was said that this trial, that the evidence in this cause, had demonstrated this man's innocence to those who doubted it before; that the ordeal of trial had demonstrated his personal and judicial purity to the world. Why, then, if thus sustained by universal judgment of the public, by the foreshadowed judgment of this court appointed to try him, by his own conscience, why, thus perfectly sustained in coming pure out of the fire that tried him, with the angels of heaven to watch by him here in the furnace in which his innocence is only proved, why kneel to this court in cringing appeals? Why, Mr. President, had I yesterday to hear the same pathetic declamation, to see the same mockery of tears, that I saw and heard upon the trial of Radcliffe, the murderer? Why, upon this trial of a judge who stands upon his innocence, of a judicial officer who here says that he is innocent, who boasts that all the disclosures here have but tended to demonstrate his innocence, to redouble the faith of his friends in his innocence, and to convince even his enemies of his purity, why, if all this security of innocence was here, were the privacies of domestic life dragged into this court to move the heart of justice; crying, craven, weeping this court to have compassion upon the innocent victims of his guilt? It was bad taste; it was bad feeling. And knowing the learned, eloquent, and able counsel, as I know him, I cannot think it was the prompting of either his taste or his feeling to do it."

Judge Hubbell: "It was not my taste, and you know it."

Mr. Ryan: "I know the gentleman. I know the learned counsel well. I ought to know him well at this time of day; and I do not believe, when he said in presence of this court, that he stood here not merely as counsel, but that he stood here as the defendant's personal and judicial friend, I do not believe that he would of himself have cringed to this court, that he would have invoked the mercy of, and compassion for women and children, the dead and the unborn, to mitigate the judgment of man upon man." Judge Hubbell was acquitted.

COL. MUNN CLOSING THE CLARK MURDER CASE.

Perhaps the most important, and certainly the most hotly contested murder trial in the north west, was what is known as the LaGrange Murder Trial — tried in Chicago in the winter of 1878.

To assist the State's Attorney, the friends of the deceased, Alvaro B. Clark, employed the celebrated John Van Arman. Mrs. A. B. Clark, the wife of the deceased, and one Joseph St. Peters, the "hired man," were charged with the murder.

Hon. D. W. Munn, was attorney for Mrs. Clark. The trial lasted nearly four weeks. Over eighty witnesses were examined. In the closing speech for the defense, made by Mr. Munn, a day and a half was occupied in the delivery. The law and the facts were presented in a masterly manner; the jury and vast audience seemed entranced and spell-bound during his entire argument. With telling effect he took up the testimony of each of the witnesses, endeavoring to show wherein the testimony for the people was unworthy of belief; especially that testimony tending to show an improper intimacy between Mrs. Clark and young St. Peters, upon which the prosecution relied as showing a motive for the killing. Mr. Munn closed his remarks as follows:

"Gentlemen of the jury, I am nearly through; but for your marked attention and the earnest expression of your every countenance, which indicates to me your great desire to know the truth in the case, I should hours ago have left my client in your hands; while she is full of hope, conscious of her own innocence, I tremble with anxiety that I may have left something undone that I might have done, as her counsel. It is a terrible responsibility to have the management of such a case, where liberty, and perhaps life, is at stake. You will bear me out, gentlemen, in saying, I have done what I could against the great array of talent and of testimony brought to bear against my client. I only beg your indulgence while I examine one witness more, whom I have summoned from the spirit land. Here he comes. (The speaker lifting his eyes to the ceiling.) It is the spirit of Alvaro B. Clark — swear him not, Mr. Clerk, he is from the abode of truth. Take the stand, give the jury your name:

"Alvaro B. Clark, formerly of LaGrange."

"Do you know the prisoner?" (pointing to Mrs. Clark.)

"Do I know her! She is my wife — the mother of my children — that were left fatherless by a murderer's bullet."

"Had she anything to do, directly or indirectly, with your murder?"

"No! No! No! She is my first love. For years we traveled the path of life together in peace — devoted to each other and our little ones — I see them here. When weary with the toils of the day, she met me with a smile and loving kindness: in sickness she was devoted and kind, and at last, when I fell upon the steps of my own dwelling a corpse, she threw herself prostrate by my lifeless body and bathed my brow with tears of affection. I have watched the trial. I have heard the perjury from the lips of every witness. My darling is NOT GUILTY! NOT GUILTY!"

Gentlemen, you have heard this witness who cannot lie, will you, can you, disbelieve him? If so (turning to Mrs. Clark), here is your victim! By your verdict tear her from these three bright little ones — her three children who are now fatherless, let them be cast upon the cold charities of an unfriendly world, fatherless, motherless: but if you believe this last witness, who needs no corroboration from any earthly witness, then by your verdict lift this cloud from the mother, and let her walk forth as free as the air of heaven."

This highly dramatic style is often dangerous, but in this case was successful: and who can complain of an art when it is *the thing that does it?* Such pictures are inspirations real, and their effect lasting.

CHAPTER XXII.

STYLE OF SPEAKING.

Distinguished speakers of all ages are believed to have given as much care and attention to the art of oratory as musicians now give to cultivate the rare melody of harmonious and inspiring music.

To suppose one can enter on the field so full of genius as the lawyer finds on his early admission to practice, without some system, or plan of meeting this essential, is to believe more than men ever expect of any other business. The lucky man in commerce is one brought up from the habits of careful experience. To the trained sea captain his chart is simple. The brick layer or builder is a student of books and designs; the race-rider is one accustomed to horses, and even the woodsman has learned to handle his axe with clever skill and powerful force.

Genius alone is well likened to a rich mine of metal, that thought and skill must apply to uses and values. It is not what we know, but how we make use of that knowledge, that makes the world better, or better comprehends its beauty. A man may out-think twenty of his neighbors and let nineteen of the twenty out-do him in honor and usefulness by one actual accomplishment.

I have seen a man cradle wheat with an ease and poetry of motion, and another strike the scythe into the earth at every other clip from awkwardness. I have seen the mason evenly spread his mortar that a new hand would throw down his sleeve with a single attempt to fill his trowel. I have known the well-tuned voice of Phillips, in graceful modulation, to so charm the senses of his hearers that few could count it less than music, and no one saw the art of concealing art that he had struggled so long to master.

The art to charm the senses by pleasing speech is an enjoyment greater to the speaker once acquired than to rule an empire. Gibbon wrote his "Memoirs" six times to secure perfection. Turner walked over mountains and in the water till they colored the retina of his eyes with intensity, before committing the colors to canvas. The elegy of Gray and the "Village" of Goldsmith, with the later examples of endurance by Morse and Edison, are apt illustrations that, "the hand of the diligent maketh rich" in oratory, in science, and all useful achievements.

I am not urging the practice-before-a-looking-glass-style, but a plan of speaking of, and dealing with, subjects that will command attention, and secure a following. The method of Judge Curtis, of New York, is to think out his speeches as Sumner did. Van Arman writes incessantly during trials, while each master with consummate care the details of his case in his own peculiar way.

Both Porter and Shaffer, of New York, write all salient points of evidence with their own pens, and trust no notes to any but their own making. They commit their speeches as they go along; the former, a powerful examiner, the latter, a master of human nature, both eminently successful. Judge Beach trusts different branches to associates, and speaks from copious manuscript; while Graham reads frequently and quotes all the wisdom of the past, at command, on the topics under discussion. Emory Storrs speaks with powerful rapidity, composes on his feet, carries his hearers with rhythmical sentences, but is a trained and thorough speaker. Wirt Dexter is more deliberate, but equally effective. He is a master of modulation and emphasis, a student of fine language and rich in resources.

Colonel Breckinridge, of Lexington, is one of the most flowery speakers since the days of Crittenden, whom his style resembles as Beach resembles Beecher. Daniel Dougherty, of Pennsylvania, is as fluent in his style as Tom Marshall was in his, without the eccentricities and brilliant fancy of that high bred Kentucky orator.

Leonard Swett, of Chicago, and Colonel Broadhead, of St. Louis, form a pair of the most scholarly orators in America. Yet each could relate many struggles and bitter embarrassments in early life. They had mastered the art of advocacy in early days, but practice their art like musicians, reading and improving through years of experience. Justice Matthews and Judge Hoadly, present a strange contrast, while General Butler and Senator Conkling are as widely dissimilar. Butler wins by rarity of illustrations, Conkling by rich imagery, Matthews by his logic and intensity, Hoadly by his mastery of analysis and purely legal principles. Senator Carpenter was an ideal orator who chose his central point and built around it, graphic in style, vivid in description, it required that giant, Judge Ryan of Madison, to even approach him in argument. Stars of such brilliancy are seldom now equaled, and never excelled, in Wisconsin, that home of brilliant advocates like Vilus, Hudd, Jenkins and Hazelton.

In the circle of the several States, from Gov. Davis, of St. Paul, on the west, to the scholarly Edmunds, on the east; from the musical pathos of Judge Curtis in New York, to the picturesque imagery of Gordon and Voorhees in Indiana, and the florid style of Jeff Chandler, on the Pacific slope, or the same vigorous heart-speaker, like H. M. Furnam, of Texas, each and all have come to fame by force of earnest oratory, ripened by age, and burnished by use. They stand and speak at the bar and before the public, and in life's affairs, as actors do on the mimic stage; studying their several parts with care and diligence, applying to them their genius and experience, ripened by age and fed by inspiration, till they so please their hearers as to meet most hearty recalls and clear appreciation in large emoluments.

Tom Corwin, of Ohio, who started with Jere Black, and died young, was a master of advocacy, but a different kind of a lawyer. He won by wit. His speeches were flowery. He often captured a jury by a simple story, or a flight of eloquence. He enjoyed a joke, and made all others in hearing take an interest in his way of telling it. Large, laughing eyes, dark complexion, robust in speech and manner, for years he led the Ohio bar in eloquence and won his cases by it. He regarded his wit and manner as a mistake, and said at last that "men never respect those who always make them laugh." That "one should look wise to attain eminence." Mr. Corwin was in Congress with Henry Clay, and made many brilliant little speeches and attained national fame. His work is mentioned elsewhere.

Webster and Choate were such active rivals as to be evenly mated. In the Smith will contests in 1845, the heirs retained Rufus Choate as their lawyer, whereupon the friends of the will secured the services of Daniel Webster as their attorney. The case came to trial before the Supreme Court of Massachusetts, in July, 1847, and occupied two days. There was the greatest excitement, not only on account of the interests involved, but also on account of the fame of the two great lawyers who were to speak for and against the will. "The battle of these giants" is still remembered in this vicinity, although it occurred nearly thirty-six years ago. So great was the crowd that ladders were put up to the windows of the court house, and eager listeners stood upon them for hours. When Mr. Choate had finished his argument the conclusion was nearly unanimous among the spectators that the will would be broken; but when Mr. Webster had finished his masterly address no one doubted but that it would be sustained — so say the older men of to-day who were present at the famous trial. The jury brought in a verdict sustaining the will.

General Butler early learned the secret of Choate's success, and matched it. He defended a famous case where Choate prosecuted, and in his closing made such a masterly analysis of his opponent's style, that he mortified the immortal Rufus, and won his victory. Butler has since won many verdicts, and next to Beach and Roscoe Conkling, is to-day, 1883, the greatest living advocate in practice.

His chief resource is a large brain and long experience in hard cases. He was government counsel in the Johnson impeachment case, and the master advocate of them all. What he fails to discern in a trial is hardly worth noting. His power of logic and strategy are both marvelous. In a railroad accident case the injured man said, "It's all my fault; if I'd been inside I wouldn't have been hurt," showing clearly contributory negligence. "This was but the wailing of a disordered fancy," said Butler, "for they swear he was in his place, inside the car door — all swear it but the allies of this corporation." He won a $26,000 verdict, which, on two new trials, reached $45,000, and was affirmed and settled.

Roscoe Conkling's power is in mastery of language and force of argument. He is not a genius, like Butler, but a man of immense tact, with force of reason and logic. He is commanding, intense, graphic, and full of supreme courage, which is admired in a court room, and delights an audience. He is rapidly acquiring a fortune in his excellent practice. Had he always followed the law as devotedly as he did politics, his fame would have been greater as an advocate. Large, tall, commanding, almost imperial in bearing, he is an attractive and impressive speaker, with scarcely a peer as an orator in America.

These advocates, all successful, are each students of oratory, patient in detail, earnest in manner, effective in delivery. While their number could be greatly augmented, and perhaps should be doubled, they represent the highest order of legal eloquence and American advocates. Many others herein described are equally worthy of study, and their wisdom and art dense with interest.

Hon. Chas. S. May, of Kalamazoo, himself an excellent advocate, thus vividly describes Mr. Lincoln's style of oratory in his great campaign with Stephen A. Douglas:

Promptly at the hour appointed for the meeting, in the midst of a buzz of eager expectation and quiet applause, following through the main aisle of the hall the chairman of the evening, there entered a tall, sallow faced man with disheveled hair and lank, angular figure, dressed in plain black — and I had my first view of Abraham Lincoln. Preceded by the chairman he mounted the bare platform at the end of the hall, and after a brief, formal introduction, stood face to face with his audience. I should, perhaps, say, stooped apologetically before his audience, for, bowed forward, with his hand on a low stand where he had deposited a few scraps of newspaper memoranda, he presented a timid bashful appearance. His opening sentences were not more reassuring than his attitude. They were hesitating, involved and awkward, as he went on to depreciate his ability to follow so distinguished a speaker as Gen. Cass, of Michigan, who had spoken the night before in the same hall. Indeed, so lame and halting were his first words, and so awkward and unpromising his whole appearance that, recalling the eulogy of the party paper, I said to myself, "Can this be one of the first orators of Illinois? Is this what they call eloquence in Chicago?" But before my disappointment had time to deepen into disgust, the speaker began to recover himself, he raised himself from the table to his full height, his language began to flow more smoothly and grammatically, he began to uncoil himself in mind and body, so to speak, and very soon I was listening with rapt and deepening interest to his words.

Of the speech itself, which held that weighty and intelligent audience for more than two hours, I still retain a perfect and vivid impression. Delivered in an animated, earnest, conversational manner, with a clear and pleasant, but penetrating tenor voice, with no attempt at oratory or fine language, it was a candid, a convincing and powerful political argument, addressed to the reason and conscience of his hearers. Nothing could exceed its perfect fairness of tone and statement, and from beginning to end there was nothing to detract from its dignity — not an epithet or coarse expression, not a single attempt to provoke applause, or create a laugh by anecdote, or joke, or stale wit, or appeal to passion or prejudice Mr. Lincoln was famous as a story-teller, but he did not tell his stories in his speeches. He was full of wit and drollery but he used these in private. The innate seriousness and earnestness of the man lifted him in his public efforts to a plane above these diversions. But his logic was overwhelming. Proceeding from premises stated with the utmost fairness, and with transparent clearness, it moved to its conclusions with a force and power and thoroughness that left no room or quarter for sophistry or evasion.

In replying to the plausible and specious arguments and positions of his great rival, who was a master of political attack and fence, he had abundant opportunity to display his great power of analysis and his keen discernment of the weak points of his adversary. I remember, too, that he had a quaint and original way of putting things. Coming to a particularly untruthful and audacious proposition of his opponent, he said: "Now, it is exceedingly difficult to answer such an argument as this. It gains strength and plausibility, paradoxical as it may seem, from its very unreasonableness, for when a man like Judge Douglas makes such a proposition, a man who has been so long in public life and in a position to know, it is natural for men to say, 'This thing looks so all wrong and preposterous to us that we may be mistaken after all, for *he* must see something that we *don't* see." A spontaneous burst of quiet but general applause showed that the audience appreciated the keen, fine point.

I will not undertake in this brief article to give even the substance of this great speech. Mr. Lincoln had momentous questions to discuss — questions of Liberty, of Slavery, of Patriotism — and he treated them in a way I have never seen surpassed. Of all our great political speakers of this generation — and I have heard them all — he has been to me the model stump orator. Discarding all the tricks and artifices and stock expressions so common in this style of address, he literally reasoned with the people, and lifted them up to the plane of his own patriotic and moral earnestness. While it was not eloquence in the traditional and technical sense, it realized the very essence and definition of eloquence — persuasion.

RUFUS CHOATE.

Rufus Choate was as nervous as a race-horse, quick, keen, fiery, fluent, pathetic and eloquent, tall, slim, graceful, gifted and bred to the law; he was seldom matched, save by Webster. The charm of his words was like a poem of wondrous beauty. The rhythm of his voice like sweet music. He was crafty in details, but won by power of eloquence.

A great lover of books and rare learning, he was a constant and hungry reader. Rhetorically speaking, he had the best command of language of any advocate of his day in America. His speeches are not reported. On the street he walked rapidly. His person stooped a little, but all who passed him recognized a genius of intense power and ability. His long jet black hair and piercing eyes framed a pale face of intellectual mould and distinction.

At the sound of his voice one would go nearer. Vast audiences hung on his sentences entranced. School-boys and college students especially, admired his exciting delivery and dramatic action.

A friend who heard him seventy times in four years (he was always in important cases on one side or the other), says: "I could listen to him all night. He was such an actor. No words now can be recalled, but I know he spoke as I believed, and reasoned as the common sense of the matter seemed to dictate. I remember he spoke to one at a time walking in front of the jury, but his voice was kept well modulated. The wonder of his delivery was its earnestness. The beauty of his thoughts entranced his hearers. He died early; worn out under sixty, by the rapid running of his life's machinery, but in his intensity he lived long."

DANIEL WEBSTER.

Daniel Webster, the greatest of American orators and statesmen, was a native of New Hampshire, born January, 1782, died in October, 1852, at the age of seventy-one. At the age of fifteen he entered Dartmouth College, graduated in due time at the head of his class: studied law and taught in an academy for a year. He studied law in his native village, and was admitted to practice in Boston, at the age of twenty-three. His early practice was near his home, but later at Portsmouth, and was elected to Congress in 1812. Here his remarkable powers as an orator were developed. He lived in an age of giants, and soon ranked as one of the greatest in the National Congress. Five years later he removed to Boston, and ten years later still represented Boston as a United States Senator. He was very largely employed in political life, having been twice Secretary of State. He had a strong desire for the presidency, but, like Henry Clay, was too prominent in his opinions to succeed to that station.

His chief prominence in law was his art of advocacy. In language powerful and dramatic, in delivery strong, logical and impressive, in manner dignified and majestic, his name, fame, tone, character and presence increased the strength of his well-worded sentences. In any city and any country Webster's speeches would have attracted large audiences on great occasions. Other lawyers have known a wider range of authorities, many have mastered the facts with as accurate analysis, but few men ever combined such strength of voice, power of thought, or carried such conviction with his delivery as did Daniel Webster before a jury, in argument or a Senate debate. His character and speeches stand out alone, a monument to American advocacy.

The style of Webster's speeches was in perfect harmony with his nature. He was large, heavy, labored and strong, never hurried, often grand, and occasionally sublime. But his nature was sublime. He feared only Choate, and Choate feared Webster alone. Webster won cases by logic. Choate by eloquence.

The late Senator Stevens said of Webster: "I shall never forget my first trip away from home, nor the impressions it made on me. I was quite a young man, and some business fell into my hands that carried me north. I had never been as far as Washington before, and, of course, I wanted to see what was there to be seen. I went into the Senate gallery and took my seat. I could easily pick out the prominent men by the pictures I had seen of them. Pretty soon a question came up, and the President of the Senate announced that Mr. Webster was entitled to the floor.

Of course I was very much gratified that I was to hear him. He arose and began speaking in an ordinary conversational way. I think he took his snuff occasionally. He never made a gesture from the time he opened until he closed. I thought it all sound doctrine, but I was convinced that I knew a dozen college boys who could have beaten him speaking. The next morning I picked up a paper. There was his speech headed: 'Mr. Webster's Great Speech on the Finances.' Pshaw! I thought they don't call that a great speech, do they? I saw another paper; there it was again, headed 'Mr. Webster's Great Speech on the Finances.' I went to Baltimore. There they had Mr. Webster's great speech on the finances. I reached Philadelphia, and everybody was talking about Mr. Webster's great speech on the finances. I got to New York. There everything was in a ferment over Mr. Webster's great speech on the finances. It was the same way in Boston. So I concluded that it must, indeed, be a great speech. It put me to thinking, and I made up my mind that it was not the way a man said anything, but what he said made him an orator."

CHAPTER XXIII.

THE NEW YORK BAR.

Men who earn fabulous fees and make splendid names will always be watched with a degree of curious wonder. We like to look in alone on their inner life and see how they bear the silent struggles of rising in the world, that we may better judge of their power and fame, and how they have attained them.

The present head of the American bar is not Charles O'Connor, who bore the honor so long and worthily. There is no head at present. He is aging fast, and over 70. His person was something like Choate, but for Choate's nervousness he has coolness. In presence, commanding; in style, lucid and elaborate; in trials, keen, adroit and full of the intuitive arts of a master advocate. Not so eloquent as the late James T. Brady or Rufus Choate, but combining so many traits and virtues, that he has ever been known as a model advocate. He has made all branches of law a science, and is a scientist in practice.

Charles O'Connor, now over 75, nearly out of court practice, is still one of the model advocates of America, and would have made his mark in any nation as a clear, logical and convincing reasoner, of great industry and excellent common sense, always his best weapon in winning cases.

In figure, tall, erect, dignified, ready ; with no attempt at wit, captious practices, or overbearing means of seeking victory, he first mastered his profession, next his cases, and last, his courts and juries. His voice has ever been clear with metallic ring and singular penetration. His self-poised and even-tempered action, leaves him always complete master of his sentences. He cares little for trifles, and acts, speaks and brings all evidence and law to bear directly on the merits of his cases.

In this way he is trusted, believed in and followed by a host of clients and corporations of which he has long been the trusted adviser. He is rather austere, but it is from force of habit rather than feeling of pride or haughtiness. To secure his counsel one must pass a partner or two, and be prepared for a brief visit and a large deposit in fees : the latter he never accepts from his intimate clients, it being requested by the gentlemanly time-keeper at about $100, and more every extra hour's consultation.

Wm. M. Evarts, of the O'Connor school, is his peer in training and success : wonderfully fluent, acute, far-seeing and logical : more of a national character, and less of an advocate than his competitor for a quarter of a century. He is slim, spare, with large powers of reason, and splendid ability. He wins his cases by learning all the law, and knowing all the fact that can apply to the trial, and never wearying in well-doing. No man can excel him in presentation of cases to a court of last resort.

Mr. Evarts was secretary of State under President Hayes, is an intellectual New Englander, of classical attainments, equipped in all arts of advocacy but magnetism. Mr. Evarts is a man of marked intelligence, keen insight, marvelous language and memory, whose delivery is one rapid and exhaustive train of logical reasoning, positively convincing in its manner of statement and conclusion.

He has been the attorney in more large will cases, and counsel in more matters of a national nature than any man in America. Early in the war he had charge of the Mason and Sliddell matters, later in the Geneva Award, and later represented the republican side of the Electral Commission, and in each case came out victorious. He is industrious, graceful, fluent, wise and successful. To his wonderful memory of legal principles he adds the tact and acumen of a master advocate. Without much of the magnetism of Beach, he was an excellent match for him in the great Tilton-Beecher trial in Brooklyn. His whole tact in that case could never be described better than in a single word, *kindness*. It is not an uncommon thing for him to accept a $20,000 or $50,000 fee in an important will case.

Judge John K. Porter, late of the Guiteau trial, is one of the old school lawyers of New York. He is not a large man, say about five feet nine, with fair round face, jet black eyes, short gray hair and moustache, a little bald; erect, energetic ingenious. He is subtle in the arts of court practice. He was not real well during the eleven weeks of the "meanest trial on earth," but rested under instructions of an eminent doctor, and looks fresh and quite youthful for one of sixty-three.

Judge Porter is an inveterate worker. He relies on no one but Porter, takes his own notes, continues in the same plodding, pains-taking labor that he did in the country. He carries his country genius into the city, and it is said whether he or Beach shall win depends on who has the last say to a jury.

His style with a jury is that employed by Rufus Choate — winning one at a time. The President's murderer mistook his man in Porter. The long play of words and the ingenious trap set for the assassin's vanity was sprung by the advocate when he said: "Then you mean if Mrs. Garfield had been with the President on the 2d of July you would not have shot the President?" "No, I would not," said the prisoner. "Then it was Mrs. Garfield's presence that restrained you once, and her absence that let you fire?" "Yes," said the foolish witness, and he was caught.

William A. Beach, of the Beecher case fame has an elegant office on Wall Street, high up and reached by elevator. One would not believe him to be over sixty by appearance, yet he is by his own count about seventy-three. Not as large as I expected, probably like the boy's giant that he expected to find as tall as a tree, and found but little taller than his father. But one is charmed by the manner and voice of Mr. Beach. He, too, was a country lawyer, and knows what struggles lawyers bore in an early day. Now he enjoys large fees from heavy verdicts and national fame. He is a little above medium size and height, with thin gray hair, gray eyes, small chin whiskers, and a countenance a little like Mr. Beecher's; lighting up with smiles or emotions, changeable and warm. He is social and kind, able and ingenious, gifted as a speaker, and has a way of impressing his belief upon a court and jury in telling terms. He took me by the hand in a way that said come nearer. He talks like Beecher. He is to the bar what Beecher is to the pulpit—all original, and as an advocate in New York, the noblest Roman of them all.

Chauncey Shaffer, of New York, is a lawyer of varied skill and intense application. His mastery of men, learned in the early contests of pioneer advocacy, is remarkable. He sifts the motive of human action; he is a genius with a natural rugged country way: he surprises a jury and his adversary by quaint sayings of original beauty: he relies on the sturdy sense of justice, honor and fair play, and shows a jury what they ought to do, and *must* do to be just and faithful. He removes obstacles and plants his cause on such rocky piers of evidence, that opposite argument cannot change his theory. Few men in New York are more dreaded as an adversary, or admired as associate counsel.

He is large—about five feet ten—and weighs nearly 200 pounds; broad chested, strong limbed, with smoothly shaven fleshy face, massive head, and piercing gray eyes that retain their sparkle at the age of over sixty-three. He is fluent and versatile in speech, and jokes and illustrates in ordinary suits, but never in sacred cases. *He wins his cases* by an old fashioned way of saying homely things well. And when all is said, only a half has been told. You should see him with expanded chest, his eyes, arms, face and hands alive with the fire of eloquence, that fills a court room and thrills its hearers. When this manly form is quivering with the power of a genius bursting into truths through concentrated speech, when the man is forgotten and his theme coining a climax. To see him thus is to admire a style of oratory that is rapidly passing away, which to him, has secured an excellent clientage and an enviable reputation. His recent verdict of $30,000 against the Elevated Railroad Company in New York, obtained for injuries against great odds, is a signal victory.

The following extract from Mr. Shaffer's speech in closing the Steven's Poisoning Case shows his style of jury work: "This I have taken time to demonstrate to you, gentlemen, that you should see your way clearly. Do you suppose the body had been tampered with, when it was taken by the professor to his private laboratory when it was under lock and seal: you will remember that all through the year the body of this woman committed to the earth is preserved by this arsenic within it. Nor did this body absorb the poison from the earth surrounding it. We have summoned the earth surrounding the coffin, and the earth responded, 'it is not in me.' We have called upon the dead woman's shroud, but the shroud says, 'it is not in me.' We have called upon her coffin, and the very nails and handles of that coffin, and each responds, 'arsenic is not in me.' And yet in the body of this unhappy woman, arsenic is found, sufficient to preserve the dead from decomposition or decay for a year. Standing securely upon the immutable test of arsenic we cannot err. Thus science has testified to the awful fact that this woman died from arsenious poison.

"You have heard all this chemical evidence, how arsenic passes through the system, and how it is absorbed, how it remains two to four days unless death intervenes, and how, when death intervenes, it fastens itself in the portions of the body, follows its victim and lays down in the grave to preserve the natural body. Here are the pieces. Here are the tests. There is the metalic stain. Arsenic has killed its victim. The metalic stain in tube number seven glows with the lustre of the deadly mineral. Dr. Doremus applied every test to that body, and that body through the voice of science responds: In me are the seeds of death. Four to six grains of the deadly poison have been found and preserved. One-fourth of a grain has been known to kill a person. His closing in this case was substantially as follows: "I shall make no further attempt to increase your sense of your present responsibility. I will not plant my foot upon the grave of a murdered woman and call for vengeance. Vengeance is not mine. If I could, I would not again ask you to go over the journey of pain, and review the torture, or listen to the low moans of patient agony: to the prayer for peace of one who is free, and we trust in that home above the sun, where pain and torture are no more. But I will ask you as men, as husbands and fathers, as good citizens, to be brave, to trouble not yourselves with consequences, to be daring in duty, to remember your oaths and how you are pledged to God and your country to make thorough this investigation and impartially to weigh this evidence, and arriving at the truth, the whole truth and nothing but the truth, fearlessly to declare the same, thereby discharging your whole duty to the people and to the prisoner of giving him the benefit of all reasonable doubts, and may justice be done, though the heavens fall."

Joseph Choate, of New York, a nephew of the well known Rufus Choate, is what we call a clean cut, clear headed lawyer, of excellent success in practice. Tall, erect, of fine presence and attractive voice, he is clear, lucid and forcible in trials, and wins many cases. He has rather a striking face, high forehead, blue gray eyes, brown hair, and small side beard — a man of some forty years, who handles his cases with studied care and extreme clearness. In argument to the jury Mr. Choate seems to give much time to explanation, while this may seem needlessly prolonged to many, it is *the* practice that wins a law suit. It is said of Mr. Choate that he is at times eloquent, always earnest, and that his simplicity of statement is his rare gift of reaching a jury.

Judge George M. Curtis, of New York, one of the brightest advocates of the American bar, was born in Massachusetts, June 18th, 1843. Served in the Union army in the late war. Studied law with Hon. John W. Ashmead. Was admitted on reaching his majority, and elected to the State Legislature where he took a high rank. Was, later, Assistant Corporation Attorney of New York, and still later served a six years term as Judge of the Marine Court.

In practice, few men of his age have been so prominent in important cases. He has appeared in fifteen murder cases, in which none of the accused were hung, and all but four absolutely cleared.

He defended Helmbold on a charge of insanity, and cleared him; appeared in the Frank Leslie Will Case, and the famous Buford-Elliott Kentucky case. In the Bouden Will Case he established the doctrine that a man in the last stages of Bright's disease was incompetent to make a will.

It is said that he never lost a case where he had the last say to the jury. His recent signal victory was of Neville v. Hitchcock, of the Fifth Avenue Hotel, where for a week he was opposed by Joseph Choate, a brilliant descendant of the great Boston lawyer, in which contest Judge Curtis was triumphant.

He is thoroughly at home in fraud, malpractice and insanity cases, and often makes briefs for older lawyers. If there is a born orator in New York, it is Curtis, and his style is a marvel. Never taking notes, but thinking out his subjects. He is extremely fluent and forcible as a debater and "Stump orator." Personally only forty years of age, a little over the medium height, rather heavy build, but well proportioned, with smoothly-shaven, strong face, like Napoleon's.

His clarion voice is deep and musical. Having long been an editorial writer (once on *Leslie's Pictorial*), he is ready in apt and appropriate language. His long service on the bench, makes him ready in practice, but with all his gifts of advocacy he has but one rule: "A thorough preparation in evidence and law of every case, diligence in enforcing both, with the tone, manner, and conduct of a gentleman."

He declined four times a nomination for Congress; declined a nomination for the Common Pleas, and Superior Court.

George Bliss, of New York, who has attained a national reputation through the Star Route cases, and a previous good record as United States District Attorney, began practice in New York City in 1856, where he ranks as one of the shrewdest counsel and advocates.

He is excedingly able in preparing the proofs and pleadings in intricate cases, and equally at home in argument to court or jury. Trained in a large city practice, he is a ripe scholar and industrious worker. Ready, fluent and decisive in speech, quick and keen in replies, in person below the medium height, in manner candid, and direct in reasoning, he is a marked man in a court room. His hair is thick and turning gray, eyes sharp and piercing, face warm, clean-shaven, save a short moustache; in conduct genial and companionable, he is a complete master of his subject, its arts, points and changes, and has made a fine fortune in his practice, and is still youthful and vigorous in looks and actions.

His frequent connection with political questions has done much to create a newspaper fame throughout the Union. But of this he is deserving. In practice he gets to the real meat of cases, and commits the salient parts to memory. In trials he is quiet and energetic, making accurate moves, and taking tenable positions, adheres to them with great tenacity. His success is due to constant application of good natural ability and a name for winning cases. He is one of a choice few millionaire lawyers.

David Dudley Field, a man of mature years, nearly sixty-five, tall, graceful, with side beard, worn after the English fashion, is a marked figure in the New York and Washington court rooms. Mr. Field is all original, a keen, watchful and successful trial lawyer, that aids his client's cause by his adroitness, skill, and sturdy sense of justice. He found the New York forms too cumbersome to suit a city practice, as with a keen knife he cut the knot instantly, and the whole code practice with its simple forms sprang into life and being.

This daring innovation made him early recognized as an original and comprehensive counsel. It is to him, as though he had coined the statutes of practice out of his fertile mind to suit his rapid thought and sensible conclusions that forms were often stumbling blocks to courts and a hindrance to progress in trials, without any object in the end gained in useless controversy. This single act will immortalize David Dudley Field in New York State.

CHAPTER XXIV.

THE CHICAGO BAR.

Lawyers are lost in the courts of Chicago much as they are in New York. Many are called and few are chosen. The bar is very full, and the practice exceedingly rapid. To even be known as a lawyer in Chicago requires five years residence.

Of those who have attained success and national mention are Secretary of War Lincoln, Leonard Swett, John Van Arman, E. S. Isham, Emery Storrs, Col. Munn, Ex-Senator Doolittle and Wirt Dexter, with many more less generally known outside of Illinois.

Wirt Dexter is a wealthy business lawyer who can, and often does try criminal cases. Nearly fifty, above medium size, large head, full brown beard tinged with gray, heavy brown hair, a dignified bearing, large, expressive eyes, a voice like an actor and finely modulated. His speeches are ripe in scholarly quotations, pure in diction, and exceedingly impressive. Few lawyers try a case with more skill, adroitness and energy. Born to the law, his father a judge, and trained in a large city practice he has but one ambition — to excel in his profession and acquire riches. He has done both while yet young. His services are sought for in lumber and corporation cases, and he is quite at home in any branch of practice that pays handsomely.

How does he win his cases? It is by a combined force of courage, character, work and eloquence. A large, fine commanding presence, with candid, plain farmer-like dress and appearance — exceptionally so in dress — he stands before a jury like a general in battle and expects a verdict. He is one of the counsel who win cases on their reputation; you know this is not unfrequently done. But he never trusts alone to high standing; he masters the case first, and the court afterwards.

John Van Arman, of sixty-six, a short, heavy, smooth faced man, who acquired a reputation years ago in the Conspiracy Case mentioned at length in "Modern Jury Trials," has continued to lead the Chicago bar as a criminal lawyer ever since. Although many good advocates have done the best of service, it is reserved to Van Arman to be the best known criminal lawyer in the West. He it was who ate the poisoned cake to show the jury it was not full enough of arsenic to kill defendant's husband. He it was that tried all the hooks to find one strong enough to hold a human body, and cleared another. He saved Vanderpool from a life sentence after he was in prison, and gained him trials enough to finally acquit his client of murder. He worked and measured in coal mines three days in Ohio to study his case and win it. A month or two is not an unusual thing for Mr. Van Arman to fit him for a victory. His speech in the Burch Divorce Case was a masterly effort, as all his great speeches are.

He is a born lawyer, with a genius a little like that of Benjamin F. Butler, now one of the greatest advocates in America. Far-seeing ingenuity, close examination of facts, accurate knowledge of fine practice and great will power win his cases.

Emery A. Storrs, the gifted speaker, political orator and brilliant advocate of Chicago, has a great following in jury practice. Much below medium size and height, he is not far from fifty, has a most excellent delivery, rapid and fluent almost to the bewilderment of many juries. There is no man living east or west who can speak faster or compose more rapidly. To him it is a gift to speak; as a minister or lecturer he would have had packed audiences. His voice is clear, penetrating and distinct as a triangle in a band. He is highly rhetorical and intensely dramatic in gestures, seeming to grow and expand with his theme, and magnetize his hearers. In this department — advocacy — he is a tower of strength and of great value in closing cases. Speaking is his specialty. He wins by it. He doubtless did much to elect Garfield in 1880 by his Burlington speech about the danger of a change of parties, a risk of making a new Supreme Court through nine more judges, and an increase of senators, with all the evils of the vivid picture he then portrayed. In the Babcock Conspiracy Case he made a fine argument. In the Cochrane Murder Case of Wisconsin he cleared the prisoner on the theory that "*courts and statutes were ever powerless to restrain a man from revenge when his home rights were invaded by the seducer.*"

Robert T. Lincoln, oldest son of the lamented President, lawyer and greatest of Illinois advocates, is under forty, dark hair and eyes, full short dark beard, and very young in appearance. His manner is candid, his words choice and appropriate, his briefs pointed and well arranged. He wins suits (when at Chicago) by his own industrious application and the rare skill of his associate, Mr. Isham, who has long been his law partner, and longer been one of the best lawyers in Illinois, ranking with Leonard Swett as the finest Supreme Court counselors of the northwest. Neither are much given to advocacy of late, having scarcely time in their immense higher court practice and corporation business. Both Isham and Swett have ever been brilliant advocates, both are eloquent and ingenious, but require a case and fee of considerable magnitude to tempt them from their business clientage. They each have fine offices on high floors, and charge in proportion to their practice. They are to Chicago what O'Connor and Evarts, of New York, are to their city, the leaders of their profession, and need no introduction. In the counsels of the nation where they should be, or in positions like Secretary Lincoln, they would either make a name in Washington.

Leonard Swett, of Chicago, an advocate of national fame, was born, reared and educated in Maine, and is about fifty-eight years of age; a gentleman of varied culture and learned in law; commanded a company in the Mexican war; came to Illinois in 1848 and located at Bloomington, commenced the practice of law there, and has since had a noteworthy career, becoming widely known in the State for his ability and success as an advocate, and was recognized as a leader among such distinguished lawyers and advocates as Abraham Lincoln (of whom he was an intimate friend and adviser to the day of his assassination), Douglas, Logan, Stuart, Linder, Baker, Hannagan, and others prominent at that time. He was a recognized leader in the whig, as he is now in the republican party. In personal appearance he has a fine natural presence, tall, erect, dark hair, intermingled with gray, well formed, of large frame and commanding figure, with great physical and mental energy: his face indicates refinement and culture as well as firmness and decision of character. He combines many qualites rarely found in combination. He has signalized himself by many remarkable achievements as defender, especially in criminal trials, having lost but one out of nineteen great and important murder cases in which he defended. It is only in great trials, when life is at stake, or innocence is assailed, that he rises to the importance of the occasion, and is at his best, and the great resources of his mind are brought out. He is then inspired with the highest order of eloquence. His style is a combination of all that was best in the Grecian and Oriental oratory — the compactness, perspicuity and elegance of expression of the former, and the bright coloring and vivid phrase of the latter. He is accomplished and learned in jurisprudence and political philosophy, acute and alert of mind, and a master of brilliant and lucid expression, and an ornament to the bar of this country — a beam of light in the midst of that prosaic monotony which too often hovers around our courts unrelieved by style and unadorned by eloquence. Everything is brought to bear on his life work as a lawyer. No learning or truth too great, no beauty too choice for his employment as an advocate. Vigilant, industrious and zealous, he could not but attain the success h has. His capacity is as conspicuous as his industry is untiring. The majesty of the law has in him as courageous a defender as it has an able and clear exponent. He is an orator in the highest sense; his subject matter is always excellent; his audience is charmed with the richness and vividness of his imagery, the beauty of his sentiments, and his happy illustrations of his propositions — that kind of eloquence which captivates and convinces by the force of logic well put; a brilliancy and eloquence which he sustains to the end. He is always self-possessed, and prepared for any emergency that may arise in a trial. He is one of the most successful advocates in this country. His name will live in the annals of the courts as an illustration and example of a powerful and successful advocate.

Luther L. Mills, State Attorney for Cook County, Illinois, is but little past thirty years of age, and acknowledged to be one of the most forcible advocates of his age in the west. In personal appearance and make-up, and oratorical powers he is of the Henry Clay type. He was born in Massachusetts and educated in Chicago and Ann Arbor, Michigan. He is small in stature, but strong in intellect; graceful in gesture, a clear and modulated voice, and has other qualities of a natural orator; clear, ringing and forcible speech; in style varied, logical, eloquent, pathetic, and hence impressive; vivid in statement, graphic in description. He is sagacious in argument as a prosecutor of criminals, and usually ends on a salient point, and gains an advantage. He has made his way at the bar by uniformly courteous and upright conduct, with fairness and sincerity in his management; he is always earnest, is popular with the profession and the public, and is in the true sense a natural advocate.

In the Sherry and Connolly murder trial, resulting in the hanging of both, Mr. Mills, in closing the case, said:

"And now, gentlemen of the jury, if guided by a true sense of justice, and an inflexible devotion to law, I entertain not the slightest doubt that you will upon Jeremiah Connolly and George Sherry, for the murder of Hugh McConville, inflict the extreme penalty of the law. This is no time for sentimentality. This is no time to stand upon mere sentiments, sensibilities and sympathies. The time has come in this community when law must be absolutely fearless, always executed.

" Death is indeed the solemnest incident of life. It is to prevent death that I make the request of you in behalf of the public that I now do. It is to prevent a hundred deaths, perhaps, in this community in the next twelve months; it is to tell lawless men and murderous ruffians that there is a law in this community, and they cannot trample upon that law without being punished. Through the class of men — if, indeed, there is such a class — to which Sherry and Connolly belong, your verdict will send a thrill of terror, and the murderous faces will grow white, and the burglars will be cautious how they do their crime, and the highwaymen will flee for safety into low, dark places, and away from this beautiful city. Let us then have an example, legally, justly, rightfully; the evidence and the law of this case warrant and demand it, and the blessings of the community will be showered upon your heads. Of late years human life has been altogether too cheap; a community of bargain, sale by the passion, and malice of murderers. It is a solemn thing, the fact of death; it is a solemner thing that there should be so many murders happening in the city of Chicago.

"The law must be executed; and in this case, because the crime is the most brutal murder ever perpetrated in this city, the penalty should be the very hardest in its severity. Did you ever hear or read in any records of a more atrocious, horrible and lawless conduct than that of these two men on that Saturday night that culminated in the brutal murder of Hugh McConville? You never did. It is the last day of the week. The twilight of Saturday. To-morrow will be the blessed day of our Lord, appointed by Divinity for the worship of Him, and for seeking to obtain from Him such inspiration as shall make men better for the days of labor after, and returning thanks to heaven, and I do believe, gentlemen of the jury, that the horrrible atrocity which characterizes this crime, and the joint guilt of these two defendants being fully submitted to absolute divine justice, so far as you can perform it in a human way, will be done unto them, and that on the morrow, in your homes, with your wives and children, you will feel like falling upon your knees in the presence of your household surroundings, and thanking heaven that you have had an opportunity, in behalf of outraged law, in behalf of the rights of human nature, in behalf of the the law of God himself, to do an act which Jehovah will approve, he who is the source and fountain of all justice and righteousness."

In the case of Dr. Charles Earll, convicted of abortion, and sentenced to the penitentiary, Mr. Mills closing was: "No man for a moment can doubt the guilt of Charles Earll of an attempt to commit an abortion. Indeed, it is almost confessed when the defense claims that the red handed abortionist was simply trifling with the girl. That he caused her death, no reasoning man using his best judgment, can for an instant doubt. What should be done with this red handed abortionist? The lesson that the jury taught the abortionest in 1879 was all too soon forgotten. Why was not that lesson obeyed? When a merciful jury let Charles Earll go with the slight punishment of one year's imprisonment, he ought to have given up the damnable, murderous business of committing abortions, but he heeded not the teaching of that lesson. He resumed the business, and he killed another girl by his bungling murderous work.

I submit, gentlemen of the jury, you are men, and citizens, and jurors, and that it is now high time to teach Charles Earll that proper punishment shall follow his horrid business of committing abortion, and murder. I submit that no light penalty is adequate. He goes about this abortion enterprise coolly and deliberately. When he takes the young girl into his hands, he plays with her life as the child plays with the bubble in the summer. What cares he for the risk that is run; what cares he for the danger staring the victim in the face? He wants money, money, money; blood money for his bread and butter.

I have said that I was honored by having a better clientage than the counsel for the defense. He defends Charles Earll well, ingeniously, skillfully, and to the best of his ability. His client is our man. The clientage I have the honor to protect is the great community, husbands, wives and children—the six hundred thousand people who are watching every movement of this great trial, and who are hanging breathless on these proceedings. We are nearly through with the case. After five long days, we shall to-night, when the curtain falls on the stage of the day, return to our homes. Each one of us this night will gather the true, loving wife, and the fond little children around the fireplace, and there shall be great welcome for each man's heart, and before the blazing beauty of the fire there shall be read, some sermon by, and of the christ child, for the children, or something from that noblest book of books, the bible of our faith, and then around the dear old mother's knee the little ones in white dresses for the night shall say their prayers, and quietly go to their rest; and in the secret ear of her who is the genius of your heart's idolatory, you will whisper the secret of the life of the last few days, and then I trust you will be able in all solemnity to offer a prayer of thanksgiving to the God who protects us all, because you have done your duty as men, and as jurors; because by punishing a red handed abortionist, you have vindicated the law and protected the honor of home, and have put the strong right arm of your verdict around the sanctity of woman.

In the John Lamb case, accused, once convicted of the murder of police officer Roce, in 1879, Mr. Mills said in closing: "Gentlemen, I make an appeal to you, not in behalf of the police department; not in behalf of any gentlemen connected with it, like the noble Dixon, and the good Seavey, and all the brave officers who knew and loved Albert Roce; I make no appeal to you in behalf of that wrinkled, grey haired old mother in Ohio, who to-night will sit with head bent over her knees, looking into the dying embers of the old fire place, waiting for the returning steps that never will come back, and craving, perhaps, a sweet mother song of love, which was a blessing over her child's cradle, and now as a bright benediction over his grave. For indeed, when the young wife dies, like the lily in the heat of the day, and the violet children are hidden in the valley, and the hoary headed sire dies in ripeness of years, there remains often times the dear old mother; and so Roce's mother now remains, but not alone for her do I plead; I plead for law; I plead for the protection of human life; I plead for the honor of this people; I plead for the men, the women, and the little children that to-night are in danger from the masked ruffians who infest our towns, and so I beg of you, gentlemen, to have your verdict quick, sharp and decisive. Let it come like a thunderbolt— quicker than the flash of lightning, which, in the heat of the summer, God makes use of to purify the air from pestilential vapors, and make way for the glory of the coming of the rainbow of peace.

Hon. James R. Doolittle, of Chicago, advocate, jurist and statesman, is a man of national fame. He has been counsel, judge, United States Senator, and is now an advocate. He was born, reared and educated in Central New York, and is somewhere in the sixties. In personal appearance he is tall, erect, grey hair and beard; a large frame and great physical and mental energy. He has signalized himself by many remarkable achievements in the higher courts. It is only in great trials that he is at his best, and the great resources of his mind are brought out. He then pours out strains of the highest order of eloquence; idea follows idea, principle succeeds principle, illustration accompanies illustration with rapidity. He is an accomplished orator, and an able and effective advocate; he states his cause in winning language — of which he is master — and in an engaging manner; then inveighs in telling and in tones which resound through the room against his client's opponent. His subject-matter is always excellent, and his audience is charmed with the richness of his fancy, the beauty and force of his sentiment, his happy illustration and his persuasive logic and eloquence by which minds are controlled. His gestures are easy, appropriate and graceful; there is nothing turgid or mysterious in his style; the grace and propriety of his delivery are equal to the copiousness and felicity of his diction. The tones of his well modulated voice are clear and full, and his manner and action are energetic without verging on that extravagance which is unpleasant. He is a successful advocate.

In the Forsythe case, just ended, Mr. Doolittle recovered $40,000 in personal fees, the largest fee ever awarded any lawyer by a jury.

Col. Daniel W. Munn, of Chicago, is an able and successful criminal lawyer, and a rhetorical advocate. He was born and educated in Vermont; is about fifty years of age. He is of large frame, erect, with dark hair, eyes and complexion; with a commanding and impressive presence; an earnest, impassioned and eloquent speaker, with a clear, ringing voice and other good qualities of an orator. In style he is logical, vivid and forcible.

His success as a criminal lawyer, in defending and prosecuting, is marked and noteworthy; he is sagacious in the management of his cases, and enjoys a large practice; has accumulated a competency, and attained success in the prime of life. He has been a legislator and army officer, and is still in the full vigor of early manhood.

A paragraph from Munn's speech in the late Dunn murder case, shows his florid style of imagery:

"A miracle that Dunn was not killed, as great as any miracle in Holy Writ — equal to that of Joshua, who reached up and took the sun by its golden bit, and the moon by its silver bridle, and stayed the course of time! As great as the preservation of Daniel in the lion's den. Daniel came out untouched and unharmed, while Dunn was mangled and wounded by the *brute* that was in *that* den of pollution — that house of prostitution, with a bar and restaurant attached, the doors of which are open night and day — never entered by virtuous women and but few respectable men — presided over by the self-acknowledged tramp, gambler and vagrant: "Appetite Bill."

William P. Black, of the law firm of Dent & Black, of Chicago, is among the younger lawyers of that city taking prominent rank for oratorical ability and as advocate. He is of the age of forty years, and has been at the bar some sixteen years, having completed his law studies after serving in the late Civil War. He is six feet in height, erect, with black hair, now somewhat silvered; has an easy bearing and good address, and a fine flow of language. He is versatile and logical in speech, and comes directly to the point, laying down his propositions clearly, and sustaining them with great clearness and fine power of expression; demonstrating his views very clearly, and sustaining them by all the arguments which can be brought to bear in his favor. He is quick to perceive the drift of evidence, and to take hold of any strong points which arise, and readily applies authorities. He decides promptly what course to pursue, and thinks while on his feet. He distinguishes with great skill the arguments and authorities produced by an adversary; discerns the weight of authorities, and is apt in applying them, and in driving home whatever tells in his favor. He is also ready with his pen, which he has been accustomed to use. His voice is unusually good. It is clear and pleasing, and he can make himself heard in the largest halls, having distinct enunciation. His general preparation for work at the bar enables him to go into a wide range of practice. His speech, when he is thoroughly aroused, is logic on fire. His practice has been mainly in civil cases; but he has acquitted himself well when engaged before the criminal courts.

CHAPTER XXV.

THE CINCINNATI BAR.

Judge Geo. A. Hoadly, present candidate for governor, the peer of Stanley Matthews, and other bright lights of southern Ohio, is of medium size, over fifty. Yet quite young in appearance, with dark eyes, smoothly shaven features, save a black mustache. He is the idol of young lawyers in his native city, of genial manners, kindly speech; clear knowledge of general practice, especially corporation cases; a man of far seeing and comprehensive methods, he wins by thoroughness and cleverness. Few men bring to a trial so many resources, wisdom, sagacity, plain sense and sturdy integrity. He is not eloquent, and yet a great speaker. In the famous Bible in the Schools Case, his argument was masterly and effective. If asked how he succeeds in practice, but one answer will be given by those who know him, by all honest arts, save eloquence. Judge Hoadly is a born and trained advocate, with cultivated powers and combined resources. He reads, studies, and reflects upon the works of great men. He masters the methods of many men, and is willing to learn, even at his stage of life, wherever new arts in practice are to be acquired. He believes that with no one man lives all the knowledge of practice, and so thinking, seeks to widen his field of information by every available source. He is a great listener, and learns much from the *other* side of litigations.

Edgar A. Johnson, his law partner, and younger in years, with something of Mr. Hoadly's appearance, is stronger in build, and, unlike the former, uses brief notes in lieu of copious ones. He is a pleasing speaker, and attracts crowds of listeners. A man of broad culture, he is so full of his subject while speaking, that he has hardly room for use of notes, and follows the extreme Southern style of oratory. Vivid and descriptive, composed from the subject where his words and sentences seem born in sight of his hearers. With that earnestness of purpose and intrepid courage, he wins by effects that advocates often neglect—intense belief in a cause, coupled with intense application. One cannot help feeling that Edgar A. Johnson is trying each case as if it were his last, and on which hang and *center all his reputation as a speaker forever*.

Thomas D. Lincoln, a relation of the lamented and greatest of all our lawyer presidents, is a lawyer of Cincinnati, that greatly resembles his namesake, of whom he is justly proud, and with whom he has tried many cases. He is nearly sixty, and stout built. Like the great martyr, Thomas is powerful in body, rugged in speech, and honest in convictions. He speaks with notes, grows intensely pathetic, in the natural interest he takes in his cases. His feelings moves other hearts as well as his own, and often leads to that towering style of carrying away a jury by flights of indignity, bursts of eloquence, or touches of pathos. It is said that on one occasion his jury half rose to their feet, and cheered by the manner as plainly as though they had orally expressed approval of his sentiments, and that he knew where to stop, at just that winning point of his argument. Few lawyers know this golden secret—and fewer practice it. It is not always that an advocate does his very best, seldom do men rise to the sublimity of eloquence, the greatest of all aids in winning cases. But with a jury, once at such a summit, to leave them, by all means is wise.

John McSweeny, of Wooster, Ohio, is an advocate of unusual power with a jury. Age, experience and natural talents as a speaker, with a sympathetic nature, add to his efforts in criminal cases, which are largely his specialty. Large, tall, strong lunged and well modulated voice, he is ardent in debate, full of apt quotations, dramatic in delivery, and spares no pains to discover the gist of the controversy, and press it with great energy to the court and jury. He wins his cases. He overcomes obstacles. He creates defenses. He argues from example, and illustrates fluently, telling occasional stories, but always as if by chance. He employs notes very sparingly, and generally speaks from memory. He has a habit of putting his intense and overmastering belief before the jury in convincing words. Once retained in a case, he forms a clear theory, and adheres to it; believing it to be the duty of counsel, and not of clients, to shape their defenses in jury trials.

In the famous Gov. Scott case, tried within the year 1882, at Napoleon, Ohio, Mr. McSweeny was extremely happy in explaining the shooting by illustration. The governor had gone hurriedly to a drug store to bring his son home late one Christmas night, where he was in bad and dangerous company, and had refused a request of Mrs. Scott to return at bed-time. Some remark had reached Gov. Scott of his son's danger, and that some rough boys might kill him, and he rose hurriedly, threw on a fall overcoat, and reached the store with hands in his pocket, and one hand involuntarily on his revolver. He demanded his son, and the clerk blocked the way to the back room, and refused to let him pass. A second demand, and, as Mr. Scott says, he lost all consciousness till he saw the clerk at his feet, fatally shot in the body, and bleeding. He stooped and raised the wounded youth, who was very much smaller than himself, and saw that he was fast dying. He surrendered himself at once, and was soon tried for murder. Mr. McSweeny defended. A companion pistol was produced. It went off at the slightest touch. In the trial, McSweeny handed the coat and pistol to an expert witness to attempt to withdraw it hurriedly, claiming it would go off unaided. Failing to get an expert to experiment, he himself took the pistol, and *three times* in succession, drew it from his pocket, and each time the discharge accompanied the withdrawal. On this theory of accidental shooting (excellently elucidated), Gov. Scott was saved from the gallows. The price of such services is beyond estimate. It secured McSweeny a place in the Star Route Cases, where his success was not so marked.

CHAPTER XXVI.

THE WASHINGTON BAR.

Walter D. Davidge, of Washington, D. C., is the leading advocate of the National Capital. A man of fifty years, with silvery hair, looking near sixty. Of medium size and build, graceful in carriage, dignified in manner; subtle and wise as a reasoner and debater, with a power of plausible language that takes and convinces a court or jury. He is gifted in defenses, and his real gift is *insight*. He labors insiduously, but has an intuitive belief in nearly all his victories. Cool, collected, not eloquent, but legally strong and commanding, he seizes the strong points of his cases, and holds them to the court and jury with determined earnestness. He has an admirable practice.

His manner is directness itself. His words are strong Saxon, his industry and personal popularity are worthy acquirements, and secure him a large clientage. He was in the Garfield assassin case, and called the President murderer many new names that made the villian dislike him, next to Judge Porter, the worst of all men living in Washington. He was retained with a $10,000 fee in this suit, by the Attorney-General. But he had already made a fortune in his profession.

Enoch Totten, of Washington, D. C., is about fifty-five years of age; a man of fine presence and impressive manner, a busy lawyer and hard worker. It is said he has the largest number of cases on the Supreme Court docket of any other counsel. He rarely indulges in eloquence, but always makes a strong, legal argument, forcibly applied to the facts in dispute. There is a native terseness and directness in his words and manner that compels attention. He owes his success partly to ability, but more to hard work. He was a colonel during the war, and has built up his practice since 1865. Few men of his years have seen more active practice, and few excel him in preparing cases for a court of Judges. He is one of that class of advocates who exhausts both sides of a question, and never leaves his adversary with a fresh, unbeaten path to follow on either side of a controversy. This thoroughness begets confidence, and he is really a strong man in a legal contest in any case before any tribunal.

Richard T. Merrick, of an old Maryland family, has won a bright name in Washington courts, and become very prominent in the Star Route cases; is about fifty years of age; rather below the medium height and size; courteous in manner—a born gentleman in every sense of the word. A hard student and a brilliant advocate; fiery and impetuous in debate; quick at retort, rhetorically eloquent in the highest degree. He uses fine, flowery language, and is hence a favorite with juries.

With a clear, ringing voice he commands large audiences, and is personally very popular, especially with younger members of the bar, to whom he is generous and obliging on all occasions. Such men are favorites, and when he comes into court, he carries an air of summer sunshine that pleases people. He was counsel for John H. Surratt, also for Samuel J. Tilden before the electoral commission, where he made the most profound and eloquent argument that was made on his side of the case, as well as the most elaborate. Although liberal and generous, he was well to do, and has a large and lucrative practice in and about Washington and Baltimore.

Other bright lights adorn the Washington bar, including Col. Ingersoll, whose home is located there; but of the Colonel, so much is said that no new thing is likely to be told of his style of advocacy. At a risk of repeating some things, I will say that he is very large, a blond, very bald, clean shaven, portly face, laughing eyes, jovial manner, witty, full of intense, original sayings wonderfully magnetic and fascinating in style, manner and language, a high liver, an earnest speaker who uses frequent illustrations, and grows sarcastic and pathetic by quick successions, turning a point for a smile, or drawing tears of sympathy, as by the wave of his generous hand.

He is not so profound in law as he is fluent in words, and powerful in graphic illustrations. The most popular of all lecturers, he of course, attracts large hearers when he appears in court trials. A natural advocate he may be called a gifted speaker on almost all themes and occasions. He grew to prominence in Illinois, and acquired a national reputation at Cincinnati in 1876, by his masterly speech that placed James G. Blaine before the convention as a candidate for the Presidency.

CHAPTER XXVII.

THE SOUTHERN BAR.

John G. Carlisle, of Kentucky, is in his 48th year. He is a trifle above medium height, weighs 140 pounds, and stands erect. He has a well knit body, fairly full chest and an elastic step. His hair is a light brown. The crown of his head is bald, and a small tuft of hair only prevents that baldness reaching from crown to forehead. The latter is fairly high and broad, projecting slightly above the eyes. With an extraordinary pale face for a background, his bright blue eyes are given unusual lustre by heavy and over-dark eyebrows. His nose is large, and would be generally called straight, but has a slightly raised bridge, and his nostrils swell out full. His mouth is generous in width, and is outlined by compressed, yet not thin lips. His chin is prominent enough to show stability of character without indicating obstinacy. His face is clean shaven and its pallid whiteness is marked by strong lines and prominent cheek bones. His features are not those of a handsome man, but of an intelligent being who has devoted his years since boyhood to constant, serious thought.

Like the majority of the men of worth in this new country, he comes of humble birth. His father was a farmer of Kenton county, Kentucky, but a few miles from Covington, and was unable to give his son any education other than that afforded by a rural school which was open only during the winters. During the remaining months of the year, young Carlisle worked on his father's farm.

From the time of his admission to the bar until now, Mr. Carlisle has managed an immense law practice. He has two partners, the junior member being his eldest son. Their law offices are in Covington, and in them is one of the finest libraries in the State. The practice of the firm takes Mr. Carlisle into every portion of Kentucky, and there is not a session of the Kentucky Court of Appeals which does not find him there as counsel on one side or the other of the most important cases.

In no sense is he a trickster. He has no taste for "working up" a case. He takes the evidence as it exists, divests it entirely of irrelevant points, arranges it in the most methodical and effective manner, and to it applies the principles of common and statute law. His rapidity in examining evidence and records, and rejecting the unimportant and misleading, is phenomenal. His memory of names, dates and figures, is marvelous. His powers of condensation, and his command of terse, vigorous, and yet smooth flowing sentences, make his speeches as interesting and effective as a Latin epic poem. Never in a speech, judicial or political, was he known to indulge in anecdote, jest, sarcasm or apt quotation. Seriousness, directness and simplicity are the features of all his public utterances. The Louisville attorney often quoted illustrates Carlisle's abilities as a lawyer by the following story: "He has never changed his style or manner. He has a remarkably sweet voice, and there is something about the man that is inexpressibly winning. He spoke before the Court of Appeals a few years ago on a murder case when I was there. His argument lasted nearly two hours, and when it was concluded, presiding Judge Cofer asked his brother judges to adjourn for the day. A lawyer who had a case set for the day, asked why the court was to be adjourned. Cofer crisply replied: 'I hate to have a good thing spoiled, as would be the case if any other man followed Carlisle.'" In Washington, when his arduous duties permit him, he is studying his law cases, preparing his briefs and forwarding them with advice about the conduct of suits, to his partners in Kentucky. He is regarded as the strongest constitutional lawyer of any democrat in either house. When Thurman was in Congress, they were equally consulted, but now Carlisle's opinions are democratic statutes.

Thomas J. Semmes, a prominent advocate of New Orleans, is a man of medium size, age about fifty-five years, whose manner is pleasing, with a voice clear and flexible, plausible and ingenius in argument, at times extremely vigorous. Selecting a few salient points of his cases, he relies on them, and never lumbers his arguments with little matters. He wins his cases on the central merits without much regard to finer details. His courtly bearing and general good practice has made him prominent throughout the State. He has been attorney general, and is one of the most popular and successful advocates of Louisiana. His high character, learning and integrity, with many graces of oratory, has made him powerful with courts and juries.

Judge William Wirt Howe, a tall, slender, but graceful, attorney, of cultivated manners and large business practice in New Orleans, is nearly forty-eight, an erudite scholar, a jurist and writer of State reputation; though a pleasing speaker, he relies more on the law of his cases. and a certain *tact* of winning easy victories.

On the bench, his reported opinions rank as of the best in his State. He has served as associate justice of the Supreme Court, but from choice returned to a lucrative practice.

In voice, style and manner, he is of the real Southern type of advocates. Courteous and considerate to others, firm and determined in duty, his decorum and urbane bearing make many friends and an increasing line of large cases.

Gustave A. Breaux, a native of Louisiana, of French extraction, aged fifty-four, is a tall man of powerful frame, full of the characteristic animation and activity of his native race. Studious, and attentive to business, careful and painstaking with his cases, he has built up a large and lucrative practice in New Orleans. Eschewing all attempt at merely ornate speaking, his arguments are marked by excellent points and forcible logic, which are his means of winning court or jury cases.

He has served as State Senator and member of the State Constitutional Convention, with credit and distinction. His share of city practice is not wholly confined to French settlers, of whom his city is a favorite home in the South-west, but a general business with a good clientage.

Besides the brilliant array of southern Ohio lawyers, and their equally distinguished Kentucky rivals who practice in the southern States in important cases, there are a vast number more over the entire south, known to fame in their native States, kept from national note by lack of a metropolitan press to tell of their victories; it is only occasionally that one like Judge Campbell of New Orleans, Senator Harris, of Georgia, General Rodman or Colonel Breckinridge, of Lexington, William Garrard, of Savannah, or Isaac Colwell, of Louisville, become noted in national cases. The growth of fame at the bar—with but few exceptions—in America, has been confined to men of eastern and southern cities. The peculiar love of eloquence that inspired Clay, Calhoun, Crittenden, Marshall and Prentiss, has left a host of bright lights unnoticed in remoter regions where the press penetrates, but seldom sends out accounts of trials and speeches. Most of the southern advocates, since the rebellion, who had formerly practiced south of Kentucky, have won renown by removal to large cities, or election to national positions.

It is said that Ben Hill, Jr., is a promising successor to his distinguished father, and one of the rising advocates of Atlanta, Georgia, whose competitors are Chandler, Thompson, Millage and Lester, with the usual complement of able attorneys in different sections of that long, large State. That L. P. Walker, of Huntsville, Alabama, David Clapton, of Montazuma, in the same State, Ed. Baxter, of Nashville, and Judge McGrath, of Charleston, South Carolina, are all able and thoroughly successful advocates, who would make their mark in any of the cities like New York, Boston, Cincinnati or Chicago, where associate press dispatches tell the world daily every event of interest. In this respect the Southern bar labors under great disadvantages, something, perhaps, in the line of compensation for their excellent climate and congenial fields for oratory. A section where more attention is given to good speeches than any other country of our continent.

Judge David Carter, Chief Justice of the Supreme Court of the District of Columbia, is about sixty-seven, over six feet high, over 250 pounds in weight, brown hair, imperial beard, high forehead, prominent features, original in thought and full of quaint sayings. A man of positive convictions, and as a judge, frequently in the absence of what he conceives to be law, will apply principles of common sense. He has a slight impediment in his speech, and possesses native reason in a large degree. On this and his commanding presence, he has made his reputation. In his native State, Ohio, he was a powerful lawyer, and succeeded in business law and became wealthy. He is an off-hand speaker, and full of directness.

Judge John A. Campbell, a distinguished jurist and advocate of New Orleans, before the war was one of the brilliant southern lights in oratory. A man of medium size, with courtly bearing, chivalrous and high-minded in practice, full of warm sympathies and excellent legal knowledge. He had a large practice, and built up a splendid reputation as an advocate before his election as supreme court judge.

Charles S. Blackburn, the great criminal lawyer of Kentucky and southern Ohio, is over forty-five, tall, large, majestic and impressive in appearance, powerful in argument and highly rhetorical in language. He has long been a leader on the defense of murder cases. He reasons fluently, without notes; is ingenius and adroit with management of facts, and relies, with these, on powerful oratory and a wise selection of his juries. He succeeds by actual determination, and if there is a man in Ohio who can talk up a case before a jury better than Blackburn, he is not known in Cincinnati.

John G. Harris, the leading advocate of Memphis, Tennessee, is over seventy years old, rather above medium size, dark eyes and complexion, and hair fast turning gray. He is at present senator, recently re-elected, as he said, for the last term.

Senator Harris is a fine speaker, and a great favorite in his native State, where he has been for years governor and where his legal and political career has been brilliantly successful.

An orator, and born with the greatest of all the gifts of advocacy, he is eloquent. Possessing friends, clients and ability, his practice has been limited mainly to his personal ability to attend to his cases.

CHAPTER XXVIII.

PHILADELPHIA LAWYERS.

Jere Black, the Philadelphia lawyer, stern, rigid, trained and bred a genius at the bar for almost a half century. A case that Mr. Black would lose must be bad indeed. He tries his suits on logical principles, avoiding all emotion, but saving the slightest sentence in favor of his client. His practice has long been in the supreme court, and he is scarcely now an active advocate. Yet his reasons are wonderfully acute and telling. He has won his suits by intense application and long experience; besides being a born lawyer.

He was engaged in the Johnson Impeachment Trial, and counsel in nearly every important national contest at Washington for a half century. In the trial of cases Mr. Black has relied upon himself. His research in English and American decisions is remarkable, but the sterling qualities of his genius is a keenness of insight. Like the late Judge Halmer Emmons, of the United States Court, he could determine in advance the result of a long litigation. This is the proverbial gift of the renowned Philadelphia lawyers. They know the mysteries of complicated cases, and with none is this faculty more developed than with Jeremiah S. Black and Daniel Dougherty.

Daniel Dougherty, of Philadelphia, and leader of Pennsylvania bar, is gifted in words, thoughts and actions before audiences. Of medium size, dark complexion, age about fifty, in the full prime of vigorous faculties and lucrative practice.

He is noted as a ready, fluent and erudite reasoner, who combines the graphic with the beautiful in a literary point of view. He is of the Irish Pennsylvanian stock, noted for warm enthusiasm and rhetorical reasoning powers.

He is a great reader; a lover of books and fine thoughts. His manner is self-oblivion and exceedingly impressive. He enters on his subjects with careful caution and chaste sentences; reaches his argument by the most direct road, and holds absolute control of his hearers — seldom failing to convince their judgment, while he charms their senses. His voice is silvery and ringing. The arrangement of his points and paragraphs is the admiration of cultured Pennsylvanians. In his final appeal to a jury he is pathetic, and often reaches the sublime. His eloquent presentation of General Hancock to the Cincinnati Convention in 1880, has been seldom equalled in all the long line of brilliant nominating speeches of presidents. His practice is large, and largely confined to estates and matters of great importance. He is modest and unassuming. He cares little for *titles*, and prefers rather to be an able advocate and counselor, than hold any office however lucrative. His conduct at the bar is marked by that deference and innate politeness to others that commands a good share of respect to himself, and causes the younger members of the bar to all long to be a lawyer like Dougherty.

THE ALBANY BAR.

Hamilton Harris is a leading, and one of the most successful advocates at the Albany County Bar. His age is fifty-eight years. He is tall, well built, dark complexion, black hair, which he keeps cut quite short. He wears no beard. He excels in managing cases and cross-examining witnesses. Before juries his earnestness and apparent sincerity impresses his hearers. He has been District Attorney of his county, and for several times State Senator. In both stations he was especially noted and successful.

In important legislature investigations he is frequently employed. The most recent, the investigation of charges against Justice T. R. Westbrook in the winter of 1882, in which he defended the Justice, and succeeded in securing a favorable report for his client. He is resident attorney for Jay Gould and several railroad companies, and his management of cases has been unusually successful. Mr. Harris was a member of the first new capitol commission, and is engaged as the one of the most active in pushing forward the enterprise.

Rufus W. Peckham, is the second son of Judge R. W. Peckham, late of the New York Court of Appeals. Since the death of his father, which occurred at sea by the sinking of the "Villa de Havre," he has taken high rank in his profession of law.

His brother, Wheeler, was one of the counsel who accomplished the defeat and downfall of the Tweed ring, in New York City. The subject of this sketch is a tall, slender, light haired man, forty-four years of age. He is a well read lawyer and fluent speaker, but has cold and peculiar manners. His best efforts are before the higher courts. He has been engaged in very important cases of litigation, and is now the corporation counsel of Albany. His extensive practice takes him before the Court of Appeals frequently. Before the death of Lyman Tremain, he was his associate in business. He was District Attorney of this county.

Judge Amasa J. Parker is the oldest practicing lawyer in the city. Judge Countryman, his partner, is a brilliant advocate, and in a few years has gained position and renown.

Judge Ira Harris, of Albany, late U. S. Senator of New York, was exceedingly courteous and finished in address and manners. A tall, scholarly and distinguished looking advocate, whose mastery of excellent English and legal principles and purity of social life, made him exceedingly popular as a friend and counsel, and much sought for in his profession. He was notably the most refined and polished advocate in New York. He lived to be near fifty, and died lamented by the Albany and Central New York bar, as one of their model practitioners.

Matthew Hale is a fine jury lawyer, and Samuel Hand is engaged nearly all his time before the Court of Appeals in the argument of causes.

THE PORTLAND BAR.

Bion Bradbury, of Portland, has for many years past been in the front ranks of lawyers in Maine. He has enjoyed a large and lucrative practice. As an advocate, he is persuasive and convincing, and often eloquent, while his known character for integrity adds weight to his arguments. He is always courteous to witnesses, parties and the court, but he never overlooks the strong points in his cause, nor forgets the weak ones of his adversary. His manner is attractive, his voice pleasing and his arguments logical, but not heavy. He is a master of the art of enlivening a dry subject by flashes of wit, and always succeeds in holding interested attention of his auditors.

Mr. Bradbury is now about seventy years of age, erect in form, of medium height, graceful in manner, and in all respects a gentleman of the old school, a class which we fear is too rapidly disappearing.

He is widely known both at home and abroad as a wise and safe counselor, an able and eloquent advocate, and is actively engaged in the management of cases, both in the State and United States court. He carries his years lightly. He has been the honored president of the Cumberland bar, and he has always been a leader among men.

Sewall C. Strout, of Portland, is one of the foremost lawyers of Maine. He is in the front ranks of the profession, a leader. Respected by bench, bar and people. He enjoys a large and lucrative practice, the reward of the closest attention to business. He is a lawyer in the largest and best sense of the term, giving his whole time and energies to his chosen and loved profession.

As a counselor, he has no superior in Maine; he is wise and safe; as an examiner he is cool, keen, incisive and powerful; and while always courteous, the reluctant and untruthful witness, in the end, always yields the truth to him.

As an advocate, he is persuasive and convincing, and at times eloquent. He is a deep thinker, and while strong in debate, he never spends time on trivial matters. His high standing with the courts, and his character for integrity and fairness, adds weight to his arguments. He never overlooks the strong points in his cause, nor the weak ones of his adversary.

He is industrious and painstaking in the preparation of his cases, and wise and sagacious in the management of them, and when he has decided to undertake a case, his client is assured that all will be done for him that a safe, well equipped and conscientious lawyer can do.

His manner is attractive, his voice pleasing, and his mind logical, but never tedious. He understands the art of so dressing up a dry subject that it shall appear interesting and attractive, and always succeeds in fastening and holding the attention of his audience.

Mr. Strout is now about fifty-four years of age, erect, of medium height, graceful, and impresses one at sight with his affibility, kindness of heart and power.

He is a man of large and varied experience, of fine presence and deservedly popular; he is known throughout the State as an able and high minded lawyer.

CHAPTER XXIX.

THE MICHIGAN BAR.

This being a State of common law practice, with an unusually able supreme court, and the home of many distinguished advocates, it is a delicate task to mention some and omit others. But there are certain admitted leaders, whose traits of character and manner of practice would be instructive, and pleasant to remember. Of those that are most frequently mentioned in Detroit to-day, will be heard the names of G. V. N. Lothrop, the polished and urbane speaker, whose eloquence alone has made him victor in many a hard fought contest. He wins by a style like Cicero possessed — the art of pleasing many men. He is now nearly seventy.

Judge Shipman, his once sharp competitor, has ceased trying cases since his judical election, except on rare occasions. He is more robust, but not less eloquent, than Mr. Lothrop. A man of genius and great knowledge of human nature.

Col. Sylvester Larned, of the same age, the silver toned orator, has won many cases, and will win many more; his power with a jury being not easily overestimated. He is of French descent, and has a large criminal court practice.

Judge Isaac Marston lately resigned a seat on the supreme bench to open law practice, and is rapidly gaining his desired object. He is much under fifty, a slim, spare, pale faced man, of pleasant speech, genial manners and wonderful reasoning powers before a jury. Coming to a full bar with ripe knowledge, he has secured an early opening, and has joined Col. Atkinson in a joint practice.

Col. John Atkinson, now one of the most prominent advocates of the State, is a rare genius; a young, rather large, well read, shrewd trial lawyer, who has an air of independence and sarcasm that is very forcible; for he cares no more for courts than opposing lawyers, and gains his points less by eloquence than sheer force of will and farseeing ingenuity. He pays great attention to libel and slander cases, and wins many of them. Being counsel for the *Evening News*, he has a means always ready to record his many victories.

Don. M. Dickinson, by far the most distinguished young lawyer in the State, is quite the reverse in his methods of those just mentioned, and yet wins large cases by a kindly affable manner, that makes him the warmest of friendships with court, jury and client. As a sagacious business lawyer, he has no superior in Michigan. He has been chairman of the State Central Committee, and is a leader of the young democracy in Detroit. Mr. Dickinson is a worker, and wins by both work and influence.

His partner, Mr. Levi Griffin, has a large trial practice, and makes it a point to get as many circuit court verdicts as possible, and is not often disappointed. His method is peculiar; if a hard case is defended or prosecuted, he wears out the other side by about twice as much evidence and examination as they look for.

Henry M. Cheever, secretary of the Detroit bar, has the reputation of being the best examiner in the State. He has won many murder cases, and always by special skill and manipulating evidence. His speeches are fully prepared, and almost committed by the work upon them, quoting largely from legal authority. He is never taken by suprise, and is exceedingly skillful.

Ashley Pond, Vanderbilt's lawyer, is at the head of the Michigan bar as a case lawyer. He has more points at his fingers end than any of his competitors. Long a Professor of Ann Arbor he has committed many principles to memory, and knows how to apply legal principles. Not so much an advocate, he is extremely able in trial practice. Hon. Otto Kirchner, late attorney-general, is mentioned elsewhere.

Alfred Russell, one of the foremost lawyers in the State, and one who goes often to Washington in supreme court work, is a gifted speaker and finished scholar. A man who wins by a long look ahead and an untiring energy, coupled with accurate ideas of practice, acquired while United States District Attorney during the years of 1866 to 1872, where he displayed coolness and ability to cope with the strongest advocates like Howard, Emmons and Van Dyke.

In the cities of the State are many gifted speakers less known and yet not less able. Men like Darwin Hughes, of Grand Rapids, of wonderful endurance and industry, who works out his cases as from Granite Marble, and brings them .to court in symmetrical order. Or Benton Hanchett, whose practice is so large that a supreme court judgship was recently refused as no temptation. He has the quality of winning cases by candor and eloquence, and is exceedingly happy with jury efforts. Still in the prime of early practice, with a bright future and a growing business. To these may be added Judge Shipman, of Coldwater, Chas. S. May, of Kalamazoo, E. L. Koon, of Hillsdale, M. J. Smiley, of Grand Rapids, A. J. Sawyer, of Ann Arbor, J. B. Moore, of Lapeer, Gov. Blair and James Gould, of Jackson, and O'Brien J. Atkinson, of Port Huron, H. H. Reilly, of Constantine, B. M. Cutcheon, of Manistee, and his brother, S. M. Cutcheon, of Detroit, all of whom are able advocates.

THE INDIANAPOLIS BAR.

Thomas A. Hendricks, eminent as an advocate, orator and statesman, is peculiarly happy before a jury, or a court of judges. He is very dignified and discreet in bearing. He speaks from notes, rather inclined to show facts to a jury than spend useless words in explanation. He goes right up to the panel, walks in between the jurors, carries a map or draft, and calls men by name familiarly, becomes at first *one* of a jury, and then returns to his place and reasons for an hour or more. But the jury remember best his explaining power. He is lucid, gifted, magnetic, great with juries. I remember hearing him two hours at a political meeting. He was strong, entertaining, and I was willing to say good. But the best had not come. He laid his notes aside, and stood silent amid great applause. He stepped to the right, as an actor at a recall. The crowd cheered again. Instead of a formal bow, the features lighted up with a look of gratification that I shall never forget, as he rolled off a five minutes period, so charged with power, pathos and real eloquence, that he seemed taller, nobler, half inspired. I shall not forget the thoughts; they were full of charity, pure principles, and expressive diction. It marked Thomas A. Hendricks as a natural orator. He represents Cicero's style of advocacy—the clear and persuasive that steals in on the senses by surprise, that captures a jury by soft, sweet sentences, and kind thoughts.

"This is the case, gentlemen," he says, and proceeds to point out on a plain map or board just what his theory is, going right along in the rows of jurymen, till he is almost one of them, for many minutes. Then he turns, reasons, argues, informs them — always talking persuasively to the end, when he warms into a strong appeal. His great object seems to be, not so much to speak about a case, as to show the jury what the case is. *Clearness, absolute clearness*, is his forte. But it must not be presumed that he is dull. Not at all. He talks as Wendell Phillips lectures, with pithy sentences. Governor Hendricks is over sixty, above the medium size, cleanly shaven, fine face and commanding manner. He is extremely cautions, and almost too much so, for a brave leader, but strong in his convictions of right and justice. For years he was a rival statesman with Gov. Morton, and once came near being a president. A man of excellent habits and pure public character that impresses all juries favorably. He is still in active practice.

Across the street from Mr. Hendricks is the office of Hon. Jos. E. McDonald, a sturdy and successful lawyer, and an attractive speaker. In Indiana, where he is best known, Mr. McDonald is called the common sense counsel. In cases of a doubtful nature, he is consulted, and, laying aside all books, he consults a half hour alone with his client, and seeks to find out fully what ought to be the rights of the controversy. If the client is wrong in his position, McDonald takes a counsel fee and withdraws at once; if right is on his side, he stands by it through every court, no matter how long the contest. This fact is so well known that it gives character to his speeches. He is thoroughly honest in convictions. He practices law from a pure love of justice. He is both a born advocate and a natural judge — bolder than most men, he never takes back what he has uttered. He is large, plain, speaks deliberately from copious notes, is emphatic, logical, not eloquent. He wins by that kind of candor that a real good large mature man of high character can command of any jury. A man of brains and common sense.

Senator Ben Harrison, of Indiana, is a speaker of unusual clearness. About five feet ten, well built, erect, and attentive to details — all fine points in practice. About fifty, with brown hair, and lighter full brown beard, worn well trimmed, and rather long; a pleasant voice, an earnest manner, and considerable magnetism. He is of the old stock of Harrisons, and stands deservedly high as an advocate in civil and criminal cases. He made a fine address in the famous Clem case, tried some years ago, for murder; but very little of his speech remains printed. He begins his trials by reading the declaration or complaint. States carefully the meaning of the charge, names the salient evidence on each side, and proceeds with the evidence which is most reasonable. Then beginning on the undisputed parts, he grows into the case, and relates the story like a romance. It is such a taking, unusual way, and so carefully told, that the telling alone is eloquent. Old family connections, long life of rectitude, and general good judgment, have done something, but clearness does most for both Choate and Harrison.

Gen. Thomas M. Browne, of Indianapolis, is an adroit and able advocate before any court or jury. Tall, of fine physique, large forehead, warm countenance, dark eyes and hair, age forty-eight, impulsive and rapid of speech, ingenious and able in arrangement of evidence, he is one of the first lawyers in his State in criminal and civil cases. Long a partner of Major Gordon, the two make an excellent team in contested suits. Largely engaged in United States Court practice, the General has time enough to run for governor or take a term in Congress. At such times he is a popular and impressive stump speaker. His ready and open manner takes with a public audience, and he is very happy as a campaigner. His *forte* is in trying jury cases for the people. Having been United States District Attorney he is quite familiar in practice, and wins a large share of cases where such lights as Harrison, Porter, Hines, McDonald and Butler are met in daily practice.

Major J. W. Gordon, of Indianapolis, the advocate of most note in criminal cases in Indiana, is nearly sev-

-enty, well formed and well preserved. A medium sized man with iron-gray hair and Napoleon beard, slightly Roman nose, sharp, keen eyes, high forehead, and ready in practice or argument. He is full of points and *objects* often, generally succeeding to get three or four new trials and as many disagreements. This is his special *forte* in practice, and he often wins by it. Witnesses move away. Some die, others forget, and sentiment changes. When defending, the Major seldom hurries his cases to trial, but generally takes his time about it. He is a great student—once a doctor, this helps him in dissecting criminal cases. He is strong, rhetorical and very graphic in trials; fertile in imagery, quaint in expression, a lover of oratory, and wedded to his profession. To try a murder case is to him a positive luxury. He will follow the details with all the interest of a discovery, and relish the happy turns with all the zeal of an enthusiast.

CHAPTER XXX.

THE MISER'S HAND.*

Griswold, once a rich merchant in Chicago, failed from the effects of the great fire, and went to Milwaukee to live on a homestead in his wife's name. Returning one day to Chicago he was arrested for the alleged concealing of property from his creditors, tried and released before the county judge, and the case was appealed to be heard by jury.

The debt was nine thousand dollars. The trial was long and bitter. Griswold was old, and if condemned would suffer a practical imprisonment for life, as the execution ran against the body. Judge Israel Holmes, of Chicago, defended, and after a forcible argument on the law and facts, concluded his address as follows:

There is a beautiful tradition of a painting, well-known in Venice; the sketch, by a great artist, of a miser's hand. It is the story of a poor young man who loved a rich young lady, the daughter of an old miser. Because of the young man's poverty, the father refused to allow the marriage to be consummated.

The young people were disconsolate and in the extreme of wretchedness. The young woman even at-

---

* Too rare to omit, although out of its order.

tempted suicide. She was rescued by an unknown friend who interceded for her lover with the old miser father. But his words were of no avail. Against all entreaty the miser remained inflexible. He would have no family of beggars for his children he said. The stranger then asked: "If the young man could put down six thousand pistoles, would you then permit the marriage?" The old man's looks said yes, but his words expressed only scorn and ridicule at the offer. The stranger turned to the table, took a small crayon from his pocket, and rapidly sketched something on a piece of parchment. He held it up to view, and the old man exclaimed: "It is my hand! It is my hand!" And sure enough it was! An open hand, with hollow palm, and anxious looking grasp; eager as if expecting to catch a shower of gold. The picture of a miser's hand with all the old man's nature woven in the wrinkles. The young man, bidden by the artist, took the sketch to the librarian of St. Mark, sold it for the required sum, and returned joyously with the money, cast it at the miser's feet, and the young people were married, and were happy.

The stranger was Michael Angelo. The sketch was preserved for centuries as a wonderful creation of genius among the treasures of Venice, and was finally destroyed in war, but its memory will never be lost. And if some Michael Angelo could give us the character of these plaintiffs, with cruel and revengeful hands, and we could see the life sketch, it would sell in the markets of men for gold enough to ransom the old merchant's liberty. But without the pencil, or the crayon sketch, you hold the power of liberty yourselves. In the name of humanity; in the name of justice: in the name of reason; stop this disgraceful chase for gold! He has borne it long. He is old. He is weary. Give him his liberty and give him his life.

In the course of nature this husband and this wife will not journey long together. We must all go soon: the judge upon the bench; the youngest and the oldest juror, the youngest and oldest advocate, and the prisoner for debt first of all must go. He is nearing the end of life's short race; torn by troubles, disheartened by care and defeat, there is but a few years left in all for him and his trusty companion; if you separate this couple in their old age, it will be worse than it would have been for the younger couple. It will be harder now, and may God save her from it, for her days will then indeed be few and full of trouble. With the husband in their prison, their grasp will soon fasten on the little she has saved for her own declining years, which will go with the ruins of their home. The fire that burned away their fortune left their honor, and this I place in your keeping; under the sublime sanction of a juror's oath of a jury's mercy, I ask you to stand as an *iron wall around their fireside, their liberty, their homestead and their honor*, and say, in spite of avarice and persecution, he is "*not* guilty." Griswold was released.

THE MEMORY LIVES.

To all who have helped me in this work I owe a debt of thanks. But to one who aided most of all, who copied and compared, was critic, office-boy and friend

I owe the most, the memory of "Louie's" life. "*Make it of little words that I can understand,*" was his advice.

He did not live to understand it all. One bright June day, when nature was in sunshine after rain, the seventh of his illness, he called his mother to place him at the window where he could see the green lawn and the garden, his pet horse and dog, and take a last fond look of familiar objects.

The words he said were full of tender meaning; "you can all live without me, but I could not live without you!" Brave words are these for one of sixteen summers, who had borne diptheria in his room alone, from choice, and then he fell asleep, and sleeps to-day in Woodmere, on a grassy slope, shaded by evergreens and covered well with flowers.   * * *

They said above his grave: "We live in a world of beauty and of tears. The trees and flowers fall down before their time, and fade and wither in their bloom, and so do lives. He that has made the trees, and fields, and flowers, controls them by His will.

"All trees are not alike — many are more beautiful than others; some more valuable. All flowers are not of equal sweetness with the rest; some are sought for, others left alone. All lives are not alike; some are nearer to us than the rest.   * * * *

"So every garden has its sweetest rose, and every household has its idol plant. The flowers that wither once, may bloom another year, but friends departed never come again. The mountain mists come down and go away, and yet some part remains. The grass drinks some, and brightens at the taste. The leaves are greener by the vapor's touch. The rose inhales it, and its sweetness grows. The wild flowers catch it and hold it in their fragrance. The earth is richer from the rain and mist. Much of it is folded in the apple and the peach to form the fruits of autumn.

So with life when taken at its prime, and so with every noble life. Sad as it is to be cut off full of promise and usefulness, *it is not* ALL *gone from us!* Some of it is woven in the scenes of home. It has *lived* there! It has left its mark upon our characters! Some part is folded in the hearts of friends, and sweetens all their memories. Much is absorbed by associates. More is blended in the thoughts of those who knew and loved its mission, and all these kindred feelings bear its lesson long after it has passed away, for "we are a part of all that we have known." * * *

"And then his going was so peaceful and so brave. As the early evening shadows came nearer, he knew he would not look upon the morrow, and called his mother to move him where he could see the sun, his brother leading out the horse, and take a last farewell of home. Thus he passed away so young. But he is not *all* gone! He has *lived* here! His *memory* remains. * * * * * *

And so in the history of many lives. "What shadows they are, and what shadows they pursue!" The memory of the deeds they do, lives on; their lives go out like sentinels relieved, to sleep; lives grown brave and useful in their state that would make others better by their reading. * * * *

It it is not my intention to particularize, and I have mentioned the different trial lawyers in this volume without a single thought of partiality, favoritism or consultation with any one: which fact will appear on a full reading of the volume, where many men not singled out are used to illustrate the value of special means employed in practice by successful advocates. Other lives are used to enforce some thought.

There is more than a single lesson to be drawn from these lives. They all have their own way and pursue it; that way embraces study, industry, art and its application; while the most successful are the best read, in men, and books, and having mastered themselves and their profession, they prove to us that "the best teachers of humanity, are the lives of great men." That success makes friends, and defeat makes enemies. That the glory of a lawyer is his strength of character. His knowledge and acumen must be forever respected. It is his lasting capital. Fires never burn it; slander cannot kill it: distance cannot destroy it; for what he owns in knowledge *is his*, is valuable, is lasting.

www.ingramcontent.com/pod-product-compliance
Lightning Source LLC
Chambersburg PA
CBHW030739230426
43667CB00007B/775